The Man
Who Went Into
the West

Other books by Byron Rogers

An Audience with an Elephant and other Encounters on the Eccentric Side
The Bank Manager and the Holy Grail: Travels to the Wilder Reaches of Wales
The Green Lane to Nowhere: The Life of an English Village
The Last Englishman: The Life of J.L. Carr (available from the Quince Tree Press)
The Lost Children (Gregynog Press)
On the Trail of the Last Human Cannonball

The endpapers illustrate details from two panels of 'The Dance of Life', the mural painted by Elsi Eldridge, wife of R.S. Thomas, reproduced by permission of the Robert Jones and Agnes Hunt Orthopaedic and District Hospital, Oswestry.

Front endpaper: detail from Panel 1: 'Man in complete harmony with nature, exemplified by Yugoslav dancers celebrating the seasonal festivals of the year with dance and music.'

Back endpaper: detail from Panel 6: 'Children play in a world of their own, oblivious of man and his machines, treating the animals as friends.'

The Man Who Went Into the West

The Life of R.S. Thomas

BY

BYRON ROGERS

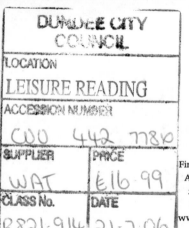

First published 2006 by
Aurum Press Limited
25 Bedford Avenue
London WC1B 3AT
www.aurumpress.co.uk

Written with the financial support of the Welsh Books Council

A catalogue record for this book is available from the British Library.

ISBN 1 84513 146 0

1 3 5 7 9 10 8 6 4 2
2006 2008 2010 2009 2007

Text design by Peter Ward
Map on p. ix by Reg Piggott
Typeset in Apollo by SX Composing DTP, Rayleigh, Essex
Printed and bound in Great Britain
by CPD (Wales) Ltd, Ebbw Vale.

R.S. Thomas drawn by his wife Elsi, 1939. The beard is the one
his mother made him remove the moment the two turned up in
Holyhead.

 CONTENTS

ACKNOWLEDGEMENTS
viii

MAP
ix

INTRODUCTION
I

1. The Makings 19

2. Holyhead: The Journey Begins 59

3. Bangor, Llandaff, Chirk 89

4. Manafon 125

5. Eglwys Fach 189

6. Aberdaron 225

7. Sarn, and Beyond 261

BIBLIOGRAPHY
317

INDEX
319

❧ACKNOWLEDGEMENTS❧

I wish to acknowledge my gratitude: to the Welsh Books Council for its financial contribution towards research which involved me crossing and recrossing Wales like an early Christian saint; to Kunjana Thomas for quotations from all poems 1945–1990; to Bloodaxe Books for quotations from *Collected Later Poems 1988–2000* (Bloodaxe, 2004); to J.M. Dent, a division of the Orion Publishing Group, for quotations from *Autobiographies*, translated by Jason Walford Davies (J.M. Dent, 1997); to Dr Raymond Garlick for letting me read and quote from the letters sent him by R.S. Thomas.

On a more personal level, to those without whose help this book could not have been written: to the Rev. Donald Allchin; to John Barnie of *Planet*; to George Behrend; to Dr Tony Brown of the R.S. Thomas Study Centre at Bangor; to Marie Carter, Health Sciences Librarian at the Robert Jones and Agnes Hunt Orthopaedic and General Hospital, Oswestry; to Ray Carter CBE, for, yet again, his book collection; to Penny Condry; to the Rev. Evelyn Davies; to Jenny Dyer; to Lord Dynevor; to Imogen Elliott and Genia Conroy, the daughters of General Pugh; to Christine Evans; to Jon Gower; to Liam Hanley; to John Harris; to Dr Glyn Tegai Hughes; to Cassie Jones; to Peter Joliffe; to Prof. Bobi Jones; to Gwyneth Lewis; to Sharon Lunney; to Dr John Marchant and his daughters Jan Spalding and Gillian Arney; to Ann Moorey; to John and Peggy Mowat; to Twm Morys; to Gareth Parry; to Alan Powers; to the Rev. Bill Pritchard; to Anne Price-Owen of the David Jones Society; to Dr John Rowlands; to Denise Rylands; to Robin Simon; to Prof. Meic Stephens; to Jonathan Stedall; to Angharad Tomos; to Rhodri and Betty Thomas; to Professor Meurig Wynn Thomas; to Gareth Williams; and to the people of Manafon, Eglwys Fach, and Aberdaron who talked to me. And to Graham Coster at Aurum, who had the nerve to commission the book.

Lastly, to someone without whom it would not have been written: to Andreas Gwydion Thomas.

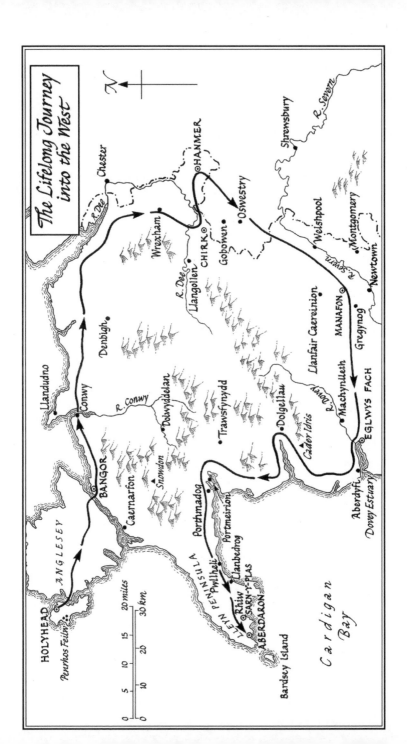

The Lifelong Journey into the West

Yes, I remember Ron Thomas, I remember him well. He was part of the background.

CASSIE JONES, classmate at Holyhead County School, 1925–31, and Victrix to his Victor Ludorum

INTRODUCTION

First there was the announcement in the classified columns of his local paper, of the sort that accompanies the passing of any man from a small rural community. It was brief, with no mention of who he was, and no initials, nothing except dates and places to distinguish him from the company in which he now found himself. 'THOMAS Ronald Stuart, died September 25th 2000. Funeral Friday September 29th. Strictly private at Pentrefelin Church. No flowers but donations if desired towards Pentrefelin Church.'

Distinguishing himself from his company had been one of his early concerns, before the poetry took care of everything. To his parents and the registrar he had been just Ronald Thomas; it was he in childhood who added the Stuart because of all the other Ronald Thomases who might be lurking in a Welsh playground, though his old friend the poet Raymond Garlick said he did it 'for euphony'. The initials came at Bangor because of all the Thomases hopeful of being included in the university's rugby Second XV. Or so he told me. What the effect on the poems, and on his reading public, might have been had he signed them Ron or Ronald Thomas is best left to psychologists. The novelist Emyr Humphreys once met a man in Penarth in South Wales who talked about a 'cousin Ronnie', though the shock of this erased all other details from Humphreys' mind.

But the mysterious beings who guard the frontiers of this world, or at least the obituary pages of the English broadsheet press, had no doubts. They accorded him the sort of space reserved for old film stars, or for those few Cabinet ministers, out of office, whose names people can still remember.

Seven-eighths of a page here, two-thirds there, in the *Times*, *Telegraph*, *Guardian*, *Independent*, so there was little room for anything else except birthdays. It was a day when Diane Abbott MP was forty-seven, and Alvin Stardust fifty-eight, when they honoured R.S. Thomas.

The strange thing was that from the headlines they seemed to be honouring different men. 'POET WHO HYMNED THE HILL-FARMERS OF NORTH WALES IN VERSE AS RUGGED AS THE TERRAIN IN WHICH THEY TENDED THEIR SHEEP.' That was *The Times*, though Thomas had never written about the farmers of North Wales, and for almost half a century had been silent on those of Mid-Wales.

'MISANTHROPE WHO CHAMPIONED THE WELSH PEOPLE AND LANGUAGE BUT WAS HIMSELF ONE OF THE FOREMOST POETS IN ENGLISH.' That was the *Telegraph,* blithely ignoring the fact that contempt for Welsh people who could no longer speak their language, that is, over 80 per cent of them, had been one of the themes of his poetry.

'RIDDLED WITH CONTRADICTIONS, HE CHARTED THE DECLINE OF MODERN LIFE AND HIS NATIVE WALES IN BLEAK POETRY, TINGED WITH FAINT SUNLIGHT.' That was the *Guardian*; alas, I wrote that obituary. But the *Independent* was on safe ground: for headline it had 'R.S. THOMAS'.

The *Telegraph* set the tone of the obituaries. From its first paragraph it was respectful, if bemused. Thomas 'was a fervent defender of Wales and the Welsh language – which made it odd that he should have been one of the best poets writing in English since the Second World War'. But it was the photographs most people would have remembered. The *Guardian* had him in his fifties posed grimly in a duffel coat against the ruins of a slate quarry (Philip Larkin was once called on by two photographers who had just visited R.S. Thomas, 'so naturally they thought I was marvellous'), but the others all used the same shot, which is one of the most remarkable portraits ever taken of a public figure.

Again in a duffel coat, but thirty years on now, gaunt and with a nimbus of wild, thinning hair, Thomas stands crouched, a huge creature cornered and about to spring, in the half-door of what appears to be the entry of a cave, his house at Sarn. It could be an illustration for one of the darker fairy tales. There is something identical, down to the half-door, to a one-eyed witch in one of Mary Tourtel's early Rupert stories in the 1930s, before Lord Beaverbrook intervened personally to stop her terrifying the readers of his *Daily Express*. As it was, the sub-editors must have thanked God for this, the *Telegraph* starting its caption with 'Thomas at home …'.

The obituary writers seemed even more delighted by the man glimpsed in his poems. The *Telegraph* with dry humour wrote, 'With a few odd exceptions – as in his poem "Suddenly" when he discerns the voice of God in a chainsaw – Thomas took headlong flight from the modern world.' But such comments must have raised more questions in readers than they answered. What was such a man doing in the late twentieth century, what had he been like?

For beyond the poems there must have been a life.

❧✝❧

In biography you do not often get a sense of what the man was like – not what he was like as a writer or a parent, but what he was like to *meet*. However many of his achievements get listed, however much of his life chronicled, friends' memories sorted, he does not walk and talk for you. For these are impressions formed in a moment, and moments get pressed down by the decades. Try to remember a dead parent, or someone you saw every day, and their outline is strangely indistinct. Think about it. The people you remember most vividly are those in whose lives you came and went. It was so with R.S. Thomas for me.

What follows is something I wrote thirty years ago. This was what he was like to meet on a March day in 1975 in

Aberdaron, when he was sixty-two years old. Think of it as a snapshot.

IT IS NOT a forthcoming entry, even for *Who's Who*. There is the name 'THOMAS, Ronald Stuart', followed by the reason for its inclusion among the major-generals and under-secretaries, 'poet'. A list of colleges, and another of church livings, follow; the books of poetry are indexed. Yet there is no record of parentage, marriage, fatherhood, not even a date of birth, and no recreations, in contrast to the blithely gardening, walking, fishing, motoring princes of his Church. *Who's Who* in fact will tell you marginally more about the private lives of Soviet politicians. But there is an address, 'The Vicarage, Aberdaron'.

It stands back from the road, above the village, and has to be the vicarage, being the biggest, bleakest house, its walls scaled with blue slates, a chain-mail against the gales from the Irish Sea. Wales ends here, at the headland which is the index finger of the Lleyn Peninsula pointing towards the island of Bardsey, graveyard of the saints.

The whole landscape has an embattled air, its few trees bent and stunted from the wind, to where, far below on the beach, earth-movers are being used to build a sea wall, the sea having encroached so much, the church, and its small graveyard, end, literally, at the beach. The church has no tower, its west wall facing the sea has no windows, and the trickle of houses beside it embouches onto the sea front. Man, you feel, is barely tolerated here, yet he has been for a long time. Thomas is the last in a recorded line of clergy dating back to 1291.

He is the first to hold the Queen's Gold Medal for Poetry. When his *Selected Poems 1946–68* appeared last year, his bemused publishers Hart-Davis MacGibbon found themselves reprinting within six weeks. 'This is quite amazing. We've never come across any of our poets being reprinted before, certainly not in six weeks.'

4

Yet with its seven electric fires straggling down the bare nave, its small slate gravestones sagging back like trees from the gales, the church of St Hywyn is not anyone's image of a poet's church. This is no place in a summer valley, no bland metaphysician's living: one cannot imagine George Herbert here, certainly not Herrick. Yet for Thomas it is all of a piece, for this is the church you would expect him to have, from the poems.

Too far for you to see
The fluke and the foot-rot and the fat maggot
Gnawing the skin from the small bones,
The sheep are grazing at Bwlch-y-Fedwen,
Arranged romantically in the usual manner
On a bleak background of bald stone.

I first met him fifteen years ago, when he held the living of Eglwys Fach, ten miles outside Aberystwyth: I was seventeen, and, briefly, a student at the university. The professor of English, Gwyn Jones, had suggested we meet, and Thomas had arranged tea in one of the hotels along the sea front. I was early, and as we had not met before I looked curiously at every passing clerical collar as the time approached. But in summer clerical collars gather like sea-gulls along the sea front at Aberystwyth. A plump parson with spectacles passed, and I hoped it wouldn't be him; when one is young there are quite definite ideas about how a poet should look. A cheery-looking man with a pipe passed. Not him either.

Then, bent a little against the wind a third man came, a very tall, lean athletic man, his face quite unlike any other I had ever seen. It had no spare flesh, so that afterwards I remembered cheek bones, forehead, chin; I did not remember lips. The face was hard, severe, almost predatory. In *Wuthering Heights* Heathcliff was posed beside Edgar Linton, the small soft friendly man of the valley: Thomas had the unnerving effect of making one feel like Edgar Linton. But the face was the face of the poems.

Acclaim for them came late. Thomas was forty-two before a London publisher brought out the collection *Song at the Year's Turning*, and even then felt the need to have John Betjeman write a preface. Betjeman wrote, 'The "name" which has the honour to introduce this fine poet to a wider public will be forgotten long before that of R.S. Thomas.' Since then his reputation had grown considerably. Kingsley Amis called him 'one of the half-dozen best poets now writing in English', and with the *Selected Poems* there was a bullish look about his stock, the *TLS* reviewer, hesitantly, beginning to use words like 'major poetry', and Professor C.B. Cox hailing a poet 'whose greatness is still not recognised'. Suddenly nobody was making the old charge any more, that Thomas was 'a limited poet'.

But it is easy to see why it was made. Thomas wrote obsessively about a way of life hardly anyone among his readers would have known, that of the hill-farmers in Mid-Wales. He wrote about religious faith when, for many, this seemed little more than whimsy. He attacked modern life, modern technology, the English encroaching into Wales, the Welsh responsible for the decline of their own culture and language. There was no comfort in his poetry, and no answers. The hill-farmer, at one point a cosmic symbol of endurance, was also greedy, joyless, physically repugnant: there was no pastoral. The absence of any answer was especially there in the religious poems, one of which, 'Earth', began,

What made us think
It was yours? Because it was signed
With your blood, God of battles?

Yet there was a grim compassion for the hill-farmer, the odd burst of lyricism when the poet was caught off guard by the beauty of the natural world, and very occasionally, like winter sunlight, moments of humour. But the tone of the poems was inevitably the bleak, comfortless, ruthlessly honest note Thomas had made his own. In spite of, or because of, this, there was a hardness about his rhythms and images that preserved him from the ranting and misanthropy into which some of his attitudes could have betrayed him.

As for the man, despite the enigmatic personal details lyric poetry compelled him to provide, he remained an intensely private figure. In twenty years of cuttings in the *Daily Telegraph* library files there was just one interview. 'It was difficult to talk to Mr Thomas,' a disgruntled reporter wrote. 'He makes it almost obsessively clear that he does not suffer fools, or foolish things, easily.'

Ronald Stuart Thomas is sixty-two. The son of a Merchant Navy officer, he was brought up in Holyhead, and educated at local schools and at Bangor University, where he read Latin. Married to the painter Elsi Eldridge, whom he met when he was a curate at Chirk and she an art teacher at Oswestry High School, they have one son, Gwydion, a lecturer at Ealing Technical College. He has held three livings, one at Manafon near the Welsh Border, one at Eglwys Fach, and the last, the most westerly of all, Aberdaron.

'I think I came here because of the sea. I'd written myself out of hill-farmers, and coming here brought me into contact with things just as elemental as them: you know, sea, sky, the wind, those sort of things.' The little joke hung in the air, there was no expression on his face.

'There are rocks out there on the headlands that are 6,000,000 years old. To see the sun casting your shadow on 6,000,000-year-old rocks ... drives you furiously to think, as they say.'

The house is cold, even austere. Cold pastels, pale waxed wood, the white skulls of sheep and dogs laid on a bleached oak chest, Miss Eldridge's pale fantasies in oil and water-colour, and, in one of the drawing rooms, the feathers and bodies of dead birds which both Thomases have picked up, and preserved, so a burglar might think himself in the house of a taxidermist with an artistic bent. In one of his poems Thomas had written about 'the strict palate' and 'the simple house', but after a half-hour of trying to be Heathcliff I asked if we might have the second bar of the electric fire. He smiled, which is to say his lips curved suddenly downward. 'My wife always says that people would freeze in our house.'

They do not entertain, nobody comes to visit ('That would create a major upset in our lives'). He takes no newspapers, there is no television. In the morning he reads: philosophy, and poets like Wallace Stevens (he once claimed to have read a poem by Wallace Stevens on every day of his adult life) and Yeats ('You have to make this admission, you couldn't write poetry without reading other poets'). In the afternoons he walks along the cliffs, birdwatching, the one great hobby of his life. In the 1960s he won some travel awards intended to widen the horizons of the recipients, only Thomas used them to go birdwatching in Spain and Sweden, and it was the first time he had been abroad ('After that I couldn't keep away. It's a good thing I can't afford to go now'). In the evenings he does his parish visiting. And so it has been all his adult life.

The loneliness is everywhere in the poems. Partly that of the priest in the lonely parish, cut off by his learning and his cloth, it is also the result of personal choice. 'I had one or two friends at Bangor, but we didn't keep in touch after. I haven't got any now. What is a friend, someone you see often? I can't afford to go sixty or seventy miles in a car to say "How do" … Don't say that, I'll have people coming to see me.'

There had been no personal influences on his life, no guiding schoolmaster or tutor; there seems to have been little contact with anyone who might be considered his peer. 'You might say I've just been unfortunate in my contacts. We never discussed poetry in my house, I never came under the influence of people who said, "You should read this." "'I'm

8

a self-made man,' said Mr Knickerbocker." It's been my disadvantage choosing this life, but I'd not have written the hill-farmer stuff if I hadn't.'

There was something enigmatic in his use of the initials of his name, was that deliberate? 'No, I think that dates from the rugby-club days at Bangor, there were quite a few Thomases in the team. They did call me Ron Thomas at theological college in the South, it was their way of being friendly.' At times Thomas can sound like a visitor to this planet, so the humour, when it comes, is disconcerting. 'Then ... then I moved North again.' How many called him by his Christian name now? 'One, perhaps two people.' The fantasy of there having been the possibility of the Rev. Ron Thomas swirled up, incredible as any St John saw coming out of the sea.

It is not the reserve, or coldness, of the man, though he is both reserved and cold, it is just the distance between you. The questions are answered politely, but the way a tired man might answer a child. There is no reason for the question, no value in its being answered, but the child has asked it so a reply comes. 'Journalism is such an unreal world, don't you think? All they'll want to know is what kind of socks he wears. Or they'll say, "Ah, he gave him a good jab there."' People, he assured me, were like that.

The effect all this has is quite amazing. The sense of the man's separation from himself, even from his talent, is such that I begin to think of the whole proceedings as fantasy; after all, why should I have come all this way to talk to a clergyman in late middle age at the end of Wales?

Knowing about the man is just another obsession of the silly modern world with its cult of personality. The poet, Thomas believes, *is* his poetry; all else is gossip and trivia. Delicately, wearily, this is impressed upon you, and with courtesy, as the child is made aware there are certain rooms not that it must not enter, but that it would not be worth its while entering. It is a formidable technique.

Yet it has to be part play, the vagueness about personal details is too deliberate. 'I have a car ... yes ... some sort of Mini.' A pause. 'A Clubman.' What did his son teach? 'I don't know ... Education, I think.' The holy island of Bardsey was bought recently by Lord Cowdray's heir: this caused a local furore. 'A Rolling Stone bought it,' said Thomas, who would have known exactly who had bought it.

Yet he has an interest in the cult of personality he deplores, only in him it seems anthropological. 'Is there a point when you start to embroider something in yourself? You're mixing with these people, you should know: is there a self-conscious strut?'

Attempts to prise some sort of personal detail from him he regards with amusement, having walked the perimeter of his mind too often not to know where the gaps come. Eventually we went on a tour of the house. More pastels, more white paint, no ornaments: Thomas gestured vaguely at the rooms, offering no explanation of their use, or occupancy. If I asked, he told me. 'Can you feel the poetry bounding out of the walls?' he asked slyly. A man who recently began a poem, 'Dear parents,/I forgive you my life', would not seem to invite questions about his personal life. Had he ever suppressed a poem because of its private detail?

'The mistake people make is that the "I" is you,' he said, patiently. 'No, I wouldn't keep it back if it's good. I don't like people knowing about me, but you're prepared to wear your heart upon your sleeve if it's any good. Everyone's prepared to make a sacrifice for great art.' The wintry smile again: it is sad, the round of adjectives Thomas forces one back on: bleak, hard ... wintry.

He decided early on to become a priest. 'At seventeen, I responded to the call.' His eyes lingered mockingly to see the reaction to this. It is difficult to reconcile some of his attitudes with his calling: they are Yeatsian attitudes, arrogant, aristocratic.

'I did a television broadcast about the Resurrection from the point of view of metaphor. I said it was all to do with language, the accounts of what happened were just what people *felt* had happened. It shocked some people, I had the odd pious letter. The butchers and bakers and candlestick-makers watch television, you shouldn't really do it. If you go on television you get people leering at you in shops.'

I remember thinking at the time that would make a lovely H.M. Bateman cartoon: the Rev. R.S. Thomas being leered at in shops. But had a tension ever arisen between the two callings?

'Sometimes. If you see a bird of prey, its great beauty and speed, how much more beautiful it is than its prey, how do you equate that with the God of love? You become very conscious of this out here. You see the savagery of a winter gale, or on a calm day under the placid surface of the sea you imagine the killers there like sharks, and then you go round bleating about brotherly love ... It's just not true what Ecclesiastes says, the race *is* to the swift.'

Did this affect his preaching? 'No, I'm not there to put my own views, I'm there to put the Church's views. I'm an honest parson, I don't push things at them. I like the challenge that puts upon one, to make sense of Christianity.'

It is when he talks about the modern world that the weariness, never far away, becomes marked. 'The quality of life is deteriorating everywhere. The Welsh Tourist Board goes on enticing more and more people here, the roads get widened, the character of the country gets knocked to hell. Paths that once led down to somewhere get so worn by the tread of human feet, they are no longer beautiful. I say to my wife, "All the places we've known, have any of the changes been for the better?"' He spoke very gently.

'There are little places I know along the cliffs here. Occasionally these creatures in bikinis come. Then I just pretend not to speak English.'

Weariness, and disgust, underline most of the poems in his most recent collection, *H'm*, probably the most strangely entitled volume in English poetry. To his dramatis personae of hill-farmers and chapel deacons he here added God, a cold figure baffled by his Creation. 'It's just souring old age, I suppose. My mother used to tell my father, "Haven't you a good word to say about anyone?" And I remember this one time, he stopped and thought about it. Then he said, "No."'

But it is when he touches on traditional human pre-occupations that he is at his most bleak. 'Happiness? I don't understand this matter of happiness. I find myself saying to couples when I marry them, "I hope you'll be happy." But it's too elusive and fleeting, I'm too honest to think anything remains the same.' He quoted Ceiriog, the Welsh poet. 'The places where I used to play, the people there no longer know me.' Life is something that has to be endured: if there are values they are in the enduring.

Curiously, he is a Welsh Nationalist to the lengths of not supporting the Welsh Nationalist party because it recognises Westminster. 'Britain doesn't exist for me, it's an abstraction forced on the Welsh people. I'm just critical of any country that belongs to another country.' He paused, then said mildly, 'Even a one-eyed country like this, that's lost its self-respect.' Yet his manners are not Welsh. The formality, the reserve, the tension these bring, are those of the English upper middle class. 'I'm quite different in Welsh, I'm told I'm warmer.' The thin lips curved downwards again. He learnt Welsh in his late twenties. 'My official explanation is that I learnt it to save the souls of the Welsh people.' His wife, from Surrey, does not speak the language, nor does his son, educated at English boarding schools and Oxford.

He admits to little curiosity about people. 'It sounds bad for a parson to say that, doesn't it? I'm slightly deaf to people, I hear the sounds of nature more.' Yet he is prepared to talk to those pilgrims who trek out to see him. 'I always answer letters, I had one from a girl in America who said I had a foul reputation about answering such things. Just meaningless, I've never failed to answer one. How many do I get? Oh, not many, about one or two a year. The big boys, Lowell, Ted Hughes, so the wise boys in London say, they must get many letters. I have lectured on my poems, I lectured a year last summer. Usually, I turn the invitations down.'

Disconcertingly the weariness extends to his own work. 'We're all much of a muchness today. There are about fifty to seventy contemporary poets capable of turning out the same sort of stuff. What I've always tried to produce is imagery, people don't give two hoots for that today.' He paused, he is given to pauses. 'As a result of this educational system we've got so many people now clamouring for attention.'

The winds were beginning to blow around the house. An old man in the village, who had pointed it out to me ('Oh, Mr Thomas, yes. Nice man. Very approachable'), had said there would be a gale. 'We get eight months of winter,' said Thomas proudly.

He got up. At sixty, he seems as athletic as men half his age. Then he said something I only remembered long after. It could not have been a slip of the tongue, Thomas is too careful with words for that. 'Let's have some lunch.' He was by the bookcase, his face away from me. 'You can answer the rest of your questions later.'

This appeared on 7 November 1975, in the *Daily Telegraph* magazine, which I had with some difficulty persuaded to commission it.

There were two things I did not mention. The first was the absence of Elsi Thomas. He apologised for this, saying the side effects of an operation for a thyroid condition had resulted in a swollen appearance, of which she was very conscious. The ill health that was to dog her for the rest of her life, and make her a recluse, had started.

The second thing was a question he asked as I was about to leave. We were standing by my car when he asked it. 'This journalism, Byron, what's it really like?' I said it could be an interesting life, but precarious: people got sacked, and disappeared as in Stalin's Russia. He nodded, and then said, 'That's one thing about the Church, it does take care of you.'

I did not mention these because they were things I did not wish to know. They suggested the vulnerability of a man of whom I was in awe.

Six days after the article's publication I got a letter, on headed notepaper and neatly stapled, from someone who had been one of his parishioners at Manafon. Cynric Mytton-Davies, son of a Dartmoor prison governor, was in the 1950s a reporter and columnist on the *Montgomeryshire County Times*, and a man with literary ambitions. Mytton-Davies had liked the article ('I enjoyed reading it because I found it so absolutely authentic'). He had not liked Thomas; in fact, as he put it, he could not stand the man. This is another snapshot, only in someone else's album.

He had known Thomas, Mytton-Davies said.

As well, that is, as most people were able to get to know him, for he was Rector of Manafon when I first came to live here, two miles away. That was in 1950, when he was as unknown a poet as I am. He called 'professionally' one evening shortly after our arrival, and hardly said a word all evening. I had to do all the talking. On discovering that he, like me, wrote poetry, I thought we might have something in common, but he completely froze on the subject ...

A few years later a poem of mine was included in the PEN Anthology, and I was invited to London to the publication party. I drove up, and outside Stratford on Avon I saw Thomas with his car on the grass verge and the bonnet up. Naturally I stopped and asked if he were in trouble. He replied with a cold, thin, bored 'No.' I said that seeing his car with the bonnet open I thought something might be wrong, and that I might be able to help or to get help for him. Again that thin, disdainful 'No.' I tried another friendly approach: 'I wonder if we are bound for the same place, the PEN party to launch their anthology?' From a great mental height he looked down at me and replied, 'I wouldn't go to such a thing.' That quite finished me. I drove off, leaving him there …

Yes, I can endorse everything you wrote … You brought him to life just as I found him, withdrawn, supercilious, disdainful, almost contemptuous; self-sufficient, and very much a show-off where the Welsh language is concerned (*plus royaliste que le roi*). He is a very cold fish, seemingly quite devoid of warmth and friendliness. I haven't seen him for years, and it won't break my heart if I never see him again …

About twenty years later, when I thought the dust might have cleared, I mentioned this roadside meeting to Thomas. 'I'm not usually that witty,' he said.

But at the time I was apprehensive. For how would he, someone who had been very kind to me when I was young, react? This was when things got really bizarre. I had, as promised, sent a copy to him, and I have his letter in front of me now, written in the usual wild hand. *And he too had liked the article* ('I admired the quality of the journalism').

Only he had started his letter like this. 'Dear Byron, Thank you for sending me your fantasy on the vicar of Aberdaron. If I were less extraverted I would be able to tell you how accurate it is …' You might like to read the last sentence again. I have been puzzling over that, and laughing at the deliberate irony, for thirty years. Thomas extraverted?

In the article I had described his face as 'hard, severe, almost predatory'. Thomas ended his letter, 'Yours sincerely, Nimrod.' Even as Nimrod the mighty hunter before the Lord …

The one effect of something welcomed as character assassination by someone who knew, and disliked him, had been to make its subject laugh. You may by now have some idea of the problems involved in writing this biography.

🌿✛🌿

Before I started on it, and was hesitating, I kept pestering Thomas's son Gwydion for 'papers'. What did I mean by 'papers'? Manuscripts, early drafts of poems. There were none. His father had written with a waste-paper basket beside him, and the fact that some poems survived at all was because his mother had retrieved and ironed them. Diaries, I said. His father had never kept a diary. Letters? Sold. Photographs? There were no photographs. All families, I muttered, had something.

I must have got under his skin, for one day I turned up at their last family home at Sarn, near Aberdaron, and there were four bulging plastic supermarket bags filled by his mother and stored in the attic. These were all that were left, he said, from her attempts to classify the universe. In one of these a bottle of air freshener had been spilt, so the unnatural reek of something called Forest Glade arose, of the sort that was never in any forest or glade, out of the strangest, and most poignant, collection of objects ever assembled. This was the personal archive of those two long and industrious lives.

Gwydion Thomas had compiled an inventory of just one bag. That, as he said, gave a pretty good insight into the home life of his parents.

The skull of a hare. An envelope from L. Garvin, Honey Merchants, containing grey mullet scales. A cheese box containing a puffin's beak, together with a Windsor and Newton leaflet containing advice on the control of moth damage to paint brushes. An envelope containing snow bunting feathers. A list of mills in Merionethshire. An envelope containing bits of old silver foil ('from Aunt Ethel').

Letter from Elsi Thomas to Ronald and Gwydion Thomas

on the subject of euthanasia. Copy of will. Envelope containing birth and marriage certificates. Envelope containing Gwydion Thomas's exam certificates. A book of phone numbers – containing *none*. An exercise book containing a hair prescription from a Dr Ferguson of Bromsgrove. An exercise book containing a list of paintings sold to Spink 1968–78.

Envelope containing grass seeds. Envelope containing an adder's skin. Poem 'The Betrothal' by RST, and photo of RST. *Queen* Christmas issue, 1968. Carol by RST. Large photo, sheep in a slate pen. Postcard of the Nanteos Cup. Letter to the AA (containing feathers). Envelope containing four-leaf clover from Manafon garden. Two copies of the *Daily Telegraph* magazine, 7 November 1975, Byron Rogers on RST, together with letter from Byron. So from somewhere they had got a second copy. Various brown envelopes (empty). Envelope containing a single dead prawn.

That was when I decided to write his biography.

Carmarthen, February 2006

ONE

The Makings

Shall I sonnet-sing you about myself?
Do I live in a house you would like to see?
Is it scant of gear, has it store of pelf?
Unlock my heart with a sonnet-key?

Invite the world, as my betters have done?
'Take notice: this building remains on view,
Its suites of reception every one,
Its private apartment and bedroom too;

For a ticket, apply to the Publisher.'
No: thanking the public I must decline.
A peep through my window, if folk prefer;
But, please you, no foot over threshold of mine!

ROBERT BROWNING, 'The House'

The singer has gone. Remember the songs.

RAYMOND GARLICK, poet and friend

A red flag flies over the lives of poets. In their lifetimes they resist the prospect of biography. In death they frustrate it. The biographer Peter Ackroyd was forbidden by the estate of T.S. Eliot to quote from the poet's correspondence or from his published work, 'except for purposes of fair comment in a critical context'. The life and the poems, like fissile material, must be kept apart. When the first selection of Wilfred Owen's poems appeared in 1920, their editor Siegfried Sassoon wrote that there should never be a biography. 'All that was strongest in Wilfred Owen survives in his poems; any superficial impressions of his personality, any records of his conversation, behaviour, or appearance, would be irrelevant and unseemly.'

It is as if they fear the life, the sheer ordinariness of experience, might diminish the art. The old Yeats, looking back over the splendours of his early verse, wrote in 'The Circus Animals' Desertion',

> Those masterful images because complete
> Grew in pure mind, but out of what began?
> A mound of refuse or the sweepings of a street,
> Old kettles, old bottles, and a broken can,
> Old iron, old bones, old rags, that raving slut
> Who keeps the till ...

But the life is the raw material out of which the poems come. Philip Larkin's long-suffering girlfriend Monica Jones told his biographer Andrew Motion, 'He cared a tenth as much about what happened around him as what was happening inside him.' The irony is that such a man, an intensely private individual, then wrote, often recklessly, about his own relationships, despairs, joy, and not within the decent obscurity of fiction but in the nakedness of poetry. And poetry, as Alan Bennett said, is a public-address system.

The more personal it is the more the poet goes to extremes when he faces the certainty that he will no longer be in control of its raw material. Larkin gave instructions in his will that his papers and diaries be shredded (also his copies of *Swish* and *Nasty Nymphos*, or whatever they were). Hardy burned his, and those of his first wife, but then had a brainwave. His first biography, by the second Mrs Hardy, appeared with remarkable speed, the first volume within months of his death, and it came with the imprimatur of being the authorised and definitive version. Only Hardy had taken one further pre-caution: he had written it himself, then burned the manu-script. The Hardys seem at the end to have had more bonfires than the retreating SS, the last being when the second burned the first Mrs Hardy's corsets.

R.S. Thomas had an even more complicated revenge on his future biographers. He wrote, not one, but four auto-biographies, if you count *The Year in Lleyn*, only he wrote the longest of these, *Neb*, 'Nobody', in the third person, referring to himself in turn as 'he' or 'the rector', then, like Caesar, as 'R.S.'. And, if this were not enough of a discouragement, he wrote it, and two others, in Welsh, which he always described as his second language, and into which most of his admirers could not, or would not, venture. His fourth attempt at auto-biography, *An Autobiographical Essay*, he wrote in English for the University of Arkansas.

And he wrote them in a very peculiar way. In 1972, in *Y Llwybrau Gynt*, 'The Paths Gone By', his first attempt at autobiography, he describes his marriage, a major event in anyone's life: 'Having been curate of Chirk, between Wrexham and Oswestry, for four years, I decided to get married.' And that is it. No background, not even a name. After those painstaking details about place and time, it is as though the future Mrs Thomas had been either recruited by mail order like a Frontier bride, or conjured out of flowers like the lady in the mediaeval Welsh fairy tale.

In *Neb*, thirteen years later, he is more forthcoming. His future bride, he reveals, also lived in Chirk (actually she lived just across the landing from him in the large house in which they both lodged, he in the nursery under a mural she had painted of angels tumbling out of heaven), and had a car (it was, of all things, an open-topped Bentley). And with that the window on his life again bangs to.

In 1994, R.S. Thomas not only refused to see his first biographer Justin Wintle, but told Marianne Macdonald of the

Independent on Sunday, 'I don't want fingers poked into my life. I don't know what they can unearth. I've never murdered anybody or robbed a bank.' His nervousness was understandable, given the fact that for over half a century he himself had been poking fingers into his own life. *I don't know what they can unearth ...*

It is probably just as well that he did not rob a bank. Had he done so, he might have written about it something like this: 'I had been vicar of Eglwys Fach for three years when, seeing the National Westminster bank in Carmarthen, twenty-three miles from Swansea, I went in, and robbed it.' The autobiographies, as his son says, are so curiously impersonal and unsentimental they seem to be a smokescreen around his life.

All right, the experience would have been there, somewhere, if only as metaphor, in the 1,500 poems; everything is there ... somewhere, for the man wrote nothing but autobiography. Some are startlingly honest, if oblique, so the effect, as Max Beerbohm said of Beau Brummell, is of a man looking life straight in the face out of the corners of his eyes. The prose and poem sequence *The Echoes Return Slow*, though in elaborate code, tells you more than you might like to know about his mother, his wife, himself.

His poetry turned on his life, probably more so than that of any contemporary poet, as the poet endlessly examined himself as human being, son, husband, father, Welshman, parson, Christian. Yet the man who did this in verse was at startling variance with the various Thomases some remembered. Compare Mytton-Davies's impressions with those of Jon Gower, arts correspondent for Radio Wales, who met the poet when he, Gower, was in his teens. He had met three very funny men, he said. One was Lenny Bruce, another was Ken Dodd. The third was R.S. Thomas. And now compare this with the Ogre of Wales, a name that stuck after the photograph appeared of the grim figure looking over the half-door. 'When they decide you are an ogre they find the right photograph,' said Thomas equably after I had told him that the man in the photograph looked off his rocker. I got the impression that he didn't mind this too much.

'My father had this public persona at which he worked long and hard all his life,' said Gwydion Thomas. 'If someone could reveal "the real R.S.", whoever that was, it would be a great achievement. Most of his critics were, and still are, lazy repeaters of the usual hoary commonplaces. My father was an actor.'

The prospect of writing the biography of such a man is, or was, as terrifying as it would have been for him. For few accounts of a modern life have had to be based so squarely on the testimonies of those who to some extent shared it, and from where I sit I can see three notebooks, the size of ledgers, which contain these. Biography is usually presented as a seamless narrative: with R.S. Thomas this could not be so.

But there was a life, and what follows is what made it possible in the first place for me to write about it.

These were the makings.

❧✢❧

'It was the most wonderfully bizarre thing. I was doing my Cambridge English finals, and it was Practical Criticism. And then I opened the paper.'

It was a May morning in 1977, of the sort that those who have known them never forget. They relive them over and over again, and not in memory but in nightmare, as the Welsh poet and academic W.J. Gruffydd did most of his life, and R.S. Thomas *'hyd nes ei fod yn ddyn canol oed ...'* ('Until he was a middle-aged man,' he recalled in *Neb*, 'he continued to have this dream about being compelled to sit an examination without having prepared for it'). Just like all the others in those night watches, reliving ...

The sense of entrapment, and despair, as age has its last

revenge on youth. Then silence, a huge arched silence broken by a cough which sets off a second and a third, then by the creaking of shoes as a man in a black gown walks up and down, up and down. And then for a moment, nearby, by the rasp of nylon, no more than a sigh, as some girl undergraduate in white blouse and black skirt crosses her legs.

So it was for me, and perhaps for you, this waste of time on a May morning. And so it might have been in 1977 for Sharon Young, from Luton, except that then she opened her Practical Criticism paper. What followed has probably never happened before in the public examination of English literature as an academic subject.

She was twenty-one, and completing three years of reading English at the University of Cambridge, an experience, she would say later, which left her unable to write a letter for years. Poems had been dissected, ironies and ambiguities explored, metaphors pegged out, all with practised rigour. For this was the home of Practical Criticism, where the only certainty was the words on the page. Anything else, the possibility that something, some experience, had led up to those words, and that someone, a creature of flesh and blood, had written them, was, they had been taught, the biographical fallacy. She began to read the first poem for analysis.

> Nineteen years now
> Under the same roof
> Eating our bread,
> Using the same air;
> Sighing, if one sighs,
> Meeting the other's
> Words with a look
> That thaws suspicion.
>
> Nineteen years now
> Sharing life's table.
> And not to be the first

To call the meal long
We balance it thoughtfully
On the tip of the tongue,
Careful to maintain
The strict palate.

Nineteen years now
Keeping simple house,
Opening the door
To friend and stranger;
Opening the womb
Softly to let enter
The one child
With his huge hunger.

'I must have said "Jesus Christ". I mean, when you're young the strangeness of life is commonplace, but this was beyond even that. *I knew the people that poem was about.* I even knew what they had for breakfast.

'At the time it was brazil nuts, eaten dry with a lot of vitamin B on them. And water, pints and pints of water. I knew they didn't speak at breakfast. And as for opening the door to strangers, it was very, very rarely people did visit, amazingly rarely in fact, and even then they were unwelcome. I remember the way the poet would say, "Oh, visitors." There was a dread of the knock at the door. For I knew the poet, not as a public figure, but as someone within the family.'

She knew the one child with his huge hunger best of all: she was living with him, and would later become his second wife.

It is the stuff of fantasy, which no writer of fiction would dare invent. Imagine Hardy's maid in an examination hall staring at 'Woman much missed, how you call to me, call to me', when she herself had lived through those terrible years at Max Gate and knew what things had been really like between Hardy and the 'woman much missed'.

But things were even worse for Sharon Young, small and pretty and just out of school, who had found herself part of a soap opera on her introduction to the family she was reading about. The poet, brooding on the collapse of his son's first marriage, had refused to talk to her and stormed out of the room into which she had been brought. This had stunned her.

'How could he have been so cross with someone he didn't know, and me so young? I was nineteen. His wife told me later that it had upset his view of himself, that he didn't want local people to know about me and his son. And these were the 1970s ...'

Later, when he had decided to talk to her, as her husband recorded in some autobiographical notes written for their son, 'He went into full *Wuthering Heights* mode, and took her off onto the edge of the cliff in a howling gale to try and deliver her a lecture on morals and the position of the Rector.' All this, she remembered, went through her mind that May morning.

'Even his appearance had been a shock. I'd always thought poets should have a more sensitive look, not that I'd met any. There weren't many poets around in Luton. And this man was rugged. He was still craggily good-looking then, he had this huge energy and held himself upright, with those very piercing eyes and that lovely bone structure.

'Also I knew the poems, I'd been reading them since I was fifteen. I thought them wonderful, which was why meeting him was so startling. It told me something about the mystery of art that I'd never been taught, what at that time I didn't even want to know, that some people had an ability to create work that was not of their personality at all. For a man with such personal difficulties to write such sublime poetry ... it was just as though something came through at times.'

But time was passing, and the question, she noted distractedly, was an important one, with forty-five minutes allocated for it. She was rescued by the Cambridge School of English.

'That was what made it even more bizarre, the fact that any intrusion of biography was then absolute anathema.'

So in the margins she carefully wrote 'Syntax', then 'Metaphor', then 'Imagery'. Thirty years on, Sharon Lunney, a death counsellor and careers adviser in Kew, cannot remember another word she wrote that May morning, except for a title and a name. The poem was 'Anniversary', the poet R.S. Thomas, later her father-in-law.

⋇

A Saturday afternoon in Kew, a day of rain and, for me, of long frantic attempts to find somewhere, anywhere, to park among the residents' spaces. Rhodri Thomas, R.S.'s grandson, a young City lawyer, and his mother Sharon were talking about the poet. Rhodri, a very tall young man ('I get that from him'), seemed more amused by the situation than anything.

'I did my course work on him for A level, it seemed a good idea to take advantage. I phoned him up and he seemed very surprised by the whole affair. I'd taken poems from his early, middle and later periods, so I asked him, "What are they about then?" I thought I knew, but I assumed I was on to a winner if I could write, "The poet said …" What *did* he say? I dunno, it was seven years ago, and it's been wiped off the computer. But I do remember that he was quite vague. Still I got $24\frac{1}{2}$ out of 25.'

This was the sort of access about which scholars can only dream. At poetry readings Thomas rarely answered questions.

'I liked him. I mean, he wasn't your ordinary grandpa, there was no hair towsing or anything like that. But it was always nice to see him, he was *so* different there were no parallels I could draw on. I remember him in his study, making forts out of books for me when I was three or four, so bang, I could knock them down. The idea of Lego and things like that must have completely baffled him, and he'd usually wander off, getting bored. Later, he'd play cricket with me, hitting massive sixes so that muggins had to go and find the tennis ball in the undergrowth. The cricket, that was pretty much every day, for there was no TV. And I think that was it, that was just about his whole contribution to family life.'

'Both of them liked the book dropping,' said his mother. 'There'd be roars of laughter, and, briefly, this mutual admiration society. But there was no understanding on R.S.'s part that this was a person, he found it difficult to focus on anything that wasn't himself. There'd been a truce between him and me as soon as Rhodri was on the way, but the only time he offered to take him out anywhere, Rhodri was two I think, he took him up the coast road from Sarn to fetch milk from the farm. He brought him back after five minutes. "I'm off now."'

'Didn't he buy a bow and arrow once?'

'Oh yes, and he must have tried it out in the garden by aiming at a rabbit. For he hit the rabbit. He was contrite for months after that.'

'I'm not sure he ever did find out how to do the family interaction thing,' says Rhodri Thomas. 'But he tried, he tried quite hard. He used to send me lots of books about birds, for he had this idea that every boy should have a hobby. Took me on one of the six-mile walks he went on every afternoon. Every afternoon. I was bored senseless. When I was a bit older there'd be pontoon. Huge stakes, three matches the maximum bet. And if things were very festive, the Sanatogen would come out.

'The last time I met him was at a hotel near Bangor. That was just a few months before his death, when he was banging into things in his car. I had a girlfriend with me, and he did his best, his best not to frighten her, that is.' Rhodri Thomas burst out laughing.

The people at school always knew he was my grandfather, for there'd be a new collection of poems and I'd be suddenly flush. 'Where did the cash come from?' 'Grandpa's poems.' He was very generous with royalties. I always called him Grandpa, though he tried very hard, signing cards "Taid", the Welsh for granddad, but it never caught on. You know, I never heard him speak Welsh, and he never brought it up with me. His accent was very English.'

His mother said, 'We'd have these slightly veiled conversations about what was going on when the Meibion Glyndwr were burning cottages. He'd put this big sign up, "CARTREF R.S. THOMAS". R.S. Thomas's home. That was because he didn't trust them to be that well organised, and didn't want his own house burned down. Elsi, my mother-in-law, put a sign up in the garden, "DANGER, POISONOUS SNAKES".'

'She was very sweet, my grandmother,' said Rhodri. 'Until I was eight I used to have her bed at Sarn, but then I saw her climbing this rickety ladder to the attic and I thought, this can't go on. She was very small. I was bigger than her when I was ten.'

'She was just like a little bird,' said his mother. 'With me and R.S., there was an absence of a relationship, but I think Elsi grew fond of me. If I could get her quietly on her own there'd be long fireside chats. She understood R.S. inside out, and he wasn't completely clueless about her, but to him women were from another part of the universe. One of the things she couldn't understand was that he was completely uninterested in her as a painter, so there was a whole area of her he ignored. She complained about that, not in a bitter way, more "bloody typical". She used to call him the Big Bo Bear. But she was very fond of Rhodri, she'd bring him things. Once she brought him a dead vole.'

'Just before a meal. Traumatised the crap out of me. She was always bringing sheep skulls and dead birds in. And knitting things for me. And every Christmas there'd be a card with these bespoke drawings of animals on it.'

His mother broke in. 'As for my father-in-law, he never

talked to me, he didn't know how, though occasionally he'd talk *at* me, usually about Kierkegaard or something, which was his usual idea of after-dinner talk. It wasn't necessary to him to know who, or what, Gwydion was, or who I was. But sometimes he and Elsi, they'd get on a roll and there'd be reminiscences, usually about Manafon. Then they'd get slightly snidey, and be very happy together. There were times when I warmed to him, he had such a lovely sense of humour and of mockery, he could bring down pomposity, even his own on occasion. He was fond of denigrating the well-known, and himself. It was he who coined "famous Seamus", long before Heaney got the Nobel Prize. About himself he was very disparaging. "Oh, it's all going in the bin." And he'd actually write his poems with a waste-paper basket beside him.

'I heard him say once when someone was coming to see him, "This nice middle-aged woman is coming 300 miles just to see the great man." And when she'd gone he said, "Fancy her going round with a hair-cut that showed her ears." I had this very strong feeling that he was ashamed of the humbleness of his upbringing, and had this desire to rise in the world, though he would never have admitted to it. He was a snob, he worried about how to behave and took a lot of notice of the old school. I think he'd have liked to have had Nancy Mitford as a sister. But he never understood himself, though he thought about himself all the time.

'He and Elsi had this very odd imposed way of behaviour. "We're both very nice middle-class artists, and I'm a vicar." It was impossible to be relaxed about them, they weren't normal, they wouldn't allow themselves to be relaxed. So there were these huge silences. And all those unspoken feelings, what they were, God only knows. But small talk was vulgar. And a lot of life is vulgar. So being with them was very odd, for life is about the mundane. When they came here we tried to make things as comfortable as we could for them, for we knew they didn't like London. We used to take them to Kew Gardens, and

I'd make queen cakes for them. He loved buns. He loved fudge too, which he used to make himself, but after she died that stopped.'

'D'you remember, he used to make toffee? Real tooth-breaking stuff,' said Rhodri. 'What did I inherit from my grandfather? The solitariness, I like to be alone every now and then. But he liked being alone all the time. Beyond that, nothing. Me, I'm a city boy, I like clubs and taxis at five in the morning. You don't get too many of them on the Lleyn. When I was small, North Wales was north of beyond, and that house, Sarn, was so craggy compared to Barton Road, Luton.'

'It was bitterly cold there,' said Sharon Lunney. 'They had central heating put in, but then they pulled it out.'

'*They pulled the central heating out?*'

'Oh yes, Elsi didn't like the way the radiators looked.'

When his mother was out of hearing Rhodri Thomas said that there was one thing about Sarn, it did have a powerful effect on young women. A bit like Wuthering Heights really. He grinned.

'You know, if you wanted to, you could make this a real tale of giggles. I mean, there was my father. He wasn't at all the sort of son R.S. wanted. R.S. would have liked someone who played Swallows and Amazons all the time, and didn't go near girls until he was thirty, when he'd meet one and marry her immediately. And it didn't turn out like that …'

❧✛❧

There was something that must have been a cause for speculation for those reading the *Telegraph* obituary that September morning in 2000. There was nothing exceptional about it, it was the house style of the newspaper to end its obituaries so. 'He married first, in 1936, Mildred Eldridge, an artist; they had a son.' But here, in context, the little statement, always poignant, became fascinating. For he was already a public figure, this child of the poems.

When I was a child and the soft flesh was forming
Quietly as snow on the bare boughs of bone,
My father brought me trout from the green river
From whose chill lips the water song has flown.

Dull grew their eyes, the beautiful blithe garland
Of stipples faded, as light shocked the brain:
They were the first sweet sacrifice I tasted,
A young god, ignorant of the blood's stain.

'Song for Gwydion'

This was the small child in his beauty. In other poems there were glimpses of the growing boy, as in this from *The Echoes Return Slow*.

He was sometimes a bad boy,
slovenly, vain, dishonest.
Yet I remember his lips
how they were soft and

wet, when I kissed him
goodnight, and a shadow
moving away from the bed's
head, that might have been God's.

What had it been like to be the child of the poems? The question was answered in 2004, when the magazine *New Welsh Review* published an interview with Gwydion Thomas by Prof. Walford Davies of Aberystwyth. R.S.'s autobiographies had revealed little personal detail: this did, only it was not what the poet's admirers may have wanted to hear. It was the first time his son had gone on record.

From the very beginning ('You will recall my father late in life airily claiming that he never knew what I did, or where I was, both of which of course were quite untrue') R.S. Thomas is presented as a bizarre figure ('[He] said he could smell evil when he used to get off the train in London. I rather like the smell ...'), a man self-obsessed and indifferent to anyone other than himself ('He was possessed of that most irritating ability to be at once overbearingly opinionated and unflinchingly irresponsible'). This was a startling portrait, most startling to those who had actually known Thomas. The poet Raymond Garlick, one of his oldest friends, said, 'I should be very sad if my own son wrote about me like that.'

Gwydion Thomas's replies were based on a long testament he had already felt obliged to put on record for his own son ('to let him understand why our family is so barmy'), and were the first glimpse of the inside of that guarded little world out of which the poems came.

'I went to see him once, at Eglwys Fach. I knew he was in.' There was a small mischievous pause as Raymond Garlick remembered the moment. 'There was a chain across the gate.'

Rhodri Thomas, for whom it was written, put his father's testament away unread in a drawer, and two years on had still not opened it. 'I'm afraid there'll be too much character assassination.'

For in the course of his interview Gwydion Thomas said of the Wintle biography written without the cooperation of R.S., 'I cannot conceive how he thought there was any point in writing the book without speaking to me. R.S, and others, may not have relished his project; I might have transformed it.'

They had a son.

⚜

KRAKKKK.

That was the first rabbit. I opened the shotgun, and pulled the cartridge out: it must count as one of the strangest starts to any biographical quest.

33

I was at Sarn, the cottage on the cliffs of the Lleyn Peninsula to which his parents retired, to meet Gwydion Thomas, and to talk about the possibility of this book. As he is his father's literary executor it all turned on him, otherwise there would have been no quotation from the poems. A college lecturer who took early retirement, he now lives in Thailand with his third wife, a Thai woman, and the two were in Britain for an emergency major operation on their two-year-old daughter. This had been a success, the worry which had hung over them for most of her short life had gone, so Gwydion had been left with the two secondary concerns of his middle age. One was the threat of a road to replace the one along the coast that had collapsed: this was planned to tear through the woodland above Sarn. The other was rabbits.

They were unhurriedly eating their way through his mother's small kitchen plot. He had tried everything, even buying a mail-order Chinese air rifle, but there were so many rabbits that the doorstep above which R.S. had posed for the photograph was often filled with their small, curious faces. Which was when Gwydion Thomas on the telephone to me had become suddenly fascinated by biography: the would-be Boswell had a shotgun.

KRAKKK. And that was the second rabbit. In the carrot rows the survivors moved over the corpse and resumed eating.

'I can't go on with this, it's a massacre.'

The last time I had seen him was forty years ago. I was waiting at the bus-stop with his father at Eglwys Fach near Aberystwyth, when a small athletic shape on a bicycle came out of nowhere, going like the wind. He grinned at us, so I turned to Thomas and asked who that was. 'Gwydion,' he said, the way someone might refer to some minor natural disaster. Home for the holidays from his English boarding school, he was a very good-looking boy then, with golden hair. When very young, he must have been like a small god, as his father duly noted in his 'Song for Gwydion'.

'Only I can't remember him catching the trout,' said Gwydion Thomas. 'That was my grandfather Tommy, when he stayed with us at Manafon.'

Now a bald, thick-set man in a black singlet, he looked like an off-duty bouncer, and his eyes, like theirs, were never still. Actually, which was even more disconcerting, they glittered.

'Why do you want to write this book?'

'Your father was kind to me when I was young.'

'Oh dear.'

You must think of what follows as the family photo-album which, in the case of the Thomas family, does not exist. 'I am not in the business of being the Keeper of the Holy Grail,' he said quietly at the outset. Like the Ancient Mariner, the son had a tale to tell.

This was the long grief of Gwydion Thomas in the house called Sarn.

When I was eight years old my parents sent me to boarding school in England. We were living in Manafon, which was a very special place for me. I grew up in a house without electricity, a place of freezing fog, which in summer burst into life, and there were hayfields with curlews and lapwings' eggs. Mine was a magical childhood. And they sent me away.

Imagine it, being told to piss off for twelve weeks at a time, and they didn't even have the excuse that my father had gone away to school, or his father before him. This was a boy from Holyhead doing it to his son. At the time they told me it was because I didn't have any friends. I had lots of friends. Later R.S. talked about the unsuitability of the boys I was growing up with, and then in his autobiography about the unsuitability of the schools. But by the time we'd moved to Eglwys Fach there were some very suitable schools, even some in Aberystwyth teaching through the medium of Welsh, which he never once tried to teach me.

I kept at him and there was the time when he actually said, 'If you hadn't gone away we wouldn't have had the time to write and paint.' With my parents it wasn't just the pram in the hall which was the enemy of promise. My parents didn't want the pram anywhere in the house. Someone had to pay the price for tramping round those cold vicarages with those two leading the high artistic life. The only thing was, I paid it.

Later things became nastier. 'Why did you send me to that fucking school?' I used to throw it up at him all the time. 'Oh, you were bored in Manafon, and you would never have gone to Oxford.' But it did get to 'Your mother wouldn't have had the time.' '*So it was a bad mistake to have had a child.*' I really used to go for the jugular. 'Oh no.' My mother would go quiet at that point. R.S. was the problem, but he was quite upset by it, he didn't want emotion in his life, and I never gave up throwing it at him.

I don't know why he did it. My mother had to teach so they could afford the fees, and the result must have been a great disappointment to him. He writes about me being deceitful in some poem, but I told him deceit was the only way to survive in an English boarding school. Think of the terror at eight of not being able to read Virgil. At eight years old.

As he talked he was moving about with his small daughter in his arms. At one point, still carrying her, still talking, he prepared, and served, a full Thai meal of five or six dishes. I have always considered myself a good short-order cook, but I had never encountered one like him before. And all the time the monologue continued.

I've thought about this a lot, and the only explanation I've been able to come up with was that R.S. was a snob. My grandmother Peggy, she wasn't posh, she'd been brought

up by clergy, and my grandfather, the seaman Tommy, he
certainly wasn't posh. But R.S. was reinventing himself as
an English gentleman.

He tried to invent himself as other things later, like a
Welsh nationalist, but he went too far with that one. He
taught himself Welsh, but such an academic Welsh he
found he couldn't talk to most Welshmen. I know he
believed he was bound hand and foot by the English
language, but basically he was an English vicar in a Welsh
parish. Psychologically he could never be Welsh, I think he
was obsessed by class. Those friends they had at Eglwys
Fach ... sorry, acquaintances, they were a colonial society
with him as padre, I don't know why they didn't have a
club.

The Welsh connections he said in his autobiography that
he was building, he was never close to them. He said he
knew the Welsh poet Waldo Williams and the novelist
Islwyn Ffowc Elis, but they never came to supper. In later
life it was mostly local Welsh people who came to Sarn. And
R.S. would wander round their houses, boring people.
Wherever there was a pretty woman or a small child or a
cat, they bore the full brunt of R.S. Welsh, he said, made
him garrulous. When he was at Manafon he used to jump
behind hedges to avoid his parishioners. At Aberdaron I
suspect they used to jump behind hedges to avoid him.

And now he's like apple pie in Wales. It was one of those
lucky strokes in life that he espoused those causes that have
become national orthodoxy, like the language, housing, the
environment. That happened in the 1980s, but if he was so
keen on the language why didn't he try to teach it to me?
There was no Welsh at home, and my mother's attitude to
Welsh nationalism was that if it made him happy, then let
it. It was very much his own journey. I even think he
would have been even happier had there been nobody at all
waiting for him on the other side.

What he'd have said if my mother had learned the
language, I don't know. She did try once, she even bought a
book with various scenarios. The first was 'The Kleeneeze
man calls.' The second was 'The Kleeneeze man in the
bedroom.' She said, 'Well if that's the kind of people they
are then I want nothing to do with them.' When she did try
to speak it R.S. said with disgust, 'Elsi, you sound just like a
South Walian.' And him with all his people from South
Wales, not that we met any of them. In his lifetime I never
met any of his relations.

There were no Christmas cards or anything like that. He
wrote that my grandfather had been one of eleven, so there
had to be uncles, but the story I was told was that they'd all
died, mostly at sea. When a cousin turned up at R.S.'s
funeral, that was the first time I'd met her. Tony Brown
from the R.S. Thomas Study Centre at Bangor University
heard from somebody in South Wales, so there was this
photograph of R.S. and my mother quite possibly on their
wedding day. That was the first time I'd seen it, we hardly
had any photographs at home. Other people come on their
parents' wedding photos in family albums; I was shown
mine by a research institute.

'I'm not a family man,' he'd say. All I can think of is that
those uncles and cousins, they'd have got in the way of the
persona he was building. Here, you don't think he killed
the bloody lot off, do you? No, he couldn't change a plug.

Elsi had a brother, she had a perfectly normal family, so I
have a first cousin whom I still see. Elsi's brother, who
worked for an insurance company, he used to come and stay;
he was the only one I can remember doing so, apart from my
grandparents. R.S. would make fun of him as he used to
have to rush home whenever they went for a walk because
he couldn't pee in fields. R.S. was a great pee-er in fields.

One thing I was grateful for, he never made me read the
Bible. God, like Welsh, was off-limits in our house, my

mother'd start to yawn. But as the vicar's son I was obliged
to attend church and to listen him drone on about the evils
of fridges.

'Fridges?' And for a few moments there was a bizarre
pantomime interlude. 'He didn't?'

'Oh yes, he did, it was the Machine, you see,' said Gwydion
Thomas, letting all emotion drain out of his voice to imitate his
father's voice.

And washing machines. And televisions. This to a
congregation most of whom didn't have any of these things
and were longing for them.

We did have a vacuum cleaner once when we were at
Eglwys Fach. It was ordered from away, and stood for a
week at Glandyfi station until someone delivered it.
Eventually it got switched on. 'Hm, makes a lot of noise,
doesn't it?' And that was the end of the vacuum cleaner.
There were rolls of dust like fleece under the furniture in
our house, in rooms painted sage green, the colour of wilted
lettuce.

He was talking, partly in the garden at Sarn above the long
curve of the bay, partly inside the house, which, even on a
summer's day, was cold.

When they came here my mother did have a fridge, but it
was only the size of a ledger. Ronald would boil tea towels
in a bucket on the fire, there was no TV, no papers. No
friends either, everyone was held at arm's length. You
know, I can't remember him ringing anyone up, and if they
rang him … 'Can I come to see you?' 'When?' 'Next
month ….' 'Sorry, I've got an engagement.' But he did
write letters. There were a lot he wrote to a sick lady in
Manchester, which were sent back to me after her death.

They were all the same, 'I hope you're feeling better. It's very cold here. Saw a blackbird yesterday.' Hundreds of letters, I sold them for a great deal of money.

Elsi did get out of the house. She did extramural classes, driving to Aberystwyth and even New Quay. But as for R.S. he followed an absolutely rigid routine, day after day, decade after decade. Eight o'clock, breakfast. At one point it was baked beans, but that changed. Then he'd disappear, 'to study', as he put it. Reading and writing. He was an autodidact, you must remember, totally alone. And he wrote every day. In time that mounts up.

That's why he was so surprised to find there were over 1,000 in the *Collected Poems*, I don't think it had ever dawned on him how many there were. He used to say, 'I'm a lyric poet, and the inspiration has dried up.' Then he'd write 500 more. He wrote on his knees on torn-up bits of paper and notebooks, sitting at an old desk, a waste-paper basket at his feet. His whole life was crammed into that desk, and when it got too full things got crammed into a suitcase. He wrote quickly and rarely corrected what he'd written, there were very few crossings out. Almost all was done in his head. But he used to throw manuscripts away, and next morning my mother would retrieve them from the waste-paper basket and iron them out.

So it went on, day after day. Eleven a.m., bread and cheese. Then more reading and writing. In the afternoons he'd fiddle about with the grass, at one stage he had a scythe. Then from five to eight he'd visit the sick. Eight o'clock, supper. Ten, bed. Apart from the visits to the sick, he was a very idle priest. He was almost incapable of being with other people.

'I don't care if nobody reads my poems.' 'What are you publishing them for then?' 'H'm.' It was always 'H'm.' Elsi used to say, 'If he had a bad review he'd be cross as a bat for days.' From the start he used to give me the books as they appeared, but I didn't read them then. For long periods I didn't want the cadences of his voice within my head. I couldn't get away from the voice, I didn't want it there. I started reading them when I was selling books in the early eighties. *Stones of the Field* was fetching between £500 to £600 even then. *H'm*, which appeared in a very small edition, that's fetching a lot now. But I never read them when I was young. I never read anything by him. You could say I discovered him in my forties.

His *Collected Poems* was my idea. He was moaning at me, 'I've been mooching ...' Mooching was a favourite word of his, it was what he did, wandering about, always on his own. 'I was mooching around a bookseller's in Bangor and saw a big hole in the Ts, except for Charles Tomlinson. I don't care.' Like hell. So I said it would be a good idea to bring out the *Collected Poems,* to keep what I thought were the decent poems in print. 'You go ahead then.' And that was that, it took me the best part of a year. I remember thinking, it's going to be a problem if I listen to him, he'll want to weight it towards the later stuff. I've never liked those, especially the ones with God in them. When I'd finished I asked him, 'Do you want to see it?' He said, 'No.' And he never mentioned it to me from that day to this.

But there was a posh limited edition, which he agreed to sign. I brought the copies to him. 'This is the book I made for you.' He said, 'H'm.' Whether he thought he was being funny, I don't know. Never thanked me. When the second royalty cheque came I said, 'Mind if I have half?' 'No, no, help yourself.'

He was very odd about money. He was overdrawn once, and Elsi said, 'He'll kill himself.' When I was at university he insisted on going through my bank accounts each term. Once I had an overdraft. 'You are a *debt-or*.' At the same time he could be very generous. He gave me money towards a house, he helped with Rhodri's education.

But what fascinated me, doing the book, was the way he had suddenly discovered his voice. One moment there'd been this romantic Fiona MacLeod stuff, and the next there's *The Stones of the Field*. And it starts to happen at the time of his marriage, something made him grow up. He'd met a brain, a slightly bizarre brain, but well read, much more so than him in the early days.

Elsi introduced him to a whole range of poets, Chesterton, Belloc, whom of course she'd met. Hardy. The Edward Thomas books in our house, they were her books. She was also well informed about Eric Gill, and the Arts and Crafts Movement. There weren't many people she hadn't heard of, but there were enormous gaps in his reading. He used to say, 'I've never knowingly read an English novel.' When I found out that Thomas Love Peacock had married the daughter of the vicar of Eglwys Fach I went on to read all his books, R.S. didn't.

'When she met him my mother was rising thirty, four years older than he was. She was quite eccentrically dressed, she loved long waisted skirts of red flannel, shirts Hamlet might have worn, and great black cloaks. She'd knocked about a bit, she'd been to the Royal College of Art where she'd won the Prix de Rome travelling scholarship, she'd moved in quite exalted circles. And she had this open-topped Bentley of all things; her father, a jeweller, was not badly off. She and a woman friend went off to Scotland in it, having put olive oil on their faces as a sun cream. At the end they had to chip the stuff off.

My mother was a small, tough woman, she had the most amazing hands, very slender but incredibly strong. She loved gardens and could transform the tips they found in those vicarages. She was this odd mixture of sensibility and ruthlessness. When the coast road below Sarn was collapsing she was at the council's throats with letters, she knew what she was up to. R.S. would have been hopeless.

He wouldn't have been able to cope with the road, he would have issued a single statement, thinking everyone would agree, then nothing. He couldn't deal with a bishop, let alone a committee. He was unable to argue, he was much less formidable than people thought, and very nervous in public, even in preaching. He had this way of sweeping his hand back from his left eye to his hair. It was a nervousness about poise.

Quite what she saw in him I don't know, probably someone romantic and polite. There would have been lots of opening of doors. And he had all these dreams of living on islands, which would have appealed to Elsi. At one stage he actually thought of giving everything up to live as a farmer on an island, and him a man who was even more cack-handed and incompetent than 'Leave it to me, Peg. Crash', his father Tommy, whose life was a series of DIY disasters. If I am a victim, I am a victim of other people's dreams.

One of the odd things is that since he's died I've had to think about him a lot, so there's a greater familiarity than we ever had. When I think about him at Manafon, say, he was just a bloody nuisance, he'd sent me away to school at which he then turned up in terrible cars. Such things matter in boarding schools.

By Eglwys Fach we hardly ever spoke. I'd got this girlfriend who was at the local sec mod, and he said three things. 'She's a village girl. I can't have you canoodling with her, I'm the vicar.' Then, 'You don't know the family.' Another time, 'Do you take her in your arms?' Yet much later he used to write to her.

When I was older there was a sort of little ritual. Before Sunday lunch he'd have a glass of the elderflower sherry my mother'd made and he'd talk at me for twenty minutes, a bit like the Mekon coming down to tell one what life was like on Venus. But the things I wanted to know about he wouldn't discuss, like whether his father Tommy had

43

screwed girls in every port. 'Oh, I suppose he was a man of the world.' 'What does that mean, yes?' 'I don't know.'

I did try to have literary conversations with him. I'd leave books around the house for him to find, and then he'd tell me that Randall Jarrell was 'unsatisfactory'. And that was it. All you'd get from him about himself was that he was no good. As for his contemporaries, his disregard for them was absolute, apart from Geoffrey Hill and bits of Ted Hughes. The rest might have been writing for Christmas cards.

Why didn't he read more? He had this extraordinary Stalinist approach, there were all these books he just *wouldn't* read. And if something got a review, that ruled it out altogether. Yet he'd trawl Pwllheli public library looking for things to read, and his choices were very odd, books about penguins and whales. I used to drop little bundles of books outside his room, then he'd read them, and when I went back to university my mother would say she'd found him crawling up the stairs to fish books out of my room. I gave him the mediaeval history *Montaillou*, he was very fond of that.

I don't remember him without affection, but what was he *for*? I never asked him for advice about anything. I mean, given his life, what did he know about? Elsi'd been around, but she was a bit dated. But him I'd never ask, like should I take this job, what did he think? A week before I married my first wife he told me he thought I was making a big mistake. I said that was a fine time to be telling me. He said, 'I thought you knew.'

He wasn't a dour monster, he could be very boyish and funny. He loved reading my comics. But he was so shy as to be impenetrable. That autobiography he wrote in Welsh, *Neb*, 'Nobody'. What utter nonsense that was, him with a wife and child. And parents. And grandparents. I couldn't read it until the translation appeared, and he never read that himself. All that sentimentality and in the third person, it was his way of shedding responsibility. He didn't mention at the end being shut up here with my mother with her feet in a cardboard box. I am very cross about that. My mother hadn't a clue. By then she was very ill.

Poetry was all right, there he could spend all his time exploring his odd nature. He blamed his knotted-up personality on his mother, and whatever had happened, she seemed to have caused him a lot of trouble, or at least he thought she had.

Peggy and Tommy used to take R.S. on holiday, and on arrival she used to give the landlady an envelope of money. 'When that's spent, we'll leave.' He hadn't liked that. He used to say that people like us didn't go on holiday, to which my mother would say, 'You're on holiday all the time.' We went to the Shetlands once, that well-known tourist destination. Why? For the birds, it was always for the birds. We stayed at a guest-house and every morning the landlady would ask, dragging out the vowels, 'Prunes or fruit juice?' And every morning R.S. would say, 'Neither, madam.' It passed into our family folklore. But while we were there Elsi's father died and she had to fly home, leaving me and him to the boiled mince until he could stagger out into a gale again. I was about twelve then.

Oh yes, and once we went to Norfolk, to Ickling in the middle of nowhere. R.S. spent the week trying to track bearded tits down in a swamp. Elsi found a dead mouse and painted it. But somehow R.S. met the local vicar, who told him, 'Oy married a 'Ickling girl.' Which also passed into our family folklore. Did anything make him sit up? Oh yes. Susan Griffiths, my girlfriend at Eglwys Fach, she made him sit up. And, later, all the other girls.

You can view him as a very lonely man struggling to make contact with those he loved, and failing, sometimes wantonly. Or you can turn it on its head by saying that was a very damaged man who tried to father by numbers. Then you feel sorry for him, and it's very peculiar to feel that. But I don't feel that sorry, if he hadn't been like that he wouldn't have been the poet. It was just that my mother knew what she was taking on, I didn't. Sometimes I blame her. No, not really, her illnesses were such a tragedy. I remember a letter in 1971, 'today I feel almost wholly better'.

His letters to me were a series of pronouncements, usually of birds he'd seen. He was a man incapable of love, and full of love, so with him it came roaring out. He tried to be an honourable man, but he was so fucked-up he found this difficult. He found let-outs in birdwatching and in the discipline of being a priest, but when it came to the rub-along of domestic life, he couldn't do it.

His small daughter still in his arms, Gwydion went on,

The closest we ever got to physical intimacy was when I was small, and he used to take me to school on the bar of his bike. There is a photograph of me on a swing and him behind me, but if you see it you will notice we are not touching. I only saw him touch my mother once, and that was a hand on the shoulder.

But there was pandemonium when she died. I'd only just come back to London from Sarn, and he rang me. 'She's gone, she's gone.' I told him I was coming up the next day, but when I got there he said, 'What have you come for? She's gone.'

There were a couple of very tense days, I remember he drove his car into walls several times. On the second night he talked a lot. He talked and talked, about himself mainly, and how he'd met her, and how illness had robbed her of her talent. Then he stopped and said, 'Oh well, we'll bury her tomorrow, and then you can go back to work.'

Later I told him, 'Why wouldn't you allow me to

grieve?' He said, 'What do you mean?' I said, 'Simple things, like when I got home my wife Sharon asked, "How do you feel?"' With him there was none of that, it was as though for him I didn't exist. I was very cross, but that only made him clam up even more. I said, 'She was my mum, I'm upset about it too. I miss her.' All he said was 'H'm.' I thought, this man is so damaged, there's no point. But it must have cut him to the quick.

He had, I noticed, referred to Elsi Thomas throughout as 'Elsi' or 'my mother' or 'mum', sometimes with amusement, always with affection. With his father there was a point when I asked, had he anything nice to say about him? It was like that question Thomas's own mother had asked his father. Gwydion Thomas also thought about it, then said, 'He was my dad, you only have one. I have respect for him, I'm pleased that he was very good at what he attempted to be.' 'My dad' ... it was the only time he had referred to him as anything other than 'R.S.' or, in lighter moments, 'Ronald'. In the sudden silence he went on, 'But why you are you asking me all these things?'

'Because you were *there*.'

'Only just.'

The other moment came after he produced the four plastic supermarket bags. In one I found a little children's picture-book called *Gwenno the Goat*, published in 1956, the illustrations by his mother, but the text, he told me, by R.S., though never acknowledged by him. 'It was a warm, sunny afternoon in May when Gwenno the little black and white goat opened a smoky blue eye on the world ...'

There was also the 1973 application for petrol by R.S. during the Yom Kippur War under regulations prepared but not implemented. He estimates his weekly mileage. 'Three churches to be served on Sundays, 25 miles. Other visits for funerals, sick and other visits, 40 miles. Say one visit a month to hospitals in Bangor and Caernarfon, 80 miles.'

There were notes for sermons. 'Day at hand. What better? To be [*sic*] in God everything.' Letters to his son, businesslike and brief, but with a faint humour breaking through. This in 1988:

My dear Gwydion,

Mummy said you wanted these statements from Macmillan. I enclose the Equity and Law payment for this quarter. The goshawk is still around. I think I am the only one who hasn't seen it by now. The Welsh crisis deepens as the English pour in week by week. But I have the Welsh Office's assurance that my comments on it have been noted.

Much love, Tad.

There was a letter from a Japanese admirer.

Dear Mr R.S. Thomas,

You often use 'machine', the image of idol, it seems, which is connected with science and civilisation. As you know, Japan is one of the leading 'machine' countries in the world. The machine is tremendously influencing the Japanese way of life and thinking. They can't live a single day without depending upon it, for which I am very sorry. Is Wales being machinized like Japan? I wonder.

Yours . . .

But there were no diaries, no photo albums, nothing to remind one this had once been a family. There was so little: a single photograph from the 1940s of the boy Gwydion in the swing, being watched by his unsmiling father in a cassock, some crumpled manuscripts, clearly ironed out, some of Elsi Thomas's paintings of small creatures, all of them bristling with life, a copy of Dylan Thomas's poem 'Do not go gentle into that good night', written out in R.S.'s hand, even though he had so often, and publicly, decried the man's work. And over everything the awful air-freshener smell.

And then I found the manuscript of a poem headed 'July 5, 1940', also in R.S. Thomas's hand, but with the letters smaller and rounded, the writing of a young man.

'What happened on July 5th, 1940?'

'That was the day they got married. Where did you find that?'

'In a bag.'

Unpublished by the poet, this is R.S. Thomas to his wife on their wedding day, and kept by her:

Nought I could give today
Would half compare
With the long-treasured riches that somewhere
In the deep heart are stored –
Cloud and the moon and mist and the whole hoard
Of frail, white-bubbling stars,
And the cool blessing,
Like moth or wind caressing,
Of the fair, fresh rain-dipped flowers.
And all the spells of the sea, and the new green
Of moss and fern and bracken
Before their youth is stricken,
The thoughts of the trees at eventide, the hush
In the dark corn at morning,
And the wish
In your own heart still but dawning,
All of these,
A soft weight on your hands,
I would give now;
And lastly myself made clean
And white as the wave-washed sand,
If I knew how.

It is not a good poem. In fact, with its long catalogue of

words and its literary archaisms, it is quite bad. It is also a straight lift from Edward Thomas's poem to his own wife, 'And You, Helen', which R.S. was later to include in his Faber selection from Thomas's work. This begins, 'And you, Helen, what should I give you?' and ends, after a far more unusual, far more personal, catalogue of gifts,

> And myself, too, if I could find
> Where it lay hidden, and it proved kind.

No matter. Bad poems about the intimate moments of life can be moving, not for what they are, but for what they represent (you have only to look at the inscriptions on wreaths and in the deaths columns of newspapers to see the very human abyss between words and the event).

But remarkably the man who wrote that would, within the next six years, be capable of writing:

> The church stands, built from the river stone,
> Brittle with light, as though a breath could shatter
> Its slender frame.

and, even more remarkably, this:

> Dreams clustering thick on his sallow skull,
> Dark as curls, he comes, ambling with his cattle
> From the starved pastures.

Many very young men (though Thomas was twenty-seven) could have written the wedding poem; only one could have written the others. The gap between them is as abrupt as that between the poems Wilfred Owen was writing at the start of the Great War and those he wrote at the end; but by then, as he himself wrote, he had been through the battle of Beaumont Hamel.

'Have you got anything else like this?' I asked Gwydion Thomas.

'No, that's it.'

But then he changed his mind. Some weeks later he phoned me. 'Ring this number,' he said.

※✢※

Call him the Collector, he does not want his name mentioned. It took months to set up a meeting, in the course of which there were many excuses.

'My house is in a terrible mess.'

'Oh, I won't mind.'

'You don't understand, I might want to sell it one day.'

A low room in a small cottage in the main street of a Home Counties village, with books everywhere, books on tables, on chairs, on the floor. And where no books were there were magazines, and manuscripts, and the only thing missing was furniture. That must have been around somewhere, forced beneath this weight of print, perhaps fossilised. Through this there moved a man attached by tubing to an oxygen machine, for the Collector was in poor health. It left the impression of an astronaut in an archive among the stars, which in its way was appropriate. Images of space will recur in this book.

Until then, in the absence of personal papers, I had begun to conduct what seemed to be an infinite number of personal interviews. Given Thomas's long life, most of these were with people who had known him towards the end of it, and were respectful of the great man. The few who had known the boy and the undergraduate came much later. I called on their houses, read the letters he had sent them (though he had kept none of theirs), walked through his churches, sat in the National Library of Wales copying out in pencil, as instructed by the regulations, the guarded short letters in that increasingly familiar longhand, sat in others where they didn't mind what you used, copying out poems in long-defunct magazines he had preferred to forget. I read the oddly impersonal hand-written autobiography of the woman to whom he was married for over fifty years, in which he is mainly an odd sort of hunter-gatherer, bringing back flowers and skulls for her to paint. But in all this there was no sign of the man behind the mask, nothing of the vulnerability I had glimpsed briefly, and nothing at all of him in his beginnings.

It had been a bit like a space probe in science fiction. There had been evidence of a personal life, its small details, its beginnings, but even talking to his son and grandson I had begun to despair of ever finding the home planet. And then, on a hot summer afternoon, I came on it, or rather, I came on its remains assembled on shelves. It was all here.

The first editions were here, the rarest of all, the books printed by small provincial presses, one of them above a chip shop in Carmarthen. And not just one or two, but four, five, six copies, each of which would fetch upwards of what? God alone knows, for these books were those the poet had given his wife, his son, his parents.

His first published book, *Stones of the Field*, that from the chip shop which housed the Druid Press. 'Elsi, *gyda'm holl gariad*, Ronald, *Nadolig* 1946'. Elsi, with all my love, Ronald, Christmas 1946. *Song at the Year's Turning*, Rupert Hart-Davis, his first English publisher. 'Elsi, *gyda'm holl gariad*, 1955.' *Poetry for Supper*. 'With love to my mother and father, from Ronald 1958.' *Pieta*. 'To my mother with love.' The beautiful *Laboratories of the Spirit* bound as the author's edition in coloured leather patterns by the Gregynog Press, and dedicated to the poet's son.

And that was just the beginning, for we were going back, beyond publication, to the typescript of *Spindrift, Poems and Prose Poems*, written around 1940, and bound in a dog-eared exercise-book cover, with an address, Bryn Coed, Chirk, N. Wales. There was no name on the cover, and nothing at all, apart from the address, which was where the curate had lodged, to associate it with R.S. Thomas.

These poems were amazing, with phrases like 'fragile elfin boats', and couplets like 'Beauty was born when a little wave/Lost himself in a dark sea cave.' There was a love poem, horribly fluent.

I never thought in this poor world to find
Another who had loved the things I love,
The wind, the trees, the cloud-swept sky above;
One who was beautiful and grave and kind,
Who struck no discord in my dreaming mind,
Content to live with silence as a cloak
About her every thought, or, if she spoke,
Her gentle voice was music on the wind.
And then about the ending of a day
In early spring, when the soft western breezes
Had chased the melancholy clouds afar,
As up a little hill I took my way,
I found you all alone upon your knees,
Your face uplifted, to the evening star.

This was a very romantic young man. There was a letter addressed to a 'Miss M.E. Eldridge' at Chirk, with a small yellowing photograph of a wild sea and, written on the back, 'NB. Welsh hills like shadows on the horizon.' The Welsh hills, as he reveals in his autobiographies, were very much on his mind in Chirk. On the envelope were two stamps, a halfpenny Edward VIII and a George V penny.

Moving back even further in time, there were bookplates from when he was a boy, inscribed, 'If found, dead, stolen or strayed, my address is Ronald Stuart Thomas, Kimla, Garth Road, Holyhead.' With these were some caricatures of a startling, even professional, quality. One was a perfect copy of Thomas Henry's drawings of William Brown from the books by Richmal Crompton, another of an old man with just one tooth in his head. It was extraordinary; Thomas as a boy had been a better draughtsman than many newspaper cartoonists in their pomp, but he seems never to have drawn again.

These were in a bundle which also contained a newspaper photograph of a rugby team made up of vicars from the area around Wrexham. Thomas, an unsmiling, hard-looking figure, is one of them, and the only one who looks as though he means business. There is no date, but an accompanying news paragraph refers to Hore-Belisha as Minister of Transport, so it would have been sometime between 1934 and 1937.

There were many letters. By the 1960s the famous write, writing to a man by then already famous himself, the Poet Laureate John Masefield to offer him the Queen's Medal for Poetry in 1964. But there were other, much earlier, letters, written at what was clearly a moment of crisis in Thomas's own life. On 21 June 1941, the great Scottish naturalist Frank, later Sir Frank, Fraser Darling writes from the Isle of Tanera, Ross and Cromarty. He and his wife were then farming there, in a place so remote that when people landed the two hid from them. In his letter Darling is a worried man, as anyone might be who in the middle of a world war has just had a letter from a Welsh vicar intent on becoming Robinson Crusoe, this in the interests of better birdwatching.

> What can you do with your hands? If you cannot use them in a score of different ways you could not live this kind of life at all. I should advise you to work for a year on a farm in a hard country such as Wales or the High Peak if you really intended burning your boats. But I cannot encourage you to do anything so rash as that, for in the first place you have a high calling which you must follow without backsliding. A man of God must think of that first ...

A day later Hitler invaded Russia. Thomas's letter does not

survive, but it is clear that, though newly married, he had contemplated throwing up his parish and was looking for his own island. It is an odd comment on his attitude to his calling at the time, and Darling was sufficiently disturbed to write four long pages in reply. He ends his letter: 'It is immoral and you know it. You must have a burning enthusiasm to DO, in coming to some such place as this, not merely a desire to get away from where you are ...'

So small islands were out, but the idea of doing a runner did not go away, it never did. On 11 September 1941, Seamus O'Sullivan, editor of the *Dublin Magazine*, writes in answer to what has clearly been a despairing letter from one of his newest contributors.

> From anything I have been able to learn about the present situation of the Protestant Church in Ireland, I am strongly of the opinion that it would be extremely unwise for you to make any change at the moment. A great many of the churches throughout Ireland – both in city and country districts – have been shut ... I am sorry that I cannot give you more heartening news, but I think you would really be well-advised to retain your present position for the time being.

The island of his dreams remained, it had just become bigger.

But it is O'Sullivan's last sentence which stops you in your tracks: 'You would, I fear, find that you would be more of an exile in the West of Ireland than in Wales.' This, presumably picking up on one of Thomas's own phrases, was addressed to the man whom many would come to regard as the national poet of Wales, and whose countrymen would enter him for the Nobel Prize.

The irony is that, thirty-seven years later in 1978, Thomas was writing similar letters himself, this time to his own son. 'Stuffy as it sounds you can't really escape. So you have to become absorbed in something so that it doesn't much matter where you are, so long as you can do it ...' It was then I saw the address from which that letter was written. Cape Clear Bird Observatory, Skibbereen, something too bizarre for comic invention, and I found myself reading the last sentence aloud in wonder. 'Thoughts like this go through my mind as I wander round when there are no birds to be seen.'

Time passed, and, now a great man, he was himself the light attracting moths, replying to those who had written to him as he had once written to others. 'It was nice of you to send me your play and the enclosures. Let me know if you want your play back ...' An ordinary letter from Thomas, perhaps declining some invitation, now fetches something like £100. Most invitations were declined.

'I got interested in him when his book *H'm* swam into my ken,' said the Collector. 'What a bloody stupid title, I thought, what sort of man could have chosen that? So I began to read him, and there were these incredibly deep poems constructed out of such ordinary language and so few lines. They seemed to me quite magical. So I became a collector. I had one great advantage.

'I am a bookseller by profession, and my interest in him coincided with what I suppose was a lull in the market for his books in the 1970s. So many of his books came into my hands, with nobody to sell them to, and that was when I thought to myself, I will keep these for myself. And I kept adding to them. At this stage my collection consisted of just basic copies, but then something extraordinary happened. I met his son Gwydion.

'That was when I realised the scale of what might be on offer. If I'd had a similar opportunity with another poet I'd have jumped at it, just to keep everything together, which might otherwise have been dispersed to the four winds. But in this case I got into financial difficulties, just keeping up.'

It was all here: manuscripts of poems, from their creases rescued from the waste-paper basket by his wife, and her drawings of him, bearded in one, and, earlier still, wild-haired and sharp-featured like a demon. On shelves and in files a life was opening in front of me, and I was so bemused by the scale of what I'd seen that I rang Gwydion Thomas. I just couldn't believe he had parted with all this.

The one-time young god, ignorant of the blood's stain, was in no way abashed. 'When we first met I asked the Collector what he would like. "Everything," he said.

'And that's what he got … *everything*.'

❧ TWO ❧

Holyhead:
The Journey Begins

It was Holyhead itself that made me what little of a
poet I am, a horrible little town with a glorious
expanse of cliff and coastal scenery. I shall never
outgrow my hiraeth [homesickness] for it.

R.S. THOMAS in a letter to Raymond Garlick,
24 January 1952

Beyond Anglesey is another island, at least on maps there is.
But where there were fords there are road and rail causeways
now, the high barriers around which remove all sense of a
crossing, so you can come and go and not know that you have
been on Holy Island. Yet all Wales is here, in this one place, the
late Lloyd Hughes, the former town clerk and brother of the
Cabinet minister Lord Cledwyn, once told me. It is just that it
is in miniature, as though some celestial estate agent were
inviting you to examine the model for a proposed country.
Mountain and moorland, beaches and small farms and the
inevitable ugly town, Holyhead.

Who first began
That refuse: time's waste
Growing at the edge
Of the clean sea?

'Sailors' Hospital'

But he knew the answer.

Cybi, or Kebius, for this was the early sixth century and a time of the old inflected British language, was a British, or Welsh, saint from Cornwall, when almost all Britain was British or Welsh, the two being the same thing. It was the barbarians who called the inhabitants of these islands the Welsh, a term variously interpreted as strangers or those who had been part of the Roman world. These barbarians, the English, were then just an irritating immigrant presence in the east, to escape whom was the ambition of any cultivated man, just as 1,500 years on it became that of R.S. Thomas. For just as Holy Island was a model of Wales, so his own life was a model for the distant past of his race.

It was here in the sixth century on Holy Island, where he could escape no further, that Cybi established the monastic community that eventually became Holyhead. He was one of those shadowy saints, sons of the ruling class, who wandered Wales in the ruins of the Roman Empire, planting religious communities on land given them by some local warlord with a wary eye on the newly explained hereafter. Outside these the tents and hovels of those attracted to such settlements became towns. The Welsh name for Holyhead is Caergybi, Cybi's Fort, an address R.S. Thomas used when he lived nearby in later life, happily confusing English Post Office sorters and those journalists who interviewed him.

There had been an old Roman fort on the island, and it is this that yanks the story out of folklore into history. It was given to the saint by Maelgwn the Tall, ruler of most of North Wales and one of the ten or so men we can name in the darkness of sixth-century Britain. Lecher, homicide and failed priest, Maelgwn had more reason than most to keep in with saints.

We know this because of the cleric Gildas, another of the ten, and the one writer whose work survives from that time. Without him all would be myth and genealogy; with him it became unbroken rant. Gildas did not like Maelgwn, but then

Gildas did not like any of his contemporaries. Out of that otherwise total silence the one voice howls abuse; his country-men he excoriated as Godless and cowardly, their leaders he denounced, and as for the English, their immigration turning to invasion, *as for the English* ...

'I always feel a certain sympathy with Gildas,' wrote R.S. Thomas in a letter to Raymond Garlick in 1954, and it must be the only time in 1,500 years that anyone has.

But by then Caergybi had long been Holyhead, the old name trodden down by the feet of English-speaking strangers. For most of its modern history the town has turned on strangers, ever since it stopped being the end of the world and became the port for Dublin, somewhere on the way to somewhere else. People lingered only when the sea prevented the ferries sailing, whereupon they cursed the town, and its hotels. In 1727 Jonathan Swift, on his way to his Dublin deanery, saw far more than he ever wanted to see again of Caergybi.

> Lo, here I sit at holy head,
> With muddy ale and mouldy bread;
> I'm fastened both by wind and tide,
> I see the ships at anchor ride.
> All Christian vittals stink of fish,
> I'm where my enemies would wish.

Delay and menus apart, the trouble was that he did not consider he was being shown proper respect. 'I come from being used like an emperor to being worse than a dog in Holyhead.'

R.S. Thomas, another clergyman, faced a similar problem. Fresh from his identification with Gildas, he wrote in the same letter, 'A man once said to my father when he arrived at Holyhead, "Be friendly with all, intimate with none." Sound advice. That man was not Welsh. You will not find it easy to keep your dignity among a Welsh community.' Which, given the dogma of his adult life, makes odd reading.

In 1994, in his eighties and living on Anglesey, he was interviewed by the journalist Marianne Macdonald.

As we leave to drive to Holyhead he sees us off with the friend who is staying with him. 'Terrible place,' he spits. 'Fourteen thousand people jammed on a rock.' His friend says, 'Oh, it's rather nice.' Thomas stands there grimly, his body shaking in vehement contradiction, saying nothing. 'You can turn left for Cemaes,' he tells us stubbornly. 'Or right – for Hell.'

Cemaes is a village to the north of the island, Hell is Holyhead, and R.S. Thomas was playing out his last role.

Growing up there in the 1920s must have been grim, for a town that turned on strangers was at the mercy of strangers. Any ripple of distant economic forces and political events could become a tidal wave breaking on the town. The founding of the Irish Free State in 1922 brought customs barriers and a loss of trade, and there was competition with other British ports for what remained.

Men with master's certificates took what jobs they could, as did R.S. Thomas's own father, who once had the whole world to cross under sail, and now became a second mate on the ferries, sailing back and fore to Ireland, back and fore; others became seamen. And these were the lucky ones. By the 1930s almost half of Holyhead's working male population was unemployed. I can remember my shock in 1968 at being given this figure by Lloyd Hughes. Though the numbers involved were far less, in scale this was more than Jarrow, only nobody marched from Holyhead. There was nothing they could do, except wait, for there were no other jobs, and no possibility of them. As late as 1967, of the town's twenty-one councillors, sixteen worked or had worked in shipping or on trains. And now even that is over.

The new car ferries are still there, so huge that, at anchor, they dwarf the town, but the Irish Sea itself has become a mere detail of geography, being part of the E22 Euroroute between Dublin and Sassnitz on the Baltic. Holyhead has become an incident on an arterial way: great roads tear through it from the dockside and across Anglesey, so no one need linger any more. Always bleak, it is now an irrelevance.

The chapels crouched among the terraces have closed, which once were so many and so big, it was said that had you been able to roof over all Holyhead you would have had a single Methodist chapel. It was a place, a journalist wrote, where pebbledash had come to die. Apart from the phone boxes and the people, everything is pebbledashed in Holyhead.

❧✢❧

And it was here that the five-year-old Ronald Thomas came with his parents in 1919, to a house called Kimla in Garth Road, when his father got a job with the LMS Railway Company. Kimla is of course pebbledashed.

'I remember the day we arrived: a dark wet day in December. Is there any town worse than Holyhead on a day like that? The taxi took us along the bare streets to our lodgings, with me staring despondently through the windows of the car,' he recalls in the short prose memoir *The Paths Gone By*. He wrote this in Welsh, a language he was not able to speak that wet December day.

Neither, seemingly, were his parents, though this would not have made them that unusual in the town. In E.G. Bowen's *Wales: A Study in Geography and History* a 1931 map of the distribution of the Welsh language shows a large monoglot English-speaking population in Holyhead, just as there was around that other railway terminus and port, Fishguard. Yet both were bordered by an almost entirely Welsh-speaking hinterland. It was when Thomas got to the county or grammar school, with its intake from that hinterland, that the fact that he had no Welsh at all became the reason one of his classmates remembered him.

He would be an outsider all his life. There would be the loneliness of a priest in a parish, of an Anglican priest in an overwhelmingly Nonconformist Wales, and of the poet longing to, and unable to, write in Welsh, and thus doomed to stand outside an adored tradition like a tramp at Christmas. What I hadn't realised was that even in childhood he didn't belong anywhere.

He came to supper one night when he was in his eighties and my family and I were staying on Anglesey, and at some point launched into a catalogue of his pet hates, which sometimes passed as small-talk with him in old age. That night they included (in addition to those hardy perennials the English) red sandstone and Jack Russells, there being a Jack Russell in the room. 'Is there *anything* you like, Ronald?' asked his second wife Betty. But he wasn't done. To my irritation he then launched into an attack on the South Wales Welsh, who had lost their language and their national traditions. I reminded him they had lost far more than that. Beached by industrial decline in their valleys, they were like some huge whale that was beginning to rot. But for him three-quarters of the population had to be written off. *And these were the people from whom he came.*

He was born in Cardiff on 29 March 1913, and his ancestors on both sides were from South Wales, from Merthyr and Mountain Ash, all with a background of coal-mining and pits. He refers to this in his usual oblique way in 'The Boy's Tale'. The subject is his mother,

> a girl from the tip
> Sheer coal dust
> The blue in her veins ...

This background, or any background at all, will come as a

shock to those of his admirers who are under the impression that this was a man who had stalked fully grown out of a cromlech on the moors of North Wales.

Only it gets stranger. On his father's side, a great-grandfather had actually *owned* a coal mine, having sunk the first deep pit in South Wales in partnership with the great industrialist David Davies of Llandinam, whose country house in Mid-Wales R.S. Thomas would get to know well. There was an air, he said in one of his rare references to his family (in an interview in the Welsh arts magazine *Planet* in April 1990), of the Thomases having come down in the world.

His grandfather James Thomas had accelerated this process by taking to drink, a problem he solved in the simplest way by buying a large pub in West Wales. From the windows of this, the Porth Hotel at Llandyssul, when wrestling with his problem, he would throw money down to passers-by in the street. Only R.S. Thomas did not tell *Planet* this, saying only that James had died young, leaving a widow to bring up eleven young children on next to nothing. This figure is probably wrong; his first cousin Ian Cameron, a Port Talbot solicitor, said there were eight children, four boys and four girls.

But his father Tommy, according to Thomas, had happy childhood memories of Llandyssul. In his autobiography, *Neb*, he wrote that his father as a boy had fished in the River Teify, his back against a gravestone, and may even have spoken Welsh during his time there. The note is wistful, for by then those things mattered. It is an insight into his attitude to his family that he had never asked whether this was so, and Tommy had not told him.

In his poem 'Relations' R.S. Thomas reflects, distant as an astronomer, on a world that, given those eleven or eight children, must still have been full of his uncles and aunts. Its opening may explain why his own son Gwydion met none of them:

An ordinary lot:
The sons dwindling from a rich
Father to a house in a terrace
And furniture of the cheap sort;
The daughters respectable, marrying
Approved husbands with clean shoes
And collars; as though dullness
And nonentity's quietness
Were virtues after the crazed ways
Of that huge man, their father, buying himself
Smiles, sailing his paper money
From windows of the Welsh hotel
He had purchased to drown in drink.

But one of them was drowned
Honourably. A tale has come down
From rescuers, forced to lie off
By the breakers, of men lined up
At the rail as the ship foundered,
Smoking their pipes and bantering. And he
Was of their company; his tobacco
Stings my eyes, who am ordinary too.

Uncle Edmund Thomas, younger brother to R.S.'s father, according to Ian Cameron, his nephew and R.S.'s first cousin, had drowned at sea in 1912; Cameron remembered this because it had made his own parents postpone their wedding for six months. Three of the four brothers were in the Merchant Navy, Tommy the eldest son having been sent to sea in 1898, aged sixteen, as an apprentice in sailing ships to help his widowed mother, Mary.

In his *Planet* interview Thomas mentions his widowed grandmother and says that as a boy he had stayed with her on Wandsworth Common in London. But then she, like her family the Mileses, was Welsh-speaking. His own mother, he says, had had nothing to do with the Mileses for this reason. He himself seems to have approved of them even more when his cousin Gwyn got a cricket Blue at Oxford, and bowled out Bradman. His cousin Bethan Miles, formerly a university lecturer in music at Aberystwyth, remembers Thomas in adult life calling on her parents in the town, but though Eglwys Fach was just ten miles away Gwydion Thomas cannot even remember the family. He met Bethan Miles for the first time at his father's funeral.

On the Thomases he is even more vague, even though Ian Cameron said his parents and those of R.S. were close. 'When my father died in 1963, it was Tommy and Peggy who came to Swansea to stay with my mother. After several days nothing had been heard from Ronald, my mother's nephew, but then a letter of condolence arrived. "Ronald has written – thank God," said Peggy Thomas.' R.S. would often tell his son, 'I am not a family man.'

To put this in context, the Welsh are, and seem to have always been, fascinated by their families. When I visit my cousins I just call on them, unlike the middle-class English who need to make appointments by telephone: it is the custom. But when in 1974 Ian Cameron, whose wife had just died, called in Aberdaron on his cousin Ronald, whom he had not seen in forty years, his reception, he said delicately, was disconcerting. Ronald was making jelly, and his wife, who was painting, came in with two brushes in her hands which she did not put down once during his visit.

Seated at table –
no need for the fracture
of the room's silence; noiselessly
they conversed. Thoughts mingling
were lit up, gold
particles in the mind's stream.

'He and She'

Family photographs of the Thomas family are about as rare
as portraits of Shakespeare, and I am staring at the two which
have survived of R.S.'s father, Thomas Hubert Thomas, called
Tommy Twice. I have been staring at these so long I feel I
know the man. The corners of his mouth are turned down, just
like those of his son would be at his age. He looks straight at
the camera, a fag in the corner of his mouth in one photograph,
a tall, tough man, with a straightforward, even a humorous,
look to him. In the other, the two rings of his second mate's
rank on his sleeve, he looks wary, as though he already knows
the fate that awaits him.

This fate is to be called in poem after poem as the chief
witness for the prosecution in his son's long case against his
mother. The case for the defence will never be heard. The
incidents of his sea-faring life will bob up as part of that
prosecution case, for his son hero-worshipped him. There was
the fall from the rigging off the coast of Romania, followed by
eighteen weeks on his back in hospital cared for by nurses
with whom he had not a syllable of speech in common. In *Neb*
R.S. Thomas appears to ascribe this to his grandfather, but it is
clear from the poem 'Salt' that it was Tommy. A shipwreck off
Argentina, and the drifting in an open boat for seven days,
became one of his finest poems, 'The Survivors'.

> But on the sixth day towards evening
> A bird passed. No one slept that night;
> The boat had become an ear
> Straining for the desired thunder
> Of the wrecked waves. It was dawn when it came,
> Ominous as the big guns
> Of enemy shores. The men cheered it.
> From the swell's rise one of them saw the ruins
> Of all that sea, where a lean horseman
> Rode towards them and with a rope
> Galloped them up on to the curt sand.

Would Tommy Thomas have appreciated the craft of that? The last adjective 'curt' is so perfect it makes the rest of the poem turn about it, this abrupt and prosaic moment of safety after the infinite anxieties of the previous days. It would be nice to think so, it would have meant a lot to his boy.

In *Autobiographical Essay* R.S. mentions his father's reaction to a letter he wrote home when he was a curate in Chirk. This, a lyrical description of a long walk in the Ceiriog Valley, must have startled Tommy, for he said the boy would become a poet. Ronald records this with wry pride, for though a poem by him had by then appeared in the *Dublin Magazine*, this recognition was different, it came from his father. But God alone knows what Tommy would have made of the other poems.

> My father was a passionate man,
> Wrecked after leaving the sea
> In her love's shallows.

> 'Ap Huw's Testament'

For most of his life R.S. Thomas brooded on the relationship between his parents, returning to this obsessively in his poems, and to his own part in it. 'I was the bait/That became cargo', 'the young tool in their hands/for hurting one another'. For him there were two victims, his father and himself.

> 'The hard love I had at her small breasts;
> the tight fists that pummelled me;
> the thin mouth with its teeth clenched
> on a memory.' Are all women
> like this? He said so, that man,
> my father, who had tasted their lips'
> vinegar ...

> 'Salt'

On his father's behalf in the next verse the metaphors reach an almost comic crescendo of hysteria, as he writes about the sailor in retirement.

> rejected
> by the barrenness of his wife's
> coasts, by the wind's bitterness
> off her heart.

We were out walking on Anglesey when Thomas brought the matter up, I hadn't asked him about it. You don't with a man in his eighties. His second wife, he told me, had said he shouldn't run his mother down in this way. 'But I don't consider I am running her down. I just let the pen go where it wants. I suppose the really important chaps, like Yeats, they were elusive, they didn't give much away. But I have been a parson, I do tend to labour the point.' He seemed amused by it, and grinned when he said he had put an inscription in Welsh on the tomb of his parents, a language neither spoke in adulthood.

I suppose I should have asked him more, for no parent, not even Stalin, has been castigated so relentlessly in print as Margaret Thomas of Kimla, Garth Road. Her son's poems leave you with the impression that the great monster of the twentieth century was not someone who looked down from Lenin's tomb, but the Holyhead housewife known as Peg, of whom just one photograph survives, and then only because her nephew kept it.

Among her in-laws crowded into some small front room, permed and in a twin-set, arms folded under her bust, the Wickedest Woman in the World, then probably in her seventies, stares beadily into the lens, the way a small, sharp bird might stare. Again I have found myself examining this over and over. Peggy Thomas looks, and this may have been her chief offence … *ordinary*.

In the 1950s there was a remarkable exchange between R.S. and Raymond Garlick. Before this theirs had been a formal literary friendship (it was five years before Thomas wrote suggesting they start to call each other by their Christian names). But then the two of them were commissioned to make a broadcast together in Bangor. Garlick was living in Blaenau Ffestiniog, so Thomas, who would have to pass through the town from his home to the south in Eglwys Fach, called to drive him to the studio.

'He wasn't a confiding man, and I don't know how the conversation started, but we found ourselves talking about our mothers. We both had mothers who were ... difficult, and we unburdened ourselves. His, I remember him saying, had been a strong woman, a very dominant mother, a bourgeois figure who had kept herself to herself in Holyhead, and pushed him, her only boy, on. At the end of the journey I think we were slightly ashamed, but it strengthened the friendship.'

Two poets in a tiny minivan against the vast backdrop of the mountains, each in turn slagging off his mother: it is a very Welsh scene. Thomas in his time played many roles, Welsh patriot, English gentleman, naturalist, poet, priest. But here, briefly, you see him in context.

A photograph, again one of the very few to survive, shows him aged two and a half, round-cheeked, his hair a mop of curls, one leg tucked under the other, his shoes gleaming, as beautiful as the child in Millais's *Bubbles*. I know such photographs of old, I have seen them prominent on pianos in terraced houses, on china cabinets in the glacial front rooms of farms. There is even such a photograph of me, one leg tucked under the other, shoes gleaming, another little household god delivered by his mother to a photographic studio. I am looking at it now.

Welsh mothers are notorious for 'spoiling' their male children, especially if there is just one of them, and he a pretty boy: there is even a word for the result, *spoilyn*. Dylan

Thomas's mother was still cutting the tops off his boiled eggs when he was the father of three. But such an upbringing, though wonderful, can result in monsters, whose impact, luckily, is blunted by wives and the world, though sometimes it takes a world war. The historian Gwyn Williams told me he had been taught to tie his shoelaces by the British Army on the eve of D-Day. The best thing to happen to her brother was a POW camp, said a friend: it made him realise he was not the centre of the universe. Both mother and son pay a price for this strange relationship, as inevitably the desires for control and independence clash, and love turns to resentment.

> My mother gave me the breast's milk
> Generously, but grew mean after,
> Envying me my detached laughter.

Thomas's poems in fact read like a case history for this peculiarly Welsh tragedy, in which the son's one offence is that of growing up, something that can never be forgiven or forgotten ('the thin mouth with its teeth clenched/on a memory'). In *Neb* he recalls the night before he left home to go to university at Bangor, being woken by his crying mother kissing him again and again. He was nineteen. Next day she insisted on accompanying him to his college, Bangor being all of twenty miles from Holyhead. A woman who was incapable of love, as has been suggested, would not have behaved like this. His own son saw him in similar terms: 'He was a man incapable of love, and full of love, so that with him it came roaring out.'

Her control lingered. Thomas was twenty-three when he finally left home, and, according to his son, on one of the first occasions when he brought his wife to the house, the young curate was sporting the set of ginger whiskers which feature in one of his wife's sketches of him. Elsi Thomas must have thought the whiskers picturesque, but his mother, meeting him at the door, told him to go upstairs that instant to shave. And he did. He does not mention this in the poems or the autobiography, nor does his wife in hers, but spare a thought for Elsi Thomas, with her English middle-class and metropolitan art background, finding herself among these lunatics.

But in what exactly did the offence of Peggy Thomas lie? She seems to have been a forceful woman. Justin Wintle, writing his biography of Thomas in 1995, met a very old lady who remembered so well 'a small bony woman with a terrible tongue', that an image of her in action had lingered for three-quarters of a century. The young R.S. Thomas, taking part in a church Christmas play, was for some reason bawled out by his mother in front of the full cast ('We all felt sorry for the boy').

Ten years on, the only person I met who had known the family, someone who had been in the same form as Thomas, had no recollection at all of the father. But the mother she remembered all too well, mainly because she talked all the time; Mrs Thomas, it seems, had been notorious locally. Raymond Garlick's wife, who came from Holyhead, remembered a woman 'who was something of a snob'. Her grandson Gwydion's main memory of her when he was small was that on their walks together she threatened to box the ears of any children who so much as looked at him. But then he, like his father, was beautiful. Poor Peggy.

Orphaned at six, she was brought up, her son says in *Neb*, by her aunt and uncle, a parish priest, though in *Autobiographical Essay* he says she was raised by her half-brother in Llantwit Major. *I am not a family man.*

But he had no doubts about his mother's power. In the poem 'Salt' R.S. Thomas describes his father's life at sea and the nemesis awaiting him.

> 'Evening, sailor.' Red
> lips and a tilted smile;
> the ports garlanded

with faces. Was he aware
of a vicarage garden
that was the cramped harbour
he came to?

In the vicarage garden awaiting him was his wife to be.

The uncle or half-brother, or whoever, sent her away to some kind of English boarding school in Wantage ('which had an ecclesiastical atmosphere, and as a result she had some kind of attachment to the Church'). This had damaged her, or, according to her son, she considered it had damaged her. 'She felt, thus, that she had been deprived of love,' writes Thomas, who went on to consign his own son at the age of eight to a similar fate. Damage, sustained and inflicted, was in the genes.

His mother's background, and the habits of middle-class gentility this must have induced, form the background to the moment in *The Paths Gone By* when Thomas describes her reaction to one of his grammar-school friends. 'Rhodri was from the town. He didn't talk with a pure accent. He wouldn't get up when my mother entered the room. So Rhodri was out of favour. But to me he was like a breath of fresh air from another world.' Yet he himself would react in a similar way to his own son's friends, as the relationship between the generations eerily repeated itself. In fact, reading this book in manuscript, Thomas's friend Gareth Williams was struck by the familiarity of what Gwydion Thomas had to say about his father, having encountered a similar hostility from the latter towards his own mother ('She was bonkers'). Such hostility, even if felt, is rarely expressed in Wales.

You also need to know something about Welsh small-town life to appreciate just how much of a curiosity his voice would have made young Ronald. For the rest of his life he would talk English with what he calls here 'a pure accent', by which he means not just that he had no trace of a Welsh accent: Thomas sounded posher than the Queen, posher even than his countryman Roy Jenkins, the most accomplished piece of social engineering since Frankenstein's monster. Thomas, said Professor Prys Morgan, sounded like a stage vicar in an adaptation of *Barchester Towers*. This probably did not puzzle his English admirers as much as it did his countrymen, but it startled his biographer Justin Wintle when he heard him read his poetry the first time. 'It astonishes,' he wrote, 'because its pedigree is so utterly … English. And I mean an upper-middle-class English of thirty or forty years ago. It is like listening to Alec Guinness reading late Eliot.'

It could even surprise his own son, listening for the first time to the soundtrack of a TV film about his father. Thomas was talking about poetry, which he pronounced as 'powat-ry'. 'Powat-ry?' said Gwydion Thomas. Lord David Cecil, according to his irritated pupil Kingsley Amis, always said 'pwetry'; Thomas, though with an extra syllable, had a similar upper-class drone with the dying fall of the final syllable. There was 'Muntgumry-shuh', the word shortened to four syllables, and 'moo-uh' lengthened to two for moor. Yet whenever there was a place name like Bwlch-y-Fedwen the voice dropped into soft Welsh, with every syllable pronounced, and you felt you were listening to a performance.

'He'd never say a hotel, it was always an '*otel*,' said Gwydion Thomas. 'I always felt he was an Englishman like Robert Byron or Bruce Chatwin or Richard Burton of Khartoum or wherever dressed up as a native, in his case Welsh. That he castigated the natives for sloth or immorality is in the best traditions of nineteenth-century sahibs talking about "the Burman".'

R.S. Thomas's English accent was a source of wonder to his wife's family, said her niece Ann Moorey ('It made us groan, we felt it was that of a self-made man'). 'That accent,' said Hazel Boulton in Manafon. 'When he came back to read his poems he stopped the car, and there it was again, I'd know it anywhere.'

I teased Thomas about this once, telling him he couldn't have talked like that in Holyhead, but he just grinned. The amazing thing is that, given his family background, he may well have had an English accent from earliest childhood. According to Ian Cameron, Thomas's parents had no Welsh accent of any kind, and his three aunts had been called 'the best-spoken girls in Cardiff'.

As for the rest of it, the being expected to leap to his feet when a woman entered the room, that might not have made him stand out as a boy in Camberley, but in Holyhead it would have been as though some alien life form had materialised amongst the pebbledash.

So how he managed to survive the playgrounds of the town is a mystery, given the upbringing for which his mother, he says, had been responsible, 'with consequences that weren't to the riffraff's liking'. He would not have met these in his first school, a fee-paying kindergarten, but ahead lay the grammar school (for which, after the kindergarten, he needed special coaching). According to him he was bullied, teased and tormented, but he left a vivid impression on the late Lord Cledwyn, a few forms behind him, who, when asked in a division lobby by his fellow MP Ray Carter what Thomas had been like at school, replied with a single monosyllable: 'Odd.'

He and his mother went everywhere together, as do many Welsh only children with theirs. And in his case, with his father away at sea during the Great War, 'travelling in "oils and grease" in between the rougher surfaces of the ocean' (though his first cousin thought he was on mine-sweepers), their relationship must have been even more intense, as the two of them, against a background of danger and uncertainty, trailed round the ports to wherever Tommy's ship docked. London, Liverpool, Goole.

His account of this in *Neb* is a catalogue of terrors, mostly those of the natural world. Left to sleep in a bunk in his father's cabin while his parents dined with the ship's officers, he sees cockroaches, a memory that never left him, for it surfaces in a prose gloss in *Echoes* ('The shadows from which they crawled were as dark as those where the submarines lurked'). But in the autobiography it is the indignation of the only child that surfaces at the invasion ('And the parents far away enjoying themselves'). In a Liverpool park he bends over to smell some lilac, and 'A little black fly got into his nose, almost into his brain!' In Goole wasps try to settle on his hands ('The others took no notice of them, but the wasps succeeded in ruining the pleasure of the afternoon'). And that was early childhood done.

Whether he intended it or no, this is horribly funny. Later, after he had been read fairy stories by his mother, giants (who snored) and a gorilla took up residence in his bedroom. His mother again. In one of his few dispassionate comments on her, he wrote that she had 'a nervous and anxious nature'. She kept him at home until he was seven or eight (he seems unsure) because of what he calls 'some unidentified illness again'. There had, it seems, been others. She taught him how to read and write herself (or, as he puts it in *Autobiographical Essay*, 'I learned to copy marks which was supposed to be a lesson in writing'), until the time 'when school could no longer be avoided'.

Though by now the father was home with them in Holyhead, mother and son continued their wanderings. Mrs Thomas 'had relatives in South Wales, and she would greatly enjoy visiting and being pampered by them, because she was an orphan'. It must have been a shock for the young boy, seeing the pamperer as the pampered, himself no longer the centre of attention.

It might even explain the sense of distance when he comes to write about his own son in the prose glosses to *The Echoes Return Slow*. 'The child growing imperceptibly into a boy; the strange plant that has taken root in one's private garden. The apple of his mother's eye ...' This was a man who knew all about being the apple of a mother's eye. He had been supplanted.

But his case against his mother starts, amazingly, with his own birth. This from *The Echoes Return Slow*:

> The woman was opened and sewed up, relieved of the trash that had accumulated nine months in the man's absence. Time would have its work cut out in smoothing the birth-marks in the flesh. The marks in the spirit would not heal. The dream would recur, groping his way up to the light, coming to the crack too narrow to squeeze through.

This suggests difficulties that may have required a Caesarean (he does not make this clear). How he knew this, unless she had told him, is not explained, but it is not metaphor. He told his friends John and Peggy Mowat that the circumstances of his birth had left him with a recurring dream of claustrophobia. He was eighty when he said this. 'I can't sleep with anyone. I go to sleep listening to the ten o'clock news and wake at twelve-thirty. I then wake up about fifteen times, and thresh around, pulling the bedclothes off.'

The cumulative effect of the poems about his mother is that, however much you admire R.S. Thomas, there comes a point of reaction. So many charges are made against Peggy Thomas that you begin to feel a growing sympathy for this phantom, which is what she is. There is no sense of what she was like as a human being in her son's writings. All we are told by him is that she was thin, disliked some of his schoolfriends, and was bossy and possessive, things which are little more than a catalogue. She does not walk and talk for the reader, being quoted just once, when her son asks to go out and play with some new friends from the town, the infamous Rhodri amongst them. She says contemptuously, 'What? With those?' That is all. Basically she is just a name on a charge sheet, only the case would never have gone to a jury.

The one thing her son seems to have approved of was her ability to breastfeed, but after her death even this ability is questioned, as in the 1970s, in 'It Hurts Him to Think', the nursing mother is dragged into a diatribe against the English.

> [I] sucked their speech
> in with my mother's
> infected milk.

Peggy could not speak Welsh.

In the 1980s, in 'Salt', he was referring to 'The hard love I had at her small breasts'. By then the railing had become malevolent. He published these poems, had he no idea what reaction they would prompt? In *Neb*, very much on his best behaviour in Welsh prose, he says absently, 'Strange, and perhaps crucial, is the relationship between a mother and her son.' In the poems he rants. He felt safe in the poems.

Peggy Mowat, who kept a record of Thomas's table talk, reports that, if argued with, he tended to fall silent. But then a man in a pulpit does not expect to be interrupted, no more than a lyric poet expects to be by his reading public. When I wrote out these quotations about his mother I felt a growing distaste.

The writer Philip Ziegler must have gone through a similar crisis in his biography of Mountbatten, when he revealed that from time to time he had to stop simply to remind himself that this was a great man. It is a confession a biographer has to make, that he finds himself obliged to come up for air. This was the finest lyric poet of my time, and yet in the poems he is pitiless to the point of psychosis. I found myself brooding on it.

※+※

'Was your father nuts?'

I had rung Gwydion Thomas. He, it turned out, was in Waitrose, arguing with his small daughter about how many croissants they should buy, when the question burst out of the earpiece of his mobile phone. I had not even given my name.

There was just the slightest pause. 'No, no I don't think he was nuts. What you must remember is that when you live in the sort of out of the way places that he did, you do run a risk, and I should know, I live in such places myself. Having no one to talk to except my mother, he walked round and round inside his own head. Darling, I think three's enough. Yes, put it back. So he could never have a conversation even like the one we're having now. No, he wasn't nuts, but he could get ... *deranged*. Things burst out of him. Hello, mushrooms are reduced.' The most bizarre feature of this conversation was that Gwydion Thomas seemed to take it in his stride among the organic foods and the sun-dried tomato bread.

'And he was on the whole a happy boy ...' That sentence occurs, grudgingly, in Thomas's autobiography, for he feels obliged to add, 'At least that is what he told himself after reaching adulthood.' But he has to admit, 'The days of his boyhood were without end.'

There was the sea, 'its noise, its smell, its ferocity on windy days'. Garth Road, far from the terraces and the chapels, was in the Beverly Hills of Holyhead, its neat semi-detached houses overlooking the harbour. Thomas was just old enough to have seen from his window the old romance of the last sailing ships in the 1920s, their masts like a forest beneath him as they sheltered from the storm. At night, he wrote, the flashes from the lighthouse darted through his room like the sails of a windmill.

And then there was the house called Bryn Awel, at Penrhos Feilw, an expanse of gorse, heather and wildlife on Holy Island between the South Stack lighthouse and Trearddur Bay, that holiday paradise of the Midlands English. For the young Thomas it was 'a place of magic and enchantment', which is now a nature reserve. Though he does not name them, the house belonged to the Campbell family, a widow, her two sons

Len and Colin, both close to him in age, and a daughter three years older. The family's origins were Scottish and Irish (rugby internationals were a test of loyalty, said a cousin who still lives in the area), and they, like similar families on the island, the Magees and Keegans, had been in the Irish cattle trade. Young Ronald had met them when he started at the kindergarten where the 'nice' people sent their children, so presumably the family had passed Peggy Thomas's social tests. Amongst them, and in their house, Ronald Thomas was, for once, happy. What is even more curious, he admits to this.

Neb gives the impression that, having reinvented himself as a Welsh-speaking Welshman, he is trying to write as he thinks such a man would write. The actor in him surfaces yet again, and you get all that naïve wonder, all those exclamation marks and 'Oh's. 'Oh, how he would look forward to that day ...' Little Ronald is getting ready for Guy Fawkes Night. It persists even in his description of adult experience: 'What a new experience it was to look down on the Continent at night through the small windows of the aeroplane!' Mr and Mrs Thomas on their first package tour. Given his personality and his mastery of the English language, it all sounds wrong, and is uncomfortable to read. But his earlier autobiographical fragment *The Paths Gone By*, also in Welsh, is less self-conscious because it is being written in the first person. No 'Oh's, no exclamation marks. Here his description of Bryn Awel is fresh and vivid, and without clutter.

'The boys had hiding places in the gorse where it was possible to hide completely out of sight of everyone, long tunnels leading through the gorse to some central chamber, and it was there that we sat like Red Indians to make our plans ...' Then there was the rock climbing, the swimming in bays where no one else came, and the supreme experience, 'to be out in the dark, out of the sight and care of his parents', for we are back among the pronouns of *Neb* again.

He was allowed as a boy to wander the island alone, and

not just in daylight hours, which makes you doubt the amount of parental control he was actually under. He was out and about so early he often saw the dawn rise over Snowdon, and would be picking mushrooms in the fields long before even that, often by mistake picking stones in the darkness. 'There was perfect freedom for me to go out.' Even had he woken his mother, he goes on, she would only have told him to wrap up warm, or to have something to eat first. He does not mention the nocturnal ramblings in *Neb* seventeen years later, when his attitude to his mother had hardened. That he had once been allowed this remarkable freedom would not have fitted the changed party line. Of course, being Thomas, he does not give his age when he was allowed this freedom, but he presents it in the context of boyhood, which makes it even more remarkable. It appears to contradict everything he says about his repressive mother.

There are other contradictions. The boy in *Paths* is formidable, conquering his fear to climb rocks, roaming the countryside beyond the town at night, a boy for whom the dark shadow in the field is just someone at the mushrooms before him. But in *Neb* he is nervous and imaginative. A dark running figure (some of M.R. James's most terrifying apparitions ran) vanishes in front of his eyes, and the supernatural stalks his own home.

'His parents would sometimes want to go out of an evening. "Will you be all right on your own?" Of course he would. He hated admitting anything different.' Again he does not give his age. 'After they had gone silence would take possession of the house. Slowly, he would realise he was on his own. And yet, was he? ...' And so on, through sounds of breathing in the dark.

Once he took revenge on his parents for going out, though, as he admits, they would gladly have stayed at home had he asked them. He rigged up a dummy, then placed this in a chair, so there was a figure waiting for them in the shadows at the top of the stairs when they came back. And naturally, it was poor Peggy who went upstairs first ... 'It was all quite innocent,' wrote Thomas in old age. But had he gone to the cinema in adult life he might have seen a film which was already familiar: the figure waiting at the top of the stairs is straight out of *Psycho*.

Then something far worse happened to the family. At some point, possibly in the late 1920s, Tommy Thomas began to go deaf, a hereditary condition on his mother's side. This put an end to any hopes of a captaincy, and to sea-going itself, and meant he had to take a job as foreman of a shore gang, with a marked drop in salary. Until then the family had been comfortably off, with private kindergartens and a house smart by the standards of Holyhead. Now there were problems with money and worries severe enough for Tommy Thomas to suffer from stomach trouble.

From his childhood visits to Holyhead in the 1950s Gwydion Thomas remembers three things about Kimla. The first was the absence, apart from furniture, of any possessions. 'My father used to say that Tommy Thomas had worked hard all his life, gone round the world, and had come back to Kimla with a single brass tray from Ceylon.' Nothing else? Nothing else at all. 'Actually there was also a vase from Shanghai, but that seemed to be it.'

The second thing Gwydion Thomas remembers was the debt collectors calling as assiduously as Jehovah's Witnesses. The third he remembers with amusement, and concerns his grandfather's attempts at DIY, which resulted in even fewer possessions. Though a fine cricketer, Tommy Thomas was accident prone. He loved trout-fishing and would spend days on the river at Manafon, which in practice meant days of disentangling his tackle from the trees. When his son writes about him, or his grandson talks, it is with tenderness.

Tommy Thomas is the great what might have been of the autobiographies, being, like God, an absence. Everything might

have been different, writes his son, had his father had a say in
his upbringing. But first there was the sea, and then there was
the deafness which prevented him even hearing his son's voice:
the most wistful, and by far the most personal, passages in *Neb*
are to do with this relationship that never was. 'He was a man
who had seen the world and its ways, and he would perhaps
have shared his experiences had he been able to have a normal
relationship with his son.' They shared a love of cricket and of
singing, and Thomas writes of his grief at seeing his father with
his ear pressed to the radio trying to hear the music.

At Bangor University, hearing that a faith healer was due
in the town, he persuaded his father to come with him, and
prayed beforehand in his hostel chapel, as, he puts it, he had
never prayed before. The night came, his father went up, and,
on their way to the station afterwards, said he could hear a
thrush singing. It was overwhelmingly moving for the two
of them. But for some reason, and 'slowly', to quote his son,
the deafness returned, at which point, as he tells it, Peggy
(naturally) piped up and accused him of losing his faith. As
you read this you feel so sorry for all three.

❧✠❧

But, apart from the roaming the fields at night like Spring-heeled
Jack, Thomas's childhood and youth do not seem that unfamiliar. He went to the pictures, watched the old cowboy star
Tom Mix, was nervous of bullies and even more of girls, whom
he watched from afar. In the autobiographies he portrays himself
as a sad and lonely figure, but the reality was very different. He
was a good cricketer, played on the wing for Holyhead XV, and
at school was *twice* Victor Ludorum at the County School. Eh?

Given the wimpish image he constructs of himself in the
autobiographies, to be Victor Ludorum once may be regarded
as carelessness, to be it twice looks like misfortune. Their
teenage defeats, and their triumphs, stay with most people for

the rest of their lives, so how could such a laureate write an autobiography called *Neb*?

I came on his sporting triumphs in the 1978 seventy-fifth Special Anniversary issue of the school magazine. A pupil from 1925 to 1931, 'while at school he [Thomas] distinguished himself both academically and in the field of sport ...' In neither prose nor verse does he mention any of this, but the editors of the magazine had no doubts: they were commemorating success. Not only did he win a silver cup, he was also given, of all things, a barometer for his academic prowess. It was, Thomas informed the University of Arkansas in his *Autobiographical Essay*, a very poor school.

But when they asked him for a poem for the seventy-fifth anniversary issue he obliged, and sent them one that probably had its origins in a Thomas family outing. The magazine duly printed 'On the Coast', adding proudly that it was hitherto unpublished.

> There was this sea
> and three people
> sat by it and said
> nothing.
> A ship passed
> And they thought of it
> Each to himself, of how it was fine
> There or irksome
> Or of little account.
>
> The sun shone and the sailors
> Were faces at a wet
> Window. They were going
> Home, one to his wife's lips
> Or his wife's tongue,
> One to remember
> This was not what he had seen
> From the ship's bridge.

The whirring propellor
Beat out the time, but nobody
Danced.
And three people looked
Over a slow surface at three people
Looking at them from a far shore.

To celebrate the survival of his old school Thomas could not have picked a terser, or a bleaker, poem. Yet it was printed among the expansive recollections of others, the photographs of old hockey teams and the school song printed in full ('And when once on the ocean the harbour behind/in quiet, in sunshine, in tempests unkind/Our hearts will hark back to that harbour town home/That fair haven of our youth still white girded with foam'). If you have a taste for black comedy, the seventy-fifth anniversary issue of the Holyhead school magazine is something to be treasured.

When he died they put up a plaque in the school foyer. 'R.S. Thomas. 1913–2000 Bardd/Poet'. Terseness is catching. Not that he would recognise a single building: each one he knew was pulled down by degrees in the 1960s to make way for a vastly enlarged comprehensive, literally about the ears of pupils and staff. ('It was Hell for the headmaster,' said John Rowlands. 'Each morning when he got to his school he didn't know what classrooms would be standing.' Dr Rowlands was the headmaster.)

Both school and the church Thomas attended as a boy were within five minutes' walk of Garth Road, so childhood should have been cosy and familiar. The church too has been completely demolished, and it is like writing about a time of legend. Except there is a solitary living link, possibly the most startling one of all.

Aged ninety-two, standing very tall in the old folks' home and still looking like the athlete she once was, Cassie Jones, retired schoolteacher, was Victrix Ludorum to his Victor when he came out of the starting blocks long ago. 'Yes, I remember Ron Thomas, that was what we called him. I remember him well. *He was part of the background.*'

The italics are mine, for it was so wonderful being told this. To a lyric poet all things are background, with the exception of himself. Also in the chronology of this book the only witness until now has been Thomas himself in his writings. It could not be otherwise, given the imperatives of time, but here the focusing suddenly changes. Miss Jones had been in the same class as Ron Thomas, and later was at Bangor with him.

'He was a very quiet type, quite handsome.' This was what his cousin Ian Cameron also remembered, after a visit to the family when he was fifteen, when Thomas, three years older, had taken him walking and swimming. To Cameron he was 'a young god'.

Cassie Jones said, 'He was English, Ronald Stuart Thomas, and he preferred to mix with the English, I remember that. Of course we didn't know he was a poet then, you could never get very close to him. I think we all knew his mother though. Oh God, how she talked, she was rather silly, a bit overboard. We were under the impression that she bossed him and tried to keep him to herself. I don't know whether it was shyness, but he had this very quiet voice and he mumbled. He didn't say much.

'I often wondered how he got on as a vicar.'

❧✦❧

That, too, had been his mother's doing. 'As I reached the top form,' he writes in *Autobiographical Essay*, 'there were background debates as to what I was to do. My father, a former sailing-ship apprentice in the bad old days, was against the sea. My mother, early orphaned and brought up by a half-brother who was a vicar, fancied the Church. Shy as I was, I offered no resistance.' But, being Thomas, he adds slyly, 'Is this also how God calls?'

He had been offered some job in Holyhead, of which he says only that he did not for a moment consider it (though it would be fascinating to know what it was). The possibility of holy orders brought an exam for a Church of Wales scholarship ('No one ever failed,' he purred), which meant he could go to university, something the family, given their reduced circumstances, could not have afforded otherwise.

Not that he was a regular worshipper. His mother's habit of arriving late for services, and the tension this induced, led to the attacks of 'nerves' or panic from which he suffered most of his life, and once he had to get up and leave.

But his mother at the time did think it a good career move. The only thing was, she at the turn of the century had known the Welsh Church before its disestablishment, when a priest's stipend at Hawarden was £4,000, and even at little Manafon £500 a year. The 1920 disestablishment, which ended tithes and endowments, effectively halved these stipends, so that even in the 1950s in Manafon Thomas was only earning £365. Still it was a good career move, though not in the way Peggy Thomas expected.

As her son informed the readers of *Planet* magazine in 1990, some sixty years after the decision was taken, 'It may have been a disaster for other people, but it was a blessing for me that I entered the Church. Talk about the parson's freehold! It has given me time, which is the most necessary of all to a poet.'

THREE

Bangor, Llandaff, Chirk

In 2000, a few months before his death, R.S. Thomas visited Bangor University to open the R.S. Thomas Study Centre. It must have been a very strange experience. In his youth he had studied there, doing, as he put it, 'his paltry best', who now in old age found himself part of the curriculum. On the shelves about him, in the eyrie which houses the Centre, with the town laid out for inspection far below, he would have seen his own library, for at the end he had given everything away except his books on birdwatching. But here, around him, were books that, packed and unpacked, had accompanied him from rectory to Welsh rectory. He had not written his name in any of them.

Books of Welsh poetry bought in the 1930s. The poems of Aneirin, of Llywarch Hen, Iolo Goch and Tudur Aled, from the Dark Age beginnings of the language to its high mediaeval splendour. Old books these, a bit tattered, much read, studied when Thomas himself was in his beginnings. Books of English poetry, Skelton and Robinson Jeffers, these not tattered, the second a gift 'To the Rev R.S. Thomas with gratitude and admiration'. Books not much read.

A volume of Verlaine, with, endearingly, *Teach Yourself French* next to it. Books of philosophy and theology. *God and the New Physics* by Paul Davies (Penguin 1983) with his own scribbled irritation in the margins ('You cannot have it both ways. With one voice you speak of the spontaneous production of life, next of God <u>manipulating</u> it to produce one.'). All were here, but out of place and time.

In the photographs taken that day members of the university staff surround a very old gentleman in a dark suit, very tall and straight, who, remarkably, at eighty-seven has managed to climb the stairs to the Centre. One of them told me that Thomas, seeing the college library again, seemed quite moved. Now the successors to those who had taught him stood around him with deference: a great man had called.

❧✢❧

The letter came after I had made an appeal in the *Spectator*, for, given Thomas's longevity, I had begun to think there was no one left of his generation who could remember him in his beginnings. Then the letter came, from Southport in Lancashire, from a retired clergyman, himself nearing ninety. Canon Thomas Robertson had known 'Ronnie' at Bangor.

'I remember him well, and admired him in many ways. As he and I were not particularly "Welsh" we were somewhat ostracised by other "native" students, and very much thrown together.'

I remember reading that, and putting the letter down. Canon Robertson was writing about the icon of Wales nationalism, the uncompromising champion of the language, the implacable foe of his countrymen who could not speak it.

'One of Ronnie's defences was to adopt an extra cut-glass "Oxford" accent, which only inflamed the Welsh backwoodsmen even more. Looking back it seems petty, but this Welsh gang were nauseating towards the English "foreigners". I was glad to leave there for the more spacious climes of Oxford.'

So the mystery of Thomas's amazing English accent had been solved.

'I was from Llandudno, he was from Holyhead, we were both under suspicion of being English,' said Canon Robertson. 'He didn't have a Welsh accent to begin with, much to the annoyance of these fellows who came from places down in the

Lleyn.' The Lleyn, his journey's end? 'They really persecuted him, they took every opportunity to make people laugh at him. He was outstanding in appearance, always well dressed, but they used to imitate his way of speaking. If you heard a burst of laughter it was usually because he was present. To them he was a figure of fun.

'I did admire him, but then I was an outcast too. We were semi-anglicised at home, my parents, they could speak Welsh, though we'd answer them in English. But Ronnie never spoke about his family, we were just thrown together from being the butt of the Welsh.

'What was he like? Very quiet fellow, tall and spare, quite a nice-looking fellow, but reflective, he'd come out with the odd comment that made you think. I don't remember him talking about poetry, but occasionally he'd say something about one of our set classical texts, "What a wonderful passage." It did surprise me when he became recognised as a literary figure, until I remembered one or two of the things he'd said. He was perceptive.

'But these fellows, they'd never been out of the Lleyn, Welsh Nonconformists, very narrow in their outlook, he'd call them "this lot", I remember that, it was his phrase, "this lot". I can hear him now. "Because we have a Welsh background, we don't have to be like this lot."'

Because we have a Welsh background, we don't have to be like this lot ...Very slowly I said, 'You do know that R.S. Thomas wrote his autobiography in Welsh?'

'Good Lord, Ronnie did? Well, isn't that amazing. Good heavens.'

All this came as a shock to Gwydion Thomas. It will be an even bigger one to his Welsh-speaking neighbours in the Lleyn to hear that they would not recognise, in his beginnings, the man who sixty years on would sit at their firesides. But the biggest shock of all will be to those Englishmen who in after years stopped their cars beside a wild white-haired figure on the road. T.J. Hughes, who wrote Thomas's entry in the *Dictionary of National Biography*, took some delight in describing these meetings. 'At his own account … passing tourists who happened to ask him for directions encountered the apparently baffled response "No English". He would relish the moment, returning indoors to his English wife.' *My father was an actor.*

Glyn Davies, a retired consultant psychiatrist who worked latterly at London's fashionable Priory Clinic, also wrote to me. Until he switched to medicine, he had been in the same church hostel at Bangor as Thomas. 'I liked him. Very shy man, not a good mixer, a bit awkward, kept himself apart, but he must have felt he could talk to me, even though he seemed to regard me with horror. I was captain of rugby, also of cricket, I got drunk occasionally, I went to dances. "I don't know how you can dance with those women." But at the same time I had a feeling that he wasn't attracted to religion.'

It came as a bit of a relief that no one else did write.

❧✚❧

In his various autobiographies he does not mention the bullying (in *The Paths Gone By* he does not even mention Bangor), except that at mealtimes 'one or two of them [the Welsh-speakers] would try to get him to say words like *llwy*, spoon, and then burst out laughing'. The boy, which is how at this stage he refers to himself in *Neb*, had felt no desire to learn Welsh ('unfortunately'). But earlier, without comment, he confesses to having heard the murmur 'Who does he think he is?' This is something anyone the least bit different in a small and conventional Welsh society will have heard. The Welsh do not like the unfamiliar.

But Thomas in *Neb*, written in old age, says he was also asking himself that question. 'He didn't know who he was. He was nobody.' At college, he goes on, he would go outside during student dances and look in, and it would all seem completely unreal to him. But then it would seem so to any outsider. It may have been his upbringing, for to a spoilt only child other people usually are unreal, but in adulthood loneliness and an ability to live, as he put it, in a world of his own would have added to this. The boy wandering Holy Island in the small hours, the old man with his binoculars on the high moors, these were at ease with themselves. It was other people who were a problem. As his son Gwydion said, 'He seemed to have an inability to put himself into anyone else's shoes, except God's of course.'

He could be extraordinarily rude. At Manafon, in reply to the parishioner who told him, 'What a lovely day', he said, 'We can see that.' Later at Aberdaron he would shut the door in the face of the Arts Council official who had driven miles to present him personally with a prize, and did the same to his old friend, the academic Lord Morris ('I don't want to see you today'). Once after a funeral service he vaulted the churchyard wall and was off, leaving the mourners still standing at the grave. Quite probably he did not intend to be rude, he just did not appreciate the effect his behaviour would have.

This might explain his obsessive, if distant, fascination with the matter of human personality, for what is this but something deliberately assembled to impress, and ease contact with, others? You may remember his questioning of me that day in 1975. 'Is there a point when you start to embroider something in yourself?' This he clearly felt he had not done. In 1990 in his *Planet* interview, which is a far more searching attempt at autobiography than anything he himself published, he said he was aware very early on of a social awkwardness in himself 'which led to reciprocal reactions' and which turned him into a 'loner' and, by extension, a birdwatcher.

There was something wistful in the way he said that things might have been otherwise ('had I come from a different background, which had put me in touch with educated and interesting people'). But at the same time he seemed to have come to terms with it by intellectualising this unease.

He rather grandly informed his interviewers, 'I don't think that a really creative being should try to wear a persona … [he] must be so open to experience and impressions, so alert and critical of the ideas coming to him, that he is not conscious of his own existence as a person.' What this meant in practice were those moments Elsi Thomas recorded. 'R.S. says so often that in a town, walking alone, he wonders, "Who am I, where am I, what am I doing?"' The temptation of course is to say, 'You are R.S. Thomas, and you have forgotten your shopping list', but it concerned him enough to provide the title of one of his autobiographies.

These irritate his son intensely. Speaking as the only living being qualified to do so, he said that they did not put flesh on the real family life of which he was once part. In his 2004 interview in *New Welsh Review* he went further. 'I find it typically evasive that R.S. should have written auto-biographies rather than a single one. While it may be argued that such a practice is refreshingly reflective of the multiple faces, masks and selves of a poet, I just find it at once devious and imprecise.'

What irritates him most of all is his father's use of a third-person narrative, which to him is just whimsy, and an attempt on Thomas's part to divest himself of responsibility for any-thing. His father's attempt to present himself as 'nobody' he resents. 'All that started sometime in the 1980s. If my mother had ever said anything to me about his lack of definition or purpose I'd have paid more attention, but what she used to tease him about was that he was too full of himself. They'd be driving along, he'd say something and she'd lean over and pat his tummy. "There, there, Big Bo Bear."' Bo Bear was Elsi's Teddy, which, given to her in 1914, she had for the rest of her life.

'As for the lack of a persona, my father had nothing but personae, the difficulty was keeping up with them as he shifted from one to the other. The public one was easy, that of the vexatious priest. But there were also the grumpy old man, the birdwatcher, the writer of love poems, and that dressing up as a Welshman when he did nothing to see that his wife and son spoke the language. Why? Because that would allow them access to the persona. And where did that grim Heathcliffian figure come from? He wasn't like that at all.'

Remarkably, another talented Welsh writer Goronwy Rees, from the same generation as Thomas, asked himself similar questions about personality. In childhood he had referred to himself as Mr Nobody, and would go on to ask such questions for the rest of his life. Rees starts his wonderful volume of auto-biography *A Bundle of Sensations* (Chatto and Windus 1960):

> For as long as I can remember it has always surprised and slightly bewildered me that other people should take it so much for granted that they each possess what is usually called 'a character'; that is to say, a personality with its own continuous history which can be described as objectively as the life cycle of a plant or an animal. I have never been able to find anything of that sort in my life ... I existed only in the circumstances of the moment ...

He gives it a philosophic gloss, quoting Hume on mankind ('they are nothing but a bundle of perceptions').

But, again, it horrified his daughter. In her biography of her father *Mr Nobody* (Weidenfeld and Nicolson 1994), Jenny Rees writes, 'He does not know who he is, I repeated to myself in horror; if my father does not know who he is, who are we? The very foundation of my existence was shaken.' It may be no accident that both men turned their backs on their roots. Rees, a Welsh speaker, reinvented himself as an English intel-lectual and Fellow of All Souls, though he always considered himself an outsider in that world. Thomas became a Welsh-speaking intellectual.

But at Bangor in 1932 all that was a long way into the future, and R.S. Thomas, whatever he was to say later, knew exactly who he was. He was Curtis Langdon.

⟡✣⟡

In the 1930s the Bangor college magazine *Omnibus* was a jolly publication. A new Registrar gets welcomed ('Endowed with exceptional physical vigour, [Mr E.H. Jones] in early days was a Rugby footballer of mark'); a student records a study trip abroad ('As for the actual work we did in Dijon, the Editor has advised us to skip that part'), another shares his first view of the Dolomites ('suddenly we were in Fairyland'). But amongst them there was one who sang of suicide and lost love and loneliness. And sang. And sang. And sang. The poems of Curtis Langdon dominate the magazine.

> So now in winter hateful is the sea,
> Hateful its low and melancholy roar;
> And yet most hateful is thy memory,
> My sole companion on the lonely moor.

Women abscond. Curlews may be mentioned, but only to be put firmly in their place ('I am far, far lonelier than they/For all their shrill and doleful clamouring'). An Italian soloist, deserted by his public, goes mad and kills himself. Abroad, that is. In a short story, Langdon having dropped into prose, an old couple hear the approach of their son, returning after the Great War, and put out a bowl of chrysanthemums, his favourite flower. Only he will never see the flowers, being now, of course, blind.

The poems, so recklessly derivative (the sea's melancholy roar is from 'Dover Beach'), so relentlessly fluent, were cranked out in such numbers that a new editor was heard to say that he would never publish another poem 'by that bloody Curtis Langdon', whereupon our hero changed his name to Figaro, and normal service was resumed. These were the first published writings of R.S. Thomas.

In his 1990 interview in *Planet* he says he contributed 'a lyric or two', but somehow manages to add another item to Peggy Thomas's charge sheet. 'My mother often used to ask the Boots librarian if she had anything nice for her to read. So coming from an atmosphere of Ethel M. Dell and Warwick Deeping it was not unlikely that I should choose the pen-name I did.'

In the same interview the object of the R.S. Thomas Study Centre said he did not remember his university days at Bangor with any satisfaction. From his autobiographies it appears that he read classics, sang bass in the college choir, went for long walks on his own (his landlady thought he was out with girls, and he did not disabuse her), played for the Second XV (largely, according to him, because he was prepared to pay his own fare when they played away), and was lonely most of the time.

He was, he says, hopeless with girls, but once he wrote home to tell his parents, of all people, that he was in love, only he had forgotten to ask the girl her name. At first I thought that a sweet touch, but his son saw it differently. 'That was spot on for him. Of course he wouldn't have asked her name. With him it was me, me, me all the time.' He fell a victim to card sharps, neglected his revision, and, unlike those who now study him, did not do well in his examinations: it could be the university career of Everyman.

He tells one strange story twice, in the English *Autobiographical Essay* and in *Neb*, written within a year of each other. This is the first version.

> I discovered the mountains. The peaks which had been visible thirty miles to the south-east of Caergybi were now within reach. I would catch the bus to a certain point, then,

leaving the road, climb the nearest of them and walk along the ridges of Carnedd Llywelyn and Carnedd Dafydd and down into Bethesda to catch another bus back. The first time I did this and was confronted by the whole sweep of the mountains, I stood on a small hillock and shouted, '*Mae hen wlad fy nhadau*', the Welsh national anthem, for no reason I knew.

It is a very human touch that, 'for no reason I knew'.

In the Welsh-language *Neb* he gave the moment the full Hollywood treatment. This time he sings, not shouts, and, by implication, all of the anthem, not just the one phrase which was probably all he then knew (and, alas, is all that most members of the Welsh national rugby XV, and most Welshmen, still know), 'pitching his tiny voice against the majestic mountains around him'. All it requires is a swelling sound track, and a filming helicopter to circle the hillock, and he could be Julie Andrews in *The Sound of Music*. We have lost the 'for no reason I knew'.

For the last two of his three years at Bangor he was in a hostel reserved for students intending to take holy orders (among whom were the card sharps). The Warden was Glyn Simon, later Archbishop of Wales, whom Thomas for the rest of his life would address in letters as 'Dear Warden', and with whose family he would often stay. In *Neb* he described him as being 'somewhat effeminate in manner', a comment that puzzled Simon's son, the art critic Robin Simon.

'I think that was just R.S. being odd. There was nothing effeminate about my father, he was a fastidious man, and, yes, quite small and slight. There was a joke that, prior to his enthronement at Llandaff Cathedral, he had to knock on the door and say, "We, Glyn ...", only people said that what he meant was "Wee Glyn". But he wasn't effeminate.

'R.S. never failed to send him first editions of all his books as they appeared. My father was very fond of him, though he would make jokes about the extravagant grimness of the poems. They had a chapel attached to the hostel, and my father used to get up early to pray there. The only thing was, R.S. would already be there, praying. So my father got up earlier, and R.S. got up earlier and earlier, it became a sort of contest between them. My father found his asceticism quite amusing, and as children we liked him, he had very good-looking features that seemed to have been wrought out of wood.'

None of this would seem to bear out his fellow student's comment that he was not attracted to religion, this man of twenty-two who in 1935 went south to St Michael's Theological College, Llandaff, just outside the city of Cardiff. 'I was unhappy there.'

After his chronicles of woe at home and at Bangor, this single sentence, so simple, so short, so unequivocal, could be the caption for yet another H.M. Bateman cartoon: 'Mr R.S. Thomas admits to being unhappy.' There was no sea at Llandaff (though Cardiff was a port), no mountains, no green places, and Warden Williamson, a noted pacifist, he again was 'effeminate'. As for his fellows, Thomas seems to have observed them from space. 'The students, being mostly South Walians, were, of course, friendly ...' The commas are bleak.

Archdeacon Bill Pritchard, who twenty years later was to follow Thomas there, and in turn become Rector of Manafon, remembered 'St Mike's' with mixed feelings. 'He would have met "a gilded youth" there. Many had been to Oxford, others would have been conscious of being middle-class and used to mixing with the gentry. It was a place where Welsh vicars learned to put on an English accent.' The students, brooded Thomas in *Neb*, did not take the place seriously.

A photograph of the 1936 college tennis team looks like a country-house weekend, with young men in striped blazers shown with the Warden. Amongst them is Thomas, all in white, a racquet under his arm. A big, fit hunk, the biggest and fittest-looking of them all, he does not seem in the least out of place, though there is no mention of tennis in the autobiographies.

Here he is keen to emphasise his feelings on the trains that took him home, and from which he had romantic glimpses of Wales. The railway network from north to south was a thing of borders and coasts, so Wales was a hinterland to him, a brooding, dark place, as impenetrable as the Matto Grosso: had there been a direct line through the interior everything might have been different. The efficiency of the German railway system, it has been claimed by A.J.P. Taylor, played a great part in the outbreak of the Great War; the inefficiency of the Welsh railway system played a great part in the development of R.S. Thomas.

> The line from Cardiff to Shrewsbury runs along the Marches, with the plains of England on the one side and the hill country of Wales on the other. I was often stirred on seeing these hills rising in the west. Sometimes night would fall before we reached Ludlow. Westward the sky would be ablaze, reminding one of the battles of the past. Against that radiance the hills rose dark and threatening as if full of armed men waiting for a chance to attack. To the west, therefore, there was a romantic, dangerous, mysterious land.

The Paths Gone By

The next sentence I find delightful. 'But having reached home the thing would disappear from my mind for a while.' For what were the oppression of Edward I and the sorrows of Heledd beside the presence of Peggy Thomas?

It was to have been a two-year course at Llandaff, but a Canon Lloyd of Chirk, in need of a curate, persuaded the Bishop to ordain Thomas after a year ('to my relief and the disgust of the staff'). He left with two pleasant memories of that year. One was seeing Wales beat the All Blacks ('when he reached Holyhead late that night he had completely lost his voice'). The other was seeing the violinist Kreisler play, an experience that, almost thirty years later, became the poem 'The Musician'. In the autumn of 1936 he took up his duties; he was twenty-three, and had finally left home. As he writes in *Autobiographical Essay*, 'adult life began'.

❧✠❧

Sixty years later I was staying near Chirk, and one evening, driving through the back lanes, I came on the strangest church I have ever seen. In a small hamlet, it was made of corrugated iron painted a fading green, and looked like a large hut that had absconded from an allotment patch. I mentioned this to Thomas, for I had read somewhere that his first curacy had been in Chirk.

'That would have been Halton,' he said. 'I preached my first sermon there.'

Chirk is the oddest place. A long village with some grand houses built along the old coaching road, the A5 from Shrewsbury to Holyhead, it occupies a sort of hairline fracture between Wales and England. On one side of the road is Wales, and not within ten miles, or with the usual Border shading, but immediately. The first place-names to the west of the A5 are Glyn Ceiriog, Pontfadog, and on the other side, just as abruptly, is England. Halton. St Martins. There is nowhere quite like it along the Border. Like Missouri in the American Civil War, Chirk was a place for a man to define his loyalties.

Once there had been a historical fracture, when this was a war front, the grim Marcher castles staring westward at Wales (though this did not stop Owain Glyndwr, who lived less than a mile from the Border, proclaiming himself Prince of Wales). There was also a geographical fracture that has not changed, between the English plains on one side of the road and the Welsh hills and mountains on the other. In Thomas's time the fracture would have been industrial and social as well, with, to the east, coal mines that had prompted the building of the mission church at Halton (the mines were to close in 1968). To the Welsh west there was estate after ancestral English estate, one of them, Chirk Castle, behind the great ornamental gates that are the supreme glory of cast iron.

R.S. Thomas's cousin Ian Cameron remembered a rare letter which he wrote soon after his arrival. 'He wrote to my grandmother after he had been appointed curate at Chirk, saying he had been dining with Lord Howard de Walden and had been fishing in Lord Trevor's water. My irreverent Uncle Freddie said, "The only Lord he hasn't mentioned is the bugger he's supposed to be travelling for."' His father, said Gwydion Thomas, was partial to toffs.

I remember him asking me years later, with the sort of distant interest he sometimes showed in other people, what I had been up to. I said, quietly, that I had been … er, writing speeches for the … um Prince of Wales, expecting some kind of outburst against the English state. Not a bit of it, he just nodded.

At Chirk he found lodgings in the large house that had been built in 1912 for the colliery manager Albert Wood. Here, with her parents dead, Wood's daughter Joan, then in her late twenties and teaching English and theatre at a girls' boarding school nearby, was letting out rooms to make ends meet. And it was here, having seen his vicar's library, that Thomas subscribed to a book-club and, at twenty-three, bought fifty on hire purchase, which, arriving all at once, 'made me feel I was both a scholar and well on the way to being a man of letters too' (*Autobiographical Essay*). Amongst them, he writes in *Neb*, were the first poetry books he had ever owned.

Yet a couple of years later he had amassed enough poems of his own, and was taking himself sufficiently seriously, to put together the typewritten collection called *Spindrift, Poems and Prose Poems*. Curtis's shadow hangs over the collection, the poems being more or less what he had been writing at Bangor, smooth things about loneliness, 'the enchanted West', and homesickness. 'It is the time of soft winds in the island called Holy.' Heavily derivative poems. 'Heart of my heart, was it yesterday/We thought that summer had come to stay.' The metre is that of Arnold's *Forsaken Merman* ('Children dear, was it yesterday/We heard the sweet bells over the bay?'). It is still a young man's self-absorbed poetry.

He became local chaplain to Toc H, the Christian discussion and prayer group, and, having read a pamphlet by the 'Red Dean', Hewlett Johnson of Canterbury, on how capitalism was responsible for the condition of Europe, delivered a lecture on the subject to them. Encouraged by its reception, he blithely made this into a sermon and delivered it to middle-class Chirk in the parish church, at which point the vicar duly went up the wall. From this moment Thomas dates his life-long commitment to pacificism, which for him was a simple matter of religious belief. 'This was my awakening to the general attitude of the Church to war between states, an attitude completely contrary to the teaching of Christ, who was that most unpopular creature in most circles, a pacifist' (*Autobiographical Essay*). Much later he was to sound bellicose enough, as when, referring to Wales and its troubles, he told his Lleyn neighbour Gareth Williams, 'It is better to fight than to go down', but this was metaphor. Looking back on the Second World War, he was to inform *Planet* magazine in 1990, 'I am personally indebted to the Church for affording me immunity to "National" Service.' The quotation marks were his, for, even after Munich ('my first awakening to politics'), he claimed to have seen the threat of war, as he put it, only in an English context. But this is him looking back. At the time, he went on, 'It is doubtful whether my pacifist and conscientious objections to war would have matured sufficiently to have resisted as a layman in 1939.'

He became interested in theosophy, that rich soup of lost wisdom, secret mysteries and the occult, in which Atlantis sits like a ham bone. He wrote articles on this, which came out in a magazine published in what was then British India. But at the same time this very young man, through his parish visits, was having his nose rubbed in real life and other people's misery. 'There was the paralysed woman in her bed who was convinced that she was getting better. Every time he called she would half raise an arm to show she was improving' (*Neb*). It would take decades for these experiences to work through into his poetry.

In the appropriately named *The Echoes Return Slow*, his most autobiographical collection, published in 1988, he tried to convey his sense of shock. On each page the poem is preceded by a prose gloss, only it is not quite a gloss, the two are point and counterpoint, and the result is tension. What follows could have been written by two different men, as he poses his numbed indifference against his anguish.

So he was ordained to conduct death, its shabby orchestra of sniffs and tears: the Church renowned for its pianissimo in brash scores. At the funeral of the collier's child, when his eye should have been on the book, he saw, with raised eyes, the wild drake mallard winging skyward to disappear into a neutral sky.

This is the poem that follows:

Our little boy he paint a tree.
We keep it safe for him.
There is no soil

too good for this tree, but he dead
we plant it rather in our hearts.
There is no fruit on it but his.

It is a bit awkward as the attempt to convey the Shropshire dialect drops into pidgin, but it is very moving as the child's painting becomes the parents' remembrance of him. It took

fifty years before he could write that. For the man who actually
went through that experience was at the time still writing:

> I never thought in this poor world to find
> Another who had loved the things I love,
> The wind, the trees, the cloud-swept sky above.

But he had.

Thomas tells a bizarre story of their meeting in *Autobiographical Essay*, in which he is off to catch a train when a car
stops, with two girls in it. The two ('from a neighbouring
house') are off to play golf, and they invite him to join them. The
implication is that they had not met until then. 'The daughter of
the house was driving, but my eyes were on her passenger. I
gave her that look which a man gives to the woman of his
choice.' And that, he wants the reader to believe, was that. The
train, presumably, was missed, and the rest of his life began.

What he does not say is that the driver was his landlady
Joan Wood (later Marchant) and there was no 'neighbouring
house'. Also they had already met, it would have been
impossible for them not to have done. At Bryn Coed he and
'the woman of his choice' had rooms at opposite ends of the
landing, and Ronald, as his second wife Betty put it, had fallen
on his feet. In this Englishwoman, four years his senior, he had
not only met his first real girlfriend, he had met the woman he
was to marry.

She was 'a recognised artist', as he put it, which intrigued
him ('this made me wish to become recognised as a poet').
What he does not say is how much of a recognised artist she
was. A winner of the Royal College of Art's Prix de Rome
travel scholarship, Mildred Elsie (she was to drop the -e as her
husband trekked into Welshness) Eldridge was in 1937, unlike
the unpublished poet, an artist whose work had been reviewed,
and praised, in *The Times*, *Observer*, *Morning Post*, *Daily Mail*,
and the *Manchester Guardian*.

Tommy Earp, then the best-known London art critic, wrote in *The Times* of her first one-woman show at the Beaux Arts Gallery, that 'it gives more than the promise of achievement'. At twenty-eight, the *Observer* wrote, she had already made her mark with a most personal style. Critics hailed 'A very delicate taste in colour...' '... with a paradise of her own so that all her work is other worldly'. Her three paintings at the Royal Academy exhibition were, it was reported, 'all sold as soon as they were hung'. The *Daily Mail* 'safely' expected great things from Mildred Eldridge 'one of these days'.

Yet trailing such clouds of glory, that same year, 1937, she turned up in Chirk, having got a job teaching art at Oswestry Grammar School, ten miles away. Why she did this is a mystery. 'There was always a certain withdrawal-from-the world tendency in my mother. She did go into a nunnery once, though she got out again quick,' said Gwydion Thomas. 'But she was young and pretty, and, from her various hints, I think the flight to Chirk may have been a reaction against the casting-couch tendency in the art world.'

But whatever it was, Ronald Thomas, who, with his book-club purchases, was beginning to read Belloc and Chesterton, had now encountered someone who had actually met them ('Those evenings at the Rothensteins ...'). And that someone was also, which is always a help, beautiful, with one of those long, delicate faces that photograph well. In one, her face framed by her hands, it is the large dark eyes you remember. Also she had a car. Though Thomas does not mention this, the car was the enormous open-topped Bentley, and it figures large in his first references to Elsi Eldridge in *Neb*.

'He became friendly with a girl who was lodging fairly close by ...' – conscious of the susceptibilities of his Welsh-speaking readers, he has changed the landing into 'fairly close by' – 'and who also owned a car ...'. He at the time owned a bike. In this car, he goes on, she would take him to places like Bala and Holyhead ('it was possible to go for a whole day through North Wales for four shillings [20p]'). There is no reference to the car in the poems he was then writing, though there may be in such lines as

> Still think of me sometimes when thou art gone
> Into the south, and I am left alone
> With but the wind and stars for company,
> Still think of me ...

Actually the south was Leatherhead, where she, her brother and her parents had moved from Wimbledon when her father bought a jewellery shop there in 1925. 'Which,' she wrote in her autobiography, 'many years later caused L.G. Duke to write in his catalogue of paintings, "Mildred Eldridge, daughter of a tradesman".' In her later years she may have given an impression of being mouse-like, but, as Gwydion Thomas says, you didn't mess with Elsi. Evelyn Davies, the present vicar of Aberdaron, taught at Moreton Hall, the girls' boarding school near Chirk, where Elsi Eldridge taught after Oswestry, and had got to know old girls who remembered her (and had hidden, giggling, in the bushes as the curate and the art teacher strolled hand in hand through the school grounds). In her exhibition devoted to the Thomases in Aberdaron Church, the Rev. Davies has a curious sentence. 'Her persona within the parish seems to have been very different from that of her professional life in London.'

Her one niece Ann Eldridge (later Moorey) met some schoolfriends of hers from Wimbledon High, a school she had hated, especially the sport taught there, though, relentlessly, year by year she had won the obstacle race, 'by being able to wriggle under the matting stretched along the ground through being so much thinner than anyone else'. These friends gave her niece the impression that Elsi had been one of the Bright Young Things of the 1920s.

'They thought of her as part of a set, the life and soul of the party. So where was she now? I said she'd married a vicar. R.S. wasn't that famous then, and their faces fell. Elsie Eldridge? Who had been so dizzy, talkative, so full of life, who'd gone to the RCA with all its free love … Elsie Eldridge married to a vicar? My aunt would always clam up when you asked her about that part of her life.'

There had been at least one serious love affair, with the painter Vincent Lines whom she had met at the RCA, yet this is her description of how she refused his proposal of marriage. 'Near [the artist] Tom Hennel's house, Lines [sic] and I were standing in the middle of a large blackberry bush, picking fruit for Tom's old housekeeper, when Vincent Lines suggested we should get married.' Until then the only other references have been to the two of them going to art galleries, and, once, flying kites. She goes on, 'A thorny place and a thorny problem. I had to sadden him for who could marry a person whose work one did not admire, and whose hands steamed in the cold weather?' Whatever her schoolfriends may have thought of her, she could be a very strange, if focused, young woman.

But she was tough. In old age, after a bleak hospital diagnosis, she addressed her husband and her son for whom her memoirs were written. 'Had my sailing ticket yesterday. I quite like having you around, but no need to feel you must stay because of me.' She went on,

> I think of my mother who in her 80s was told she would only live three months. Father came and sat on her bed and, in the 'endearing' way that men have, told her that when she died he would go to live with Elsie [sic]. Mother was so horrified that she said to herself, I must get better. And she did, nursing father until he died years later of senile decay, being completely unable to do anything for himself.

This toughness she had inherited. Her mother, hearing that her husband was about to run away with another woman, appeared at the station with her two small children in her arms. He stayed, which in time allowed Elsi to draw him in his coffin.

'Everyone looks rather lovely when they are dead,' she writes.

> After drawing and painting the skull of a young Frenchman, who was killed during the Franco-Prussian War, which I borrowed from the dentist in Welshpool, I hoped that even I might make a lovely skeleton ... I have a drawing of my father when he died. He was always good looking with an arched nose and very very blue eyes, but not nearly as beautiful as when the ivory skin was tautly drawn over the fine bones.

An adventurous woman, she thought nothing of spending the night alone on Box Hill in Surrey, sleeping in her car, with the owls hooting around her. She was then on her way to the village of Mickleham to fix the sign of a dragon she had painted for two old ladies who kept a tea-shop there. Practical, too. All her life she made chair covers and handkerchiefs, her own Christmas crackers, and painted her own cards for the family, usually with small birds and mice ('to keep sane one must now and again *make* something'). Her letters are a joy for the sketches and cartoons she throws in, of herself in age, hobbling through the flowers, and of R.S. Thomas in his hawser-like braces.

There is one cartoon from the time in 1980 when she and he, both hospitalised in London, were about to start their journey home. She is shown as small and slightly bent, carrying a bag marked 'Home Grown', because, refusing to eat hospital food, she had been kept alive by food parcels cooked by her son. But there is a lovely touch of mischief in her depiction of R.S. Thomas. A wild-haired, balding figure, he is shown rushing off, a suitcase marked 'Cymru' in one hand, but with a Harrods bag in the other. You can make of this what you will, but this was a woman so visual that to make a point she drew something. To draw was as natural as breathing.

> I hated all my schooldays. I only remember every term looking through the new books we had to buy to see if there were any line drawings which could be coloured ... I remember clearly and vividly having to go to the headmistress's room to be told how evil I was, to have drawn in pencil around the pattern of bunches of grapes on the white table cloth at lunch time. For this crime I got a disorder mark, and, having told me, 'You would not have done this at home', I replied, 'Yes, I think I would' for all kinds of drawings are good. For this I got a second disorder mark, a second life sentence.

The artist Denise Rylands was a girl at Moreton Hall when Elsi came to teach there. 'I can remember the night the head-mistress came to my room with the news. "I've just met this wonderful person at a cocktail party." I was thirteen. She was magic, slight and small and fine boned in white tweed. I loved her, she was so full of fun and life. And so determined. "What do you want to do when you leave here?" I said I thought I'd like to study history. "Complete waste of time. Go to art school." Which I did. We were in touch for the rest of her life, it was she who taught me to look at nature and to observe.'

The extraordinary thing is her lack of recognition today. The year 1937, when she came to Chirk and met Ronald Thomas, was to be the high-water-mark of her fame. His fame awaited him; hers dwindled in the years which followed, years of book illustration, however exquisite, and Medici Society greetings cards, also of extramural lectures to help meet their son's school fees. His mother, said Gwydion Thomas, paid an enormous price for being a parson's wife. But the matter of the two careers, the one booming, the other quietly fading, remains a mystery to her admirers.

The art historian Peter Lord, writing in *Planet* in June 1998, quoted the sculptor Constantin Brancusi who, after three months with Rodin, left the master's studio abruptly, saying, 'Nothing grows in the shadow of a tall tree.' Philip Athill of Abbott and Holder, the London picture dealers which held exhibitions of Elsi Eldridge's work, said something similar. 'It is very hard for two highly sensitive people to flourish together. One has to give.' But he then asked the question that might serve as a book title. '*Did R.S. Thomas wash up?* If he did, then the matter of her subsequent career is still a mystery. If he didn't, then there's the simple answer. If you look at a list of early twentieth-century prizewinners at the Slade you will find all these women's names. And what became of them? They just disappeared into domesticity.'

When Gwydion Thomas got divorced from his second wife and had to sell his late mother's paintings, Abbott and Holder held an exhibition in 1999. There were drawings of her husband and son, and the tiny, precise drawings of small creatures, those of her old age which had the tiny numeral 1 poignantly in the left-hand corner to show that her failing sight had obliged her to paint this with just one eye. But amongst them, survivors of another age, were the large, once so celebrated, oil paintings from the 1930s. Her public, in Philip Athill's words, 'her watercolour following, her botanical following, her polite drawing-room following', were confronted by strange other-worldly paintings, some of them sinister, others wistful, of dovecots and bee-hives and dreaming ladies in long skirts out of a time that never was. Many had had to be cleaned of chicken shit, said Athill.

'Actually it was turkey shit, and the footprints of barn owls,' said Gwydion Thomas. 'My mother had stored them in an outhouse at Aberdaron, and two-thirds of them, twenty or more, were ruined. And even then she was cross when I first managed to rescue the others. It was as though she wanted that part of her life forgotten.' But then this was a woman who said years later that, after watching and listening to the reaction of the visitors to that first exhibition at the Beaux Arts, she 'vowed never to have another one'. And never did.

Yet out of what it is tempting to call the lost years of Elsi Eldridge there rises her masterpiece, the great mural painted for the Orthopaedic Hospital at Gobowen, near Oswestry, in the 1950s. Seeing this for the first time in 1958, Stanley Spencer, himself the greatest living muralist, wrote to her. 'What we see – because of ourselves and associating, mixing and becoming one with it – is a part of ourselves. You are those hills, you are the directions they take, you are the thing that keeps the wind off those sheep, you are the scudding sky, you are the world and all this fact can only be known by your mastery in composition.' Unfortunately the mural has been taken down and is in storage, awaiting decision on a suitable site for its display.

Almost as extraordinary as Elsi's current lack of recognition is the fact that this extended to within her own marriage. Her daughter-in-law Sharon Lunney said, 'One of the things she couldn't understand was that R.S. was completely uninterested in her as a painter, so there was a whole area of her he ignored. She complained about that, not in a bitter way, more "bloody typical".' Thomas never wrote about, or even commented on, his wife's work, except that once in the poem 'The Way of It' he wrote, 'With her fingers she turns paint/into flowers.' Invited to do so once by an arts magazine, he declined, but it is the way he declined that is so strange. 'M.E. Eldridge did not discuss her work with me.' Their son, when he heard this, said, 'But this was a woman who every night after supper had to listen to him discussing his work with her, particularly the bad reviews.'

One of her earliest drawings of him came up for sale in October 2005, at Bonham's. It shows Thomas as he looked when she first met him, young, dreamy, wild haired. 'Just look at those eyes,' said Philip Athill. 'That was drawn by someone who if she's not already in love then clearly thinks him the most beautiful thing she's ever seen. It's so romantic. And intense.'

Amongst his mother's papers ('between two squashed dead mice') Gwydion Thomas came on the following note from his father, from the handwriting written about the same time. There is no name on it, just this: 'If you love me – promise never to let <u>anything</u> – however unjust it may seem – come between us – knowing that always I love you.' There is no signature.

In the rare photograph of the two there is always a space between them, but then in every photograph ever taken of Thomas there is usually a space between him and whoever else happens to be with him. In the photographs at Chirk, on walks or sitting in the snow, Thomas is the man apart.

'If you look at them he seems to be saying, "Here I am",' said Gill Arney, daughter of their former landlady Joan Wood. 'Ronald, according to my mother, was *difficult*. But then she couldn't be doing with all that depression and crumbling rocks in the poems. She used to say that all that Welshness he'd taken on had been too much for him, he'd got dizzy and even more solitary. So Elsie had been good for him, she'd given him humanity. Mind you, she must have been a bit cold herself. All those blues in her paintings and all those skulls in their house she'd picked up. I mean, she could have picked up leaves.'

But it had been a meeting of minds. They dreamt of islands together. In *Autobiographical Essay* R.S. Thomas writes, 'My painter friend, Elsi, abetted me. She shared my inner dissatisfaction with modern society. We dreamed of breaking away, and going to live in a cottage "on water and a crust".'

There was an expedition to one not long after they met, which must have meant a lot to Ronald and Elsi for each of them was still reliving it in their writings fifty years later. The only thing is, whatever they intended, their accounts read like the adventures of the Glums in the BBC comedy programme *Take It From Here*: Ron and Eth go to the Hebrides. This Ron and Eth may have been a startlingly good-looking couple, but the comedy will keep breaking in.

It had started when R.S. Thomas discovered the writings of Fiona MacLeod ('and lost my head completely'). Fiona MacLeod was actually the invention of the late-Victorian London journalist William Sharp, though Sharp never admitted this. She was a Highlands lady who wrote verse and prose (Sharp could crank it out even more than Curtis), all of it very 'Celtic' and far away, with faery realms and nature worship, and much vagueness and many raptures in, of course, the West.

> How beautiful they are,
> The lordly ones
> Who dwell in the hills,
> The hollow hills.

Unfortunately, pestered by journalists keen on interviewing this remarkable lady, Sharp had said she lived somewhere in the Hebrides. And Elsi had a car. She had by this time, luckily, traded in the Bentley.

'Elsi had an Austin Seven, which was ready for anything,' Thomas begins in *Autobiographical Essay*. This included stopping: the car's great virtue, according to its owner, was that the front wheels, sticking out in front of the bumper, formed an efficient buffer. 'Early one morning in August we set out for Scotland with vague plans in our minds. By half-past two we were crossing the border …' Which, if you look at the map, remembering there were no motorways and the old A1 went through every town, was going it some. A man I know who has driven an Austin 7 said that, with a top speed of 50, they would have been lucky to average 35mph, so by any standards it was a remarkable achievement. By night they were well into the Highlands.

We had decided to catch the MacBrayne steamer for the Outer Isles, but the road to Mallaig was under reconstruction and by the time we came in sight of the quay the boat was fast drawing away. We wandered the dockside rather at a loss. I saw a fishing boat moored there. 'Are you going to the islands?' I asked a rough-looking man in an old sailor's jersey.

'Which islands?' he asked, somewhat dauntingly.

It is a nice comic touch, the 'Which islands?' and shows how much Thomas had overdosed on Fiona MacLeod who went in for subtitles like 'A Romance of the Isles'. He might just as well have asked for a lift into the Celtic Twilight.

I took breath. 'Barra,' I said hopefully.

'Nay, I come from Soay,' he answered. Then with a canny look he said, 'I'll take you there, if you like.'

Autobiographical Essay

And with that Ronald was off. He left Elsi ('rather ungallantly') on the quay, himself bound, as he admits, for an island he had never even heard of before that moment. This again was an example of the extraordinary behaviour of which he was capable.

Remarkably, Elsi, who had driven more than 300 miles, seems to have borne him no ill will for being dumped, no more than, later, she would bear him any ill will for his two- and three-month absences birdwatching; life for R.S. Thomas would have been very different with a Welsh woman. In her memoirs she writes, 'Keep your hearts together, and your tents separate.' But she had one small revenge. She writes that as soon as the boat was well out from shore, the man produced a bottle of whisky, which he offered to Ronald, and so the two, boatman and curate, sailed, swigging, to Soay. The Rev. Thomas does not mention the whisky.

Elsi, admitting that neither of them had the slightest idea of life on the islands, caught the steamer the next day to the island of Canna. Here she was unloaded into twelve inches of sea water and left to find her own way ashore ('Having only one pair of shoes, I doubted if they would ever dry'). The next problem was to find somewhere to stay, for on the island there was just a Post Office, four crofts and the laird's house. Tourists, like mainland motorways, were a long way into the future.

> I got a bed from a woman who looked mystified. Only years later I learned that every bed in these and the Irish crofts are full of damp. This one was in a small attic room reached by ladder. The plaster of the ceiling bulged down in a great balloon so there was only just room between it and the bed.

Ronald in the meanwhile was similarly squeezed damply in under a sagging ceiling, the whole house creaking and swaying around him as its inhabitants climbed to their beds. The boatman's wife had refused to let him sleep in their house (he had heard them arguing about him), so he had been quickly passed on to a neighbour. Still, he brightened up next day at the possibility of a *ceilidh*, a traditional evening of song and recitation, and an expression of the old Celtic culture he had travelled so far to see. A man called John Macdonald was coming.

> Macdonald passed in front of the window and stood in the doorway. 'Come in, John Macdonald.' A long silence after he had settled in the best seat by the peat fire. Then, 'It's a very fine evening.' 'Very fine, John Macdonald.' And after about half an hour of that, Macdonald got up, bade them goodbye, and went home.

Neb

Even amongst his dreams Thomas had a dry sense of humour.

He needed it. In the middle of the night, unable to sleep, he looked out at the bay beneath him, listening to the rain. Having assumed he was following the setting sun, he was totally unprepared, or equipped, for rain. 'He tried to convince himself that he was in the Hebrides. But it was so different.' Which is sweet.

He says he lasted a week in his unmagical land, but Elsi says that on the second day he was back in Mallaig, frantically telegraphing her. 'Hating it, come back to Wales.' She got the telegram, but, having persuaded two fishermen to take her in rough seas to Eigg, she was far too busy being seasick. The mother of one of them gave her a room for the night. 'One cannot believe how uncomfortable a bed can be when legs cannot be stretched out.' Somehow the two did meet, extricated themselves from the Hebrides and Fiona MacLeod, and went home.

The lure of islands was never to leave him. It was three years later that he wrote to the naturalist Fraser Darling, asking him to recommend one, and for the rest of his life he would take any opportunity to watch birds on Bardsey or Ramsey, off the Welsh coast. But in 1938 there must have been a sense of relief as the Austin 7 pulled into the courtyard at Bryn Coed.

It is a lovely place, a large Arts and Crafts house with beautiful Edwardian carpentry, a grand staircase, and servants' bells. Dr John Marchant, the local doctor whom Joan Wood was to marry, was still living there when I met him, surrounded like Dr Dolittle by those of his chickens the fox had so far spared, and by white doves. A bantam cockerel paced arrogantly beside us as we walked through the rooms. It must have been a wonderful house to come back to from the damp and the dilution of dreams, with Ronald in the nursery again, Elsi across the landing, Joan in the attic, and, as important a factor as any, Peggy Thomas seventy miles away. The next year Ronald and Elsi went to the West of Ireland in a van.

He had by then had a poem published in the *Dublin*

Magazine, edited by Seamus O'Sullivan, himself a poet and author of *Twilight People.*

> Twilight people, why will you still be crying,
> Crying and calling to me out of the trees?
> For under the quiet grass the wise are lying,
> And all the strong ones are gone over the sea.

Thomas had earlier met him in Dublin on a holiday he took alone, having been given a week off by his vicar, cycling to Holyhead and the ferry. Irish poets, he records, talked a lot. But when he and Elsi went they headed into the west again, where they nervously encountered more problems with bed and breakfast. 'Crofts with grass sod roofs,' she writes, 'into which chickens burrowed, causing great havoc by falling into the room below.' Even so, she goes on, 'Alas, very many people have taken advantage of a grant and changed the roofs for Marley tiles.' Comfort was never an aesthetic option for the woman who would later tear out her central heating.

But in the late 1930s, in the background to these wanderings and these moments of quite lovely comedy, clocks to the east were ticking more and more loudly towards world war. It was raging on 5 July 1940, when Ronald Thomas and Elsi Eldridge were married.

'I think everyone was very surprised,' said Dr John Marchant. 'I don't think either one of them was a passionate person, they just got accustomed to being together, and got married. Habit does that. But I think they were perfectly happy, they matched up.' This is how Elsi, previously proposed to in a thorn-bush, describes the proposal:

> RS and I were on the moor at Bwlch-y-Fedwen, the wind blowing across the bleached grass and grey stone, and the golden plover calling when we decided that we could live together. On the same day we found a buzzard in a gin trap

on top of a pole. We were able to free it after putting a coat over its head to calm its fear. RS then threw the trap into the middle of the lake and the bird flew off strongly. I wonder what sort of creature the farmer thought had flown away with his trap.

It was, wrote R.S. Thomas, a small wedding. In the photograph supplied by the R.S. Thomas Study Centre at Bangor Elsi is wearing a large hat and is grinning, which was unusual for she was very conscious of her teeth. She also, as she reveals in her memoirs, disliked her body: some beautiful women are like that, believing themselves to be plain. Ronald is wearing a dog-collar and a three-piece suit, though it is a very hot summer: he looks grim. The Battle of Britain might have been at its height, Hitler putting the final touches to his invasion plans, but by Bala Lake R.S. Thomas was annoyed that the owner of the Goat Hotel, where the reception was held, had failed to recruit a harpist. The hotelier was an Englishman.

Unfortunately, the vicar of Chirk being opposed to the idea of a married curate, it was an end to the idyll at Bryn Coed, and the paths of two of the strangest priests in the Church in Wales were about to cross.

In 2000, the year R.S. Thomas died, the writer Lorna Sage published her autobiography *Bad Blood*, in which she takes a chainsaw to her immediate relatives, and to one of them in particular. The figure dominating its early pages is her grandfather Thomas James Meredith-Morris (a name she can bring herself to mention just once), and according to her, a drunk and an adulterer, who managed to fit in being the vicar of Hanmer in Flintshire as well. According to her again, and as a child she shared his vicarage, Meredith-Morris seduced the district nurse, then his own daughter's best schoolfriend. All this on a pushbike, which allows Lorna Sage to speculate beadily on when and where and how.

The result is black farce, which closes in like sea mist from the start.

> My grandmother never went near [the church] – except feet first in her coffin, but that was years later, when she was buried in the same grave with him. Rotting together for eternity, one flesh at the last after a lifetime's mutual loathing. In life, though, she never invaded his patch; once inside the churchyard gate he was on his own ground, in his element. He was good at funerals, being gaunt and lined, marked with mortality. He had a scar down one hollow cheek too, which Grandma had done with the carving knife one of the many times when he came home pissed and incapable.

And that is just the first paragraph.

It is so beyond any soap opera that the reader starts to wonder what more unlikely details can be piled on such a narrative. There is no need to speculate, life was to do that. When the suspicion first came that the dates tallied I scurried from book to book, checking them, for this twist in the plot was scarcely credible. But the dates did tally. In 1940, up the road from Chirk to Hanmer in the Austin 7, the newly-weds came. R.S. Thomas was Meredith-Morris's new curate.

'Some of the most eccentric people I've known have been Welsh parsons,' said Archdeacon Bill Pritchard, one of Thomas's successors at Manafon. 'Some were as mad as hatters. One kept goats in his cellar and got engaged to two women at the same time. Another employed a chef. A third styled himself B.D., and when I remonstrated with him, said this stood for Black and Decker. Welsh parishes were so isolated you could do what you liked, except commit adultery. Some vicars lived in Hell, some in Paradise, they were so isolated, so out of their class and marooned in those parishes.'

Lorna Sage, though a professor of English literature, does not mention Thomas in her autobiography, and neither Ronald nor Elsi mentions her grandfather in theirs, preferring to concentrate on the place where they now found themselves.

They who had sought the West were now in the most easterly of all Welsh parishes, 'this little rounded isthmus of North Wales sticking out into England' (Lorna Sage), 'one of those strange bits of Wales that got stranded on the other side', in Elsi's words. R.S. Thomas, homesick for islands in Chirk, now, fifteen miles even further east, became homesick for hills, and 'would gaze hopelessly at them over miles of flat, uninteresting land'. At this point he did not know the historical significance of where he was: Owain Glyndwr's wife, a Hanmer herself, was from his parish. And now war had come again to Hanmer.

the parish was in the flight path of the German aeroplanes as they made for Merseyside. Every night, weather permitting, the aeroplanes would pass overhead on their way in, and they soon started getting on the curate's nerves, not because of fear as much as despair and disgust at the thought that they were on their way to drop their fiendish loads on helpless women and children ... Although Merseyside was twenty miles as the crow flies, as he stood in the doorway with his wife to listen to the sound of bombs in the distance and to see the flames lighting up the sky, he felt the occasional puff of wind going through his hair and lifting his wife's skirt.

Neb

That last image was to stay with him all his life, and was there fifty years later in *The Echoes Return Slow*.

In the country house
doorway the wind that ruffled
the woman's skirt came
from no normal direction.

Skies were red where no
sun had ever risen
or set. He learned fear,
the instinctive fear

of the animal that finds
the foliage about its den
disarranged and comes to know
it can never go there again.

Planes, as you might expect, were very much in his mind
at the time, and 'Homo Sapiens 1941', published that October
in Cyril Connolly's *Horizon*, starts 'Murmuration of engines in
the cold caves of air'. Bombing had startled him out of his
Curtis Langdon reveries, obliging him to think about someone
other than himself, in this case the man trying to kill him, the
bomber pilot. 'And a frenzy of solitude mantles him like a
god.'

He built himself a bomb shelter, something he describes a
bit vaguely in *Neb* as 'an earthwork against the walls of the
parsonage' (I should love to have seen it, given his DIY reputation), and learned Welsh, the two activities being linked.
'Partly from a cowardly wish to get away from this in a place
where I did not belong, but more from a wish to have the
whole of Wales open to me, I began to take Welsh lessons.' He
started to look for a parish in the Welsh hinterland.

There was a possibility of Llansilin in the hills of Clwyd,
but when they got there Ronald and Elsi found a tree had
forced its way into the vicarage drawing-room, and two albino
squirrels were playing in its branches. This, as their son said,
'clearly appealed', but the Thomases for some reason did not
go to Llansilin.

Instead, in 1942, aged twenty-nine, R.S. Thomas was
appointed Rector of Manafon in Montgomeryshire, in the
heartland of what had been the old Welsh principality of
Powys, just eight miles from legendary Mathrafal, the seat of

its princes. Here the twelfth-century poet prince Owain Cyfeiliog had welcomed his soldiers home in the dawn, and in verse, after a night raid, probably on England, their spears red with blood. Of Mathrafal just one small mound remains, an abandoned caravan beside it, which can serve as a metaphor for Welsh attitudes towards their heroic past. As Thomas was four years later to remind readers of the magazine *Wales*, 'Why chant the praise of Helen when Nest remains unsung? Why lament Troy fallen, when Mathrafal lies in ruins?' In 1942 he was starting the long trek into his inheritance, which was to occupy him for the rest of his life.

Until then he had been at the edges of Wales: born in Cardiff, at one end, brought up in Holyhead at the other, a man for whom the hinterland had been something glimpsed from train windows, this priest of the Border was about to become a Welsh-speaking Welshman and, all faery realms forgotten, a poet in the English language, whose first book was to be published from a room above a chip shop.

❧ FOUR ❧

Manafon

In 1946 the poet Harri Webb, a young Oxford graduate newly demobilised, was unpacking copies of the latest book to be brought out by the Druid Press, a tiny publishing house in Carmarthen. Twenty-six years later in a special issue of *Poetry Wales* he would write about that moment, in 'the upper room above Mr Baughli's chip shop in Lammas Street, opposite the Crimean War memorial'. Webb may have forgotten the proprietor's name, which was not Baughli but Baugh (he was a man from Aberdare), but he had not forgotten the book; he never would. The special 1972 issue of *Poetry Wales* was devoted to its author. The title on the cover was *The Stones of the Field*, and this time there was a name beneath it: R.S. Thomas. It was his first book, and we are in what to me is a place of myth.

The memorial Harri Webb mentioned was the first in Britain to record the names of the ordinary soldiers who died in that, or in *any*, war. In column after column the names are there of all the soldiers of the Welsh Fusiliers who died in the Crimea, on a memorial paid for by their officers. The cost of regilding these was met in my time by Gwyn King Morgan, a local pharmacist. Remember him. And remember the local council which, sensitive to the historical significance of the memorial, built a urinal underneath it, which, flooding periodically, has now been sealed off like Hitler's bunker.

Remember too the pharmacy, just down the road, where the man made his own fireworks (they had fuses, not blue touch paper, and, let off in a bin, blew the rivets out). And, just beyond this, yet another pharmacist who made cough pastilles which he supplied to the Great Caruso. I was brought up in the town, amongst remarkable pharmacists.

The fireworks and the pastilles are long gone, but the chip shop, the West End Café, is still there, and will be till the Day of Judgment, which will be when the chip shops close in Wales. But what I did not know until I came to write this book was that in 1946 Iago Prytherch, a Welsh hill-farmer stalked through it, and out of Thomas's poetry,

The book was a vanity-press venture. Thomas and his wife paid £60 to publish it ('I never did find out whether this was too little or too much'). Whatever it was, £60 was a considerable sum of money for them; with Thomas being paid £365 a year, out of which he had to meet the wages of a nurse for his one-year-old son, this was two months' salary. Elsi Thomas drew the cover, of a tree blowing over the map of Wales (to show his allegiance, as Thomas put it). To have his book published above a chip shop may have shown his allegiance even more (shortly afterwards the upper room became a little crisp factory).

Sales of *The Stones of the Field* were poor: the publisher, writes Elsi Thomas, was not interested in distributing the books. 'We had a whole trunk of them which we sent in small packages to various bookshops. Most of the booksellers did not pay for them. One or two Welsh ones did.' Today, in its dustjacket, *The Stones of the Field* can fetch £1,000 a copy. In 1946 it cost the equivalent of 30p.

But if the publisher Keidrych Rhys had neglected the booksellers, he had not neglected the London literary editors. *John O'London's Weekly* was appreciative, if long-winded. '*The Stones of the Field* (Druid Press, 6s) by R.S. Thomas shows a Welsh poet conscious of, and using with skill, his native scene. There is Silurian cunning in his verse-craft with its subtle internal rhymes and the like.' But the *Times Literary Supplement* was shaken into directness. 'Essentially a Welshman steeped in the customs, traditions and feelings of his country, Mr Thomas has a fearful intensity and reality.' It was a small notice, but in the *TLS* of 26 April 1947 the reviewer was in no doubts that a new, and disturbing, talent had emerged.

Keidrych Rhys had two years earlier edited the Faber *Modern Welsh Poetry*, which, because he included only those by Welsh poets writing in English, managed to create a rift between them and their countrymen who wrote in the Welsh language. In the anthology there were eight poems by Rhys himself, another eight by his wife, and seven by Dylan Thomas. There were two by R.S. Thomas, which earlier he had published in *Wales*, the magazine Rhys also edited. The first of these was 'A Peasant'.

The title would have been a shock to English readers, for whom peasants start in middle Europe. In Wales, where the *gwerin*, the cultured working class, is revered (and its very existence such a shock for George Borrow), Thomas was breaking a national taboo. I have seen it suggested that he meant no offence by his choice of title. But I come from a Welsh farming family and have a fairly precise idea of how my uncles and cousins would react to being called a peasant. Beyond this there is just one other, the ultimate taboo, that of attacking a Welsh mother in print. But give him time.

To complicate things, the publisher, a farmer's son, was himself just one generation away from the land. Still, had you read only the first few lines of 'A Peasant', then the last, you might have assumed that Thomas was writing within the proprieties of a poetic convention.

> Iago Prytherch his name, though, be it allowed,
> Just an ordinary man of the bald Welsh hills,
> Who pens a few sheep in a gap of cloud.

He ends the poem,

Remember him, then, for he, too, is a winner of wars,
Enduring like a tree under the curious stars.

The Welsh poet Iolo Goch had written just such a poem
in the late fourteenth century with 'The Ploughman', and
Thomas's contemporary Roy Campbell in English 'The Serf'.
For both the agricultural labourer, humble and innocent, is
also a figure of grandeur about whom all human life turns.
'*Nid bywyd, nid byd heb ef,*' writes Iolo Goch. 'There would be
no life, no world without him.' Then, more pointedly, '*Pab nac
ymherawdr heb hwn.*' 'No pope or emperor without him.' This
is Campbell celebrating

The timeless, surly patience of the serf
That moves the nearest to the naked earth,
And ploughs down palaces, and thrones, and towers.

Thomas's poem was very different. In it he observes the
proprieties just to allow himself the drama of tearing them up.
In 'A Peasant', between the introduction and the conclusion,
you do not just see the man at long range out in the fields, you
get to meet him. As Thomas was to write in *Neb*, he had seen
such a man on a dark November day at 1,000 feet, and it had
made a deep impression on him. 'A Peasant' was 'the first of his
poems to confront the reality of what lay around him'.

The result is that you also get to *smell* the peasant. This is
not someone tidied up for symbolism, this is the genuine
article:

Docking mangels, chipping the green skin
From the yellow bones with a half-witted grin
Of satisfaction ...

You are invited into his house:

see him fixed in his chair
Motionless, except when he leans to gob in the fire.
There is something frightening in the vacancy of his
    mind.

In this there is something else to consider. Thomas was not just a poet, he was a vicar introducing you to his parishioners, taking you into farmhouses to which he, because of his cloth, had access. He may have felt obliged to add that the smell coming off Prytherch shocks 'the refined/But affected sense', but that is awkward, as though he had had a moment of unease and hurriedly added it. Perhaps it was as well that so many copies stayed in his trunk; for what would Thomas's bishop and archdeacon have made of this poem reprinted in his first collection? And what of the other poems? One was entitled 'A Priest to His People'.

Men of the hills, wantoners, men of Wales,
With your sheep and your pigs and your ponies, your
    sweaty females,
How I have hated you for your irreverence ...

When a poem starts like that, those to whom it is addressed tend not to read on.

Yet six years before the book appeared Thomas, the curate of Chirk, was still Curtis Langdon, that poet of vague images and fluid metre who longed for far-away islands. Nothing in *Spindrift* prepares the reader for *The Stones of the Field*; the poems of 1946 could have been written by another man. Something must have happened, but what?

The temptation, when change is this abrupt, is to assume some kind of personal crisis. But there had been no illness (until the last few months of his life Thomas was one of the healthiest human beings who has ever lived). Outwardly all that had happened was that in 1942 he and his wife had set out, not for the north this time, or the all-purpose west, but some thirty miles to the south in the Austin 7. They had two goats with them on the back seat. God knows where they came from, but they are a nice touch. A literate and unworldly young man of twenty-nine, possibly brooding on Pistol's anti-Welsh taunts in *Henry V* ('Not for Cadwaladr and all his goats'), may have thought them a necessary part of equipment for where he was going.

A bishop once bade farewell to the vicar of Dowlais in his Llandaff diocese with the cheerful words, 'I leave you as a missionary in the heart of Africa.' But that was in 1827 and the man's newly built church was on the roaring frontier of the Industrial Revolution in South Wales. Thomas, on the other hand, was going into the heart, and long traditions, of rural Wales, into the unchanging hills, and the past he had imagined. The man who had reconnoitred other Celtic cultures was about to try and graft himself onto his own.

When he had moved on, and was living in Eglwys Fach, Thomas came back to address the Montgomeryshire Society. He told his audience, 'I still have to resist the temptation to go back there.' But the reality was a little different. In May 1974, thirty years after Thomas had left the village, his friend John Mowat, writing up the poet's table talk as was his custom after their meetings, recorded what he had been told about a recurring nightmare. In this Thomas would dream that he had gone back there, only to wake with relief when he found this was not so.

For Manafon had been a shock.

> Scarcely a street, too few houses
> To merit the title: just a way between
> The one tavern and the one shop
> That leads nowhere and fails at the top
> Of the short hill, eaten away
> By long erosion of the green tide

Of grass creeping perpetually nearer
This last outpost of time past ...

The shop has gone. There was a school, but that closed. Only the pub, the Beehive, and the church of St Michael and All Angels remain, on opposite sides of the road, as in some old Temperance tract; the rectory has been sold, and the blacksmith gone, whom R.S. Thomas heard hammering on his anvil, the sparks flying around him. It is the Old Smithy now. But then there was always something precarious about Manafon. 'When it came time for secondary school, a bus took me to Welshpool,' said Hazel Boulton, born in Manafon in 1946. 'But a girl just two miles down the road, she was taken to Llanfair, and another girl went to Newtown. We were on the edge of everything.' Manafon, wrote R.S. Thomas in *Neb*, scarcely existed.

You hear odd stories. That part of Montgomeryshire was the Welsh equivalent of the Deep South, said Jon Gower, arts correspondent of BBC Wales: a man could easily find himself his own first cousin there. A very curious place, said Glyn Tegai Hughes, formerly warden of Gregynog, the stately home and centre for the arts five miles away; Manafon had never really progressed beyond Gwallter Mechain. This was that early nineteenth-century vicar, a poet and agricultural economist, but, according to his parishioners, a wizard. He is said to have cast a spell on one of them that had the man standing all night on a stone in the middle of the River Rhiw.

After that, said Dr Tegai Hughes, the village was understandably suspicious of its vicars. One night two drunks fired a shotgun outside R.S. Thomas's rectory, shouting, 'Come out and fight you bloody parson,' but he did not emerge, and the episode did not make it into either the poems or the autobiographies. History, wrote the Rev. Bill Pritchard in his church guide, seemed to have passed Manafon by.

Still, history did its best. A few miles down the road is Berriew, where the early seventh-century Welsh saint Beuno one fine morning heard, across the water meadows of the Severn, a man call to his dogs in a foreign tongue. The English had come. This, the most vivid anecdote in early mediaeval history, had Beuno decamping for the Lleyn Peninsula, where, 1,300 years later, R.S. Thomas was to follow him.

There is also the curious story of the burial of a cremated body, for the first time in consecrated ground, in Manafon churchyard. Done in 1878, at night, this is recorded in the burial register, the remains being those of a Londoner called Henry Crookenden, who had died three years earlier and been buried in Brompton Cemetery. From there, on the orders of a Manafon heiress, an enthusiast of cremation, then illegal, the body was exhumed and exported to Milan, where it was burned, before the much-travelled Mr Crookenden ended up in Manafon. It is not known where, but the fact that the matter went no further is yet another indication of the remoteness of the place. The question strangers usually asked about Manafon, said R.S. Thomas, was where was it ? 'No one passes through Manafon on their way to anywhere,' wrote Elsi Thomas. 'It just wasn't on the way to anywhere at all.'

The village is set in the strangest landscape. The hills crowd in on the valleys, so there are no views until you get above a certain height, around 1,000 feet, at which point there is nothing but views, the world being suddenly unrolled for you the way a carpet salesman might display his wares. But these hills are so abrupt that to drive through the lanes above Manafon is like being on a switchback ride in a fairground.

This is Eric Jones talking. He is eighty-four and once farmed the 120 acres of Llwyn Copa, a place R.S. Thomas knew well and mentions in his autobiographies. We are in the brick bungalow to which Eric retired sixteen years ago, when, as he put it, 'he came down', like some absconding angel. The car he came down in is in his garage, having, despite its age, just passed the MOT, as it has done every year for the last sixteen since the coming down.

'That's Llwyn Copa, up there.' Mr Jones is pointing across a field at some buildings. The farm is a couple of hundred yards away, it is just that it is in the sky. 'We were there all our lives, it was Dad's first farm. I suppose you could say we were R.S. Thomas's closest neighbours, except we were up there and he was down here. Dad died, so there was only Mum and me left, which was when I came down. A stranger's got the house now, a neighbour's got the land. We're at 525 feet here in Manafon. The farm is at 650 feet. And the hill behind, that's 900 feet.'

Mr Jones was speaking with a Shropshire accent, the way most Manafon people do. 'Dad could speak Welsh, but it's died out now.' At least at 650 feet it has. But a few hundred feet higher, and it is still there in the hills behind the hills, where the Welsh language, like the view, begins at 1,000 feet. In terms of distance you could be about four miles from Manafon, where, for all its Welsh place and farm names, the language has not been used in the church since the First World War. But in terms of culture you are a world away, only you have to climb to reach it.

Climate, like culture, follows the contours. 'Up there you're at the mercy of the elements,' said Megan Humphreys of Manafon. 'It's much colder and windier,' said John Jones of Penybelan farm. 'If they have snow in Manafon we have drifts up here. If it rains on them it lashes us. Not that he would have noticed the rain.'

When Gisela Chan Man Fong published *Themen und Bilder in der Dichtung von Ronald Stuart Thomas*, her Kiel University dissertation, in 1969, she speculated about the effect of continual rain on Thomas. But Dr Glyn Tegai Hughes, living just down the road, took exception to this in his review of her book in *Poetry Wales*. The annual rainfall in Manafon, he said, was very similar to that in Rome.

In the hills life was hard. 'The society R.S. Thomas came to was quite different from what'll you find today.' David Hall, a further-education lecturer, came to the village when he married into a family that had been there for four generations. 'Just before, in the 1930s, this had been an enormously depressed place, with people trying to make a living off 40 to 50 acres, where today a 200-acre farm wouldn't be enough. It was a tough time, with the old estates being broken up, and the sitting tenants buying their farms. Only they didn't think of this as an investment, they *had* to buy, for where else could they go? They didn't want miners in the 1930s. So you had a generation that hung about on these small farms, all those unmarried brothers and sisters.

'Still when he came it was the middle of the war, and things were beginning to pick up a little. Then in the 1950s the machines came, the first little grey Ferguson tractors. So of course there was the materialism he complained about, there had to be. "How much off for cash?"'

R.S. Thomas was to see this change. He saw the coming of the machine (the tractor came to Llwyn Copa in 1950), and wrote about it, delightfully, in 'Cynddylan on a Tractor', a name out of Dark Age heroic myth, chosen as the Welsh equivalent of Plantagenet, say, to give a comic irony to this picture of a farm labourer 'riding to work as a great man should'. He would never have met anyone called Cynddylan.

But there was no comedy later, for this was just the beginning of a change that would prove overwhelming. As Dr John Davies noted in *A History of Wales* (Allen Lane 1993), by 1971 there were more tractors on Welsh farms than there were Cynddylans to drive them. Mechanisation brought the end of small farms (in 1945 there were 40,000 farms, in 1971 there were scarcely half that number), so the hill country Thomas paced was being depopulated in front of his eyes. But up there he had seen it in its bleakness, and had known the last survivors. It was just that every night he had been able to come down.

Coming home was to that:
The white house in the cool grass
Membraned with shadow, the bright stretch
Of stream that was its looking glass.

And smoke growing above the roof
To a tall tree among whose boughs
The first stars renewed their theme
Of time and death and a man's vows.

'The Return'

Manafon might not have been on the way to anywhere, but Elsi Thomas had no doubts as to where she was. She may have paid a price for being a country parson's wife, as her son said, but she paid it with joy. At Manafon she had no electricity, cooked on an oil stove, with water piped from a spring across the river (when she had this tested, and went for the results, the chemist with interest asked, 'You still alive then?'), but the moment she saw the Rectory Elsi Thomas knew she was in the Garden of Eden.

'We went one spring day to look at it, it seemed like Paradise. The apple orchard beside the river was full to the brim with white Poet's Eye narcissus, red squirrels in the trees, the river only a short path's length from the back door. Living there was like living in the middle of a lovely field, the grass billowing up to the door ...' This was that grass over which her husband was to agonise in verse and parish magazine.

'My father used a scythe,' said Gwydion Thomas. 'The only thing was, he could never sharpen it properly so there was a time in his life when for him mankind was divided into two species, those who could set an edge on a scythe and those who couldn't.' In a photograph taken about 1948, a golden-haired Gwydion, aged four, beams at the camera, while in the background a sinister black-suited figure is bent double, his scythe almost flat to the ground: the Rev. Thomas is attacking the grass, as he did most afternoons. On the back of this some-one has written, 'Gwydion and the Grim Reaper'.

The Rectory, with its eleven bedrooms and three bath-rooms, and once with stables, a coach house and a paddock, is an elegant, late Georgian mansion at the end of a long drive. Thomas was often to tell his son that one of the sadnesses of his life was that the remote parishes he chose meant he could not provide his wife with the sort of house she deserved, but all three vicarages were quite grand, Manafon the grandest of all: it would not have looked out of place among the advertise-ments in *Country Life*. So quite what he had mind, short of Chatsworth, is unclear.

The Rectory was outside the village. From Elsi's memoirs you get an idea not only of its isolation but of the isolation the two of them achieved for it.

> In Manafon, where one lived as tho' in a huge field without any other houses to be seen, there was a long drive which no one ever came down. When Gwydion was very small he saw someone walking down the drive from the roadway. This so astonished him he ran out to explore, calling, 'I think I will just go to find out what is going on ...'

In a busy parish people would have been calling all the time. Here no one ever came to stay, apart from in-laws and Elsi's one niece.

When Elsi Thomas writes about Manafon her writing quickens, the memories are lyrical. Some are very gentle memories. 'One year the robin built her nest in the tub of polyanthus which was under the kitchen window. When the sun grew too hot for the chicks in the nest we had to put an umbrella up to keep them cool.' Others demonstrate the toughness of which she was capable. One minute she was raising sunshades for robins, and the next ...

Gwydion's godmother lent him [a toy] Peter Rabbit in an enchanting blue jacket, with instructions that he was not to be played with or touched. This was too much for Gwydion at four to five years, and he removed all Peter Rabbit's whiskers. Great consternation. I got Lewis the Manafon rabbit-catcher to procure a young [real] one, and I was able to give Peter Rabbit his whiskers again.

And then there was the hunt.

One morning there was a group of farmers pounding through the field after a fox. I happened to look out of the kitchen window which looked down the path to the river, and there was the fox coming up the path, men and dogs about to cross the river. Quickly I opened the kitchen door and stood behind it, the fox came in, and I shut and locked the door. The fox went through into the slate-floored dairy and stayed quietly, while men and dogs hullabalooed outside. Eventually they decided it had cut across the garden and they moved off. After a while I opened the door and left the fox to find its way back across the river.

When, at the end of her life and in poor health, she looked back in her memoirs, there were two golden times. The first was when she was a young art student, and the doors of the famous were opening to her talent, among them those of I Tatti where the great Bernard Berenson was her host in 'a lovely house with white walls and grey stone skirtings, [where] he showed me his special treasures, Madonnas, altar pieces, so many one became confused'. The painter Aubrey Waterfield, who had known D.H. Lawrence, talked about 'the alarming sight of Frieda bursting out of her bodice'. But the other golden time was her Manafon years.

'We had a Sunday school of about ten small children.' Elsi then was very much the rector's wife, and ran this.

Every Sunday they were supposed to learn and say a verse. Mostly they forgot to learn one, except some of the small and 'proper' little girls. The boys used to fall back on one line they could always remember. 'There cum a leopard and wor-shipped him.' Never having heard of a 'leper', this seemed to them a miraculous happening, a leopard prostrating itself in a flurry of rippling spots and golden colour. They never forgot it.

Ronald for some reason asked them what kind of tree was in the Garden of Eden. Tom Belan Deg leapt up, hand raised. 'Cooker, sir.'

People liked her. She was amusing, attractive ('This is a teenager's view mind, but she must have been a knock-out when she was younger,' said Eric Jones), and she had a practical side to her that endeared her to them. Eric Jones again. 'Socially she'd muck in, she'd call and bring us cakes. Once a pane in a window had gone. "I'll do that for you." She cut the glass and brought the putty. She was so totally different from him, I can't imagine him doing that.' All this is at odds with the recluse of Aberdaron and Sarn ('Here, where I see no one, speak to no one,' she writes in her memoirs).

But her Manafon years were also industrious in terms of her art. There was much painting, including one of Ronald asleep which she submitted for an exhibition at the Royal Watercolour Society. It was returned with a note saying they did not accept portraits of dead men. She did book illustra-tions, including her first in colour for Faber, to accompany some animal stories by Dorothy Richards, *A Home for Miss Fieldmouse*, which added to the church salary. Later there were the *Merry Folk of Flowerdale* and *Spindle Spider* ('not a good book to illustrate, but I tried to make the best of the spider …').

Towards the end of her life Elsi could look back on 'Manafon days when the church salary was £365 a year, and we thought that was wonderful – a £1 a day on your plate every morning, and the butcher's weekly leg of mutton five shillings'. But the reality, according to her niece Ann Moorey, was that she 'worked her butt off' to make ends meet. Commissions now, not the large canvases which had attracted such attention in the late 1930s. And, from 1950 on, extra-mural classes for the University of Wales, the Austin 7 being driven at night through the lanes to Newtown and Welshpool. These, she noted tartly, were on the Appreciation of Art, and included, at her insistence, *painting sessions*. 'Nothing so undignified had ever been approved of before (the University of Wales had not even allowed instruments to be played at Appreciation of Music classes).' But Elsi had her way, she usually did. A fellow lecturer remembered 'a small, determined lady who insisted on a certain room or a certain piece of equipment'.

His memory of Manafon, said Gwydion Thomas, was that his parents were hard at it all the time, not at work, or at least not at what he meant by work, which involved going out ('For years I thought we had to be terribly well off'). In the mornings Ronald wrote and read, Elsi painted in a room on the third floor, 'the smell of turpentine filling the air together with that of Gloire de Dijon roses'. In the afternoons she gardened, he cut the grass, which, like the poor, was to be with him all his life. In the evenings he did his parish visits. And that was the iron regimen established which lasted for the rest of their long lives.

Meals came and went with the precision of a space-launch timetable. Breakfast at eight, bread and cheese at eleven, lunch at one, tea at five, supper at eight. 'Every day without fail. Elsie [*sic*] feeding him like a robot. He is never early, never late, never cooks,' wrote Gwydion. Mutton and fish were delivered, vegetables came from the garden, milk, butter and eggs from the farms. Sunday there was the mutton boiled, Monday the mutton cold, Tuesday the mutton warmed, Wednesday mutton rissoles, Thursday a pie of eggs, tinned tomatoes, and white sauce, Friday plaice, Saturday rabbit, Sunday mutton …

Elsi Thomas made cushion covers, handkerchiefs, lampshades out of an early plastic, which she sewed and punched; she made purses out of moleskins, and berets and waistcoats out of rabbit-skins which, though these smelled, her small son was obliged to wear. She hung dead owls in the apple tree, waiting for the skeletons to emerge, when they would join the severed heads already on the mantelpiece in the hall. This, in miniature a sort of mediaeval Tower Bridge where the heads of traitors whitened, already bore the skulls of sheep and badgers, foxes, hares and stoats.

Somehow, between the cooking, the needlework and the taxidermy, she managed to illustrate the children's book *Gwenno the Goat*, based on Angharad, the offspring of the two brought from Hanmer, which Elsi had tried to milk. 'A particularly good goat, she ate everything, books, vegetables, flowers, clothes, shoes, washing and oranges,' said Gwydion Thomas.

But what was much more extraordinary was that at Manafon Elsi Thomas managed to find time to start work on her masterpiece, the 95-foot-long allegory *The Dance of Life*, which few have seen. Strictly speaking, this is not a mural but a painting on a scale not known in Britain since Benjamin Haydon, being done in oil on stretched canvas panels. Intended for two walls of the dining room in the nurses' home at Gobowen Orthopaedic Hospital, it was something which, for £900, almost three times her husband's annual stipend, and an additional £138 for materials, the Management Committee commissioned, 'the stuffy Management Committee', wrote Elsi, which is unfair.

Brought to their notice by Dr C.E. Salt, a Chirk GP, she was first called in to advise on suitable colour schemes for the wards by John Menzies, then the Hospital Secretary. He had spent some time in Sweden and had been impressed by the work being done there on the therapeutic effect of colour. An idea of the extent of her influence, of the remarkable people prepared to accommodate it, and of the glories of the NHS in its beginnings, can be seen in this letter from Menzies in 1950.

Dear Miss Eldridge,
Goodford, Kenyon and Gladstone Wards
I have this morning had a letter from the Consultant Engineer asking if it is possible for a decision to be given on the colour required for the shades on the bedside lights in the above mentioned three wards.

Bliss was it in that dawn to be alive ... The following year the Management Committee accepted her proposal for the wall painting.

The respect they accorded it can be seen in a letter from Menzies's successor, written in 1958 in reply to her complaint about the effect of escaping steam. The Secretary offered to call in a specialist firm to investigate any moisture behind the canvas.

'Britain is full of surprises,' the art critic Alan Powers was to write in 1988 in *Country Life*, *The Dance of Life* being to him 'a major work of twentieth-century mural painting'. Marina, Duchess of Kent, opening the building in 1956 and clearly startled by its scale, asked Elsi Thomas how many people had helped her, the way royalty does.

Time passed. With the redevelopment of the original building the mural was taken down, and now a modern hospital with a national reputation has been left with the problem of what to do with a great work of art that requires a huge amount of space to display. This will eventually be done. But when my wife and I visited the dining room was being used as a store-room, and we were given something like twenty minutes as a member of staff, in this case a boiler man, had to accompany us. As my wife said at the time, 'Twenty minutes? To look at an extraordinary work by an extraordinary artist who has been forgotten?' The boiler man said he sometimes came in alone just to look at it.

Its themes are complicated, each of the six panels contributing in its different way. The first celebrates innocence and the lost natural traditions of mankind, with young women at harvest singing to the bees. The mural then moves on to the experience of lurking mortality, to loss of innocence and the destruction wrought by society and science as mankind and machines show what they have made of this world, and, finally, to the need to repair this destruction.

But this comes from commentaries. To give you an idea of its visual impact let me quote from notes taken by my wife, who then did not have access to such information.

People in an orchard, a woman playing on pipes, then the bare ribs of an abandoned boat on a beach, behind which there are distant hills. Small sea-birds. Then something strange, another beach, but there is a tremendous wind and long trails of mist. Another woman plays on pipes, but others, their heads thrown back in despair, are being blown away, I could almost hear the wind. Amongst the figures is a skeleton. Then some scenes with very odd things, two priests, each praying within a lobster pot, an old land mine, a small boy freeing a bird from a cage. And then jet fighter planes of the 1950s, with parachutes fluttering down. Nearly all are in very muted colours, greys, greens, blues, just a few reds in the long skirts of the first scene and the planes in the last.

In the short time we were allowed I couldn't make out what it meant, it was like seeing something in a dream, through a mist. But what it did suggest was sound, of the wind, of voices, of the Gale of the World blowing. It was when I looked at the detail that I began to see what a master craftsman she was. A cat, back view, walks away, and I could see the ripple of muscle under the skin and over the bone. I looked closely at the little birds on the beach, something I could not do in a gallery, and I could see every brush stroke, lots of them, tiny, delicate, together making up a bird. In every hand or foot of a human you could see the strength, the sureness, the complete understanding of how this was made.

All the time people around us were shifting boxes, wheeling trolleys about, talking on the phone, against a background of faint pop music. And it seemed to me that such a painting left in those surroundings was part of the spirit of our time, when everything old and well-made is destroyed. The irony is that its present fate has become the theme of the painting.

Most of the panels were done at Manafon, where the long wall of the dining room allowed the necessary run of canvas. A small girl in the painting was the child from the village shop, but the boys were all studies of the young Gwydion Thomas. The buoys she did at Holyhead when she saw men repainting them from the inside. There was to have been a seventh panel, but the hospital decided that they needed the wall space for notice-boards and a portrait of the chairman. The matron, who does not seem to have shared in the initial enthusiasm, said that every new foot of painting was another blanket off the beds of her patients.

In his autobiography *Wild Life My Life* (Gomer 1995), the naturalist Bill Condry wrote,

the margins were illuminated as in a mediaeval manuscript by exquisite images of miscellaneous natural objects. Elsi encouraged us to bring her anything we found of interest. So we got into the habit of taking her anything we found of interest, a shell, a feather, a butterfly's wing or a wildflower or maybe some poor dead chaffinch we had picked up on the road. Next time we called, there they would be, painted with wonderful delicacy along the border of her mural.

But R.S. Thomas's only comments on this huge under-taking by his own wife concern a house move. Going to Eglwys Fach, he writes in *Autobiographical Essay*, 'was rather incon-venient for Elsi, who was halfway through an extensive mural painting for Gobowen Orthopaedic Hospital. But she coped in her usual competent way.' In *Neb* he writes that his 'poor wife' agreed to take her canvas down off the wall in Manafon, and that is all. But the themes of the painting, the abandonment of tradition, the destruction wrought by mankind en masse, the Coming of the Machine, became the themes of his later poetry. His mother's influence on his father, said Gwydion Thomas, had still to be acknowledged.

Glimpses of family life are rare. Gwydion Thomas apart, Ann Eldridge (now Moorey), Elsi's niece, is the only living eyewitness to the little closed world at the Rectory. At twelve, put into the charge of the guard, she was met at Shrewsbury station by Elsi and the Austin 7, and remembers a drive that seemed to go on for ever through winding lanes, and then the huge, echoing house. And, after that, silence.

It was not like David Balfour turning up at the House of Shaws in *Kidnapped*. The Rectory, though in need of a coat of paint, looked plainly grand, and Uncle Ronald, though distant and frightening ('I always thought of him as a great black crow'), was fascinating to a child for he scraped out every custard pan, and licked up the fairy-cake mix. Such things did lighten the silence.

But on her second night, startled by sounds, Ann Eldridge crept downstairs only to find her uncle and her aunt sitting reading at the table, with a Brahms concert on the radio. Neither spoke, neither looked up, neither even noticed as she scuttled nervously away like a little mouse. But such silences were totally at odds with the 'dizzy, talkative, full of life' Elsi the Eldridge family remembered.

Ronald Thomas on his own could be bizarrely funny. Once on a visit to the island of Skomer with the Welsh poet

Waldo Williams he was met by the writer R.M. Lockley who asked rather grandly, 'How is the Church?' 'Oh, terrible, terrible,' said Thomas. 'And Wales, how is Wales?' 'Terrible.' 'Do you have no publications there?' 'Yes, we call them graveyards.'

The poet Bobi Jones, who told me that story, believes that Thomas even parodied himself in verse. In his terrifying poem 'The Island' he has God revealing his malign designs. An island will be created on which mankind will be compelled to worship in return for poverty and sickness, after which the best of them will be thrown back into the sea. 'And that was only on one island.'

The man who wrote that, said Professor Jones firmly, was pulling the legs of his readers. Once, when I was out walking with him, we came on a feather I had never seen before. 'What's that?' Thomas looked at it carefully. 'Oh, Red Indians,' he said.

He and Elsi could even be quite funny together. Some years after her Manafon visit, Ann Eldridge, staying at Eglwys Fach, went with the two of them to call on their friends the West End dramatist N.C. Hunter and his wife. 'It was absolutely amazing, Ronald and Elsi chattered and smiled and were absolutely, totally *human*. They got tiddly and even told jokes.' But this was a shock. Together he and Elsi seemed to generate silence between them, 'Sighing, if one sighs.'

The Rev. Donald Allchin, who got to know the Thomas family later, remembered Gwydion as a young man telling him what a surprise it had been to visit other people's houses. People talked to each other there. 'Of course, there were weeks when nobody said anything in our house.'

'My feeling about Ronald and Elsi was that they were too much alike,' said Donald Allchin. 'They were so introspective I think they were both afraid of each other. If they'd pulled each other's legs it would have done them a lot of good.'

But, alone, they could. She knew just about everything

there was to be known about him, and could laugh at what she knew, even at his self-obsession.

At breakfast on my birthday he said, 'August 1st is a very special day.' While I was trying to work out why being 78 should be so very special, he continued, 'August 1st is the first day of three months' glorious unbroken bird-watching'!!

Other women might have thrown the teapot at his head; Elsi just put two exclamation marks in her memoirs. 'I think he meant it as a joke,' said Gwydion Thomas. 'The only thing is, after you've made a joke like that you pass the diamond over. My father would have forgotten the diamond.'

At times the humour turned on people they had known in Manafon, like the man, whose wife having left him, put a sign up on his gate, 'Gone for good.' In her memoirs Elsi tells R.S. Thomas's favourite joke. Two men in a car go through a traffic light at red. The passenger turns to the driver. 'Didn't you see that?' 'Oh yes, I saw it, but when you've seen one you've seen them all.' But what tells you more about the two is that this followed a conversation between them about what one saw when looking at a Corot or a Van Gogh. Once you had seen one Corot, Elsi had said, you had seen them all.

But to anyone encountering it for the first time the silence was a shock. Writing to Robert Conquest on 20 February 1962, Philip Larkin described such an occasion. 'Our friend Arsewipe Thomas suddenly was led into my room one afternoon last week, and stood there without moving or speaking ...'

I had experienced it three years earlier, when R.S. invited me to supper at Eglwys Fach, in the course of which he had a baked potato, Mrs Thomas had a baked potato, and I had a baked potato ('the strict palate'). I was uneasy from the start, eyeing the potato like an unexploded bomb, for I didn't know whether he would suddenly say grace, he was a vicar after all. But he didn't, he never did. And then the silence fell.

I was seventeen, and not used to silence, the Welsh are not. I remember I talked and talked and talked, I told anecdotes, I tried to think of the odd joke, I even, oh dear, tried to be intelligent, talking faster and faster like a variety turn dying on its feet. At one point I was aware of Thomas watching me, with an expression halfway between curiosity and amusement. Mrs Thomas did not look up from her potato. 'I don't think you realise how honoured you were,' said Gwydion Thomas. 'Nobody ever came to supper.'

There was an even more bizarre meal at which I should love to have been present. At Oxford Gwydion Thomas's acting ability brought him to the attention of Richard Burton, who later cast him in his film of *Dr Faustus*. Finding out who Gwydion was, Burton expressed a wish to meet his father, and a lunch was arranged at Woodstock. Present were Richard Burton and Elizabeth Taylor, Ronald and Elsi Thomas, and Gwydion and his girlfriend at the time. 'It was extraordinary. My mother never looked up from her plate once, Richard Burton spent the whole meal trying to chat up my girlfriend, and, during a lull in the conversation, I heard my father say, "And have you tried plaice?" He was talking about flatfish to Elizabeth Taylor.' Miss Taylor, Thomas told the Mowats, had not been his cup of tea.

But two things, apart from the tractors, shattered the silence at Manafon. The first was the arrival in 1944 of evacuees from Hackney fleeing the flying bombs, when, as billeting officer for Manafon, R.S. Thomas was himself forced to accept in the Rectory 'people who were just as barbaric as the enemy'. That is to say, the wives were young and bored, seemed to live entirely off swiss rolls, and at night would slope off to the pub, from which R.S. Thomas, with a house full of abandoned children, had to drag them away. In the end, boredom triumphing over danger, they went back to London, from which one rang up a few days later, wanting to return. Thomas refused. But the following year someone called whom he could not turn away.

In his bizarre autobiography the most bizarre passage of all is this:

As hopes that the war would not last long increased, the rector's wife expressed her desire to have a child. He had not thought seriously about the possibility. How can no one be a father to someone? But so it was, and one morning in August, 1945, after a night of thunder, he stood in a room in the hospital in Newtown to gaze at the bit of flesh lying in a cradle next to his mother's bed. This was Gwydion …

That passage offends the Manafon people who remember the family. '"The bit of flesh",' said Hazel Boulton. 'It is as though something had come which was surplus to requirements.' In her memoirs Elsi writes, 'Gwydion came to us on August 29, 1945. He was such a very lovely baby and beautiful child and young man, and still is, Madame Karczewska called him "a true poet's child".'

The trouble was, what were they to do with him? The true poet's child had a pair of lungs, and for two years did not give them a single night's uninterrupted sleep. First they got a nurse from the village, who, with her own small son, looked after him, but then he began to grow. Gillian Arney, the daughter of Joan Wood, his parents' former landlady, remembered that whenever the Thomases called on her mother, 'It was always Gwydion had done this or Gwydion had done that or he didn't toe the line. We'd go for a walk by the sea and there he'd be, running up and down the rocks. And when he got older he was beyond them.'

He, as a small boy, was left to wander the fields and to stray into farmyards, which was when, aged seven and riding on the brand-new Llwyn Copa tractor during the harvest, he found a bottle of cider. 'And finished it off. We had to take him home, he couldn't walk,' said Eric Jones. 'But that was that.' His parents, said Gwydion Thomas, may not have noticed.

He seems from an early age to have been nervous about his place in the household. His mother writes, 'When RS and I were starting off somewhere, Gwydion came running out of the house. "Did you forget me?" A very small person, probably about four years old.' Gwydion, aged sixty, over the phone line from Thailand, bawled, 'Yes, of course they'd forgotten me.' But the point is that at four it had already occurred to him. In adult life he remembers that neither of his parents sought to involve him in their interests. Elsi rarely talked about painting, R.S. never about religion, poetry, birds or the Welsh language.

Still he was diverting enough then to disrupt the schedules. Elsi writes,

> They were very lovely, those early days when he played in the hay and had houses in the empty pigsties. He could explore the fields with curlews calling all round him. One day he came running in from the fields with a curlew's egg in his hand, such a large egg. He was able to show me, two fields away, where he had found it, so that we were able to put it back in the nest. As the shadows grew longer we were sad for we should have to go back into the house soon.

Gwydion Thomas in Manafon felt that he too was in the Garden of Eden.

Then in September 1953, its gates shut on him. All three Thomases have left accounts of what happened. This is Gwydion:

> Some visits to Shrewsbury to acquire clothes and other things made me vaguely aware something was up. I had already had my curls removed a couple of years earlier when I had my tricycle, so it was not the haircut. We had been, in I think the May of that year, to Packwood [an English prep school in Shropshire], where I was introduced to a large gingery man

in plus fours with a lot of hair in his nose … I watched a lot
of boys playing cricket and running around. He asked me if
I would like to come and be one of his bunnies. 'Not likely,'
I said. But in September off to be a bunny I was dispatched
… And so started that routine of cold baths, breakfast,
prayers, Latin and maths, games, prayers, prep and tears that
is your average prep school.

He was eight, and had never been away from home.

The night before he left he ran round the houses in
Manafon, chalking 'Remember me' on the doorsteps. The
people of the village have not forgotten that, no more than he
has forgiven his parents, especially his father; his mother, he
believes, went along with his decision, though Thomas was to
give Peggy Mowat the impression that Elsi had been responsible. The party line agreed on by his parents was that the boy
had been too advanced for the village school, and the
secondary school too far away and not 'satisfactory', according
to Elsi, being full of the children of farmers. The fact that R.S.
Thomas's poetry was also full of the farmers did not occur to
them. 'There was no alternative.' Both Thomases clearly felt
guilty about what they had done.

'All those good years away at Packwood, Bradfield,
Magdalen, and Kings, and then marriage,' wrote Elsi. 'It all
seems such a waste …'

At the time they told him he was being sent away because
he had no friends, he who spent all the hours of daylight
playing with his friends. In the notes Gwydion prepared for
his son there is a long, sad, precise roll-call, like the names on
a war memorial, of those who had roamed the fields with him
and played in the river, and had even been reluctantly
admitted to the Rectory.

It was a school with a very good reputation, purred R.S.
Thomas, that enthusiast for all things Welsh, in *Neb*. 'It was a
turbulent time at first, and the little one nearly broke his heart

1. Ronald Thomas, born 29 March, 1913. His first, and possibly most successful, attempt at a smile.

2. The household god, aged two and a half.

3. Seated on the extreme left, this is the only surviving likeness of Peggy Thomas, R.S.'s mother. Seated extreme right is R.S.'s aunt Bess.
The man standing is his first cousin Ian Cameron.

4 (*right*). Tommy Thomas, R.S.'s father, second mate on the Irish ferries.

5. The young curate of Chirk, *c.* 1938.

6 (*right*). R.S. and Elsi. This, despite the gap between the two, is thought to have been taken on their wedding day, 5 July, 1940. Their son saw it for the first time at the R.S. Thomas Study Centre, Bangor.

7. R.S. and Elsi as a young married couple, Tallarn Green, *c.* 1940. The gap is wider.

THE RECTORY MANAFON

8. Manafon Rectory, the grandest of the three vicarages,
not one of which was to R.S.'s taste.

9. A new household god. Elsi with
Gwydion at Manafon, *c.* 1947.

10. On the back of this, taken
at Manafon *c.* 1948, someone has
written 'Gwydion and the Grim
Reaper'. R.S. brooded much on grass
and the bluntness of scythes.

11. Eglwys Fach church,
the pews of which the Thomases were to paint matt black.

Jennifer Dyer, Eglwys Fach W.I.

12. Elsi and R.S. at the Eglwys Fach
carnival, Festival of Wales 1958.

13. A day out. R.S. at Talyllyn,
c. 1958.

14. Gwydion Thomas during the filming of *Dr Faustus*, 1967, with one of the supporting cast. His parents had lunched with the Burtons, when R.S. and Elizabeth Taylor discussed flatfish.

15. P.C. Elfyn Pugh, R.S. and Bill Condry birdwatching on Ramsey Island, 1979, a moment of relaxation before the rutting stags closed in.

Elfyn Pugh

16. A selection of his first books.

17. Aberdaron church.

The Photolibrary Wales

18. Elsi in her garden at Sarn. 1977.

19. 'Thomas at home', as the *Telegraph* gleefully put it, leaning out of the half-door at Sarn as the Ogre of Wales.

Howard Barlow

20. Elsi's cartoon of the
two of them leaving
London for Wales after
their hospital stays,
R.S. clutching two
bags, one mischievously
marked 'Harrods', the
other 'Cymru'. *c.* 1980.

19. Elsi's cartoon of
herself in old age:
'hump-backed, gone in
the middle, spindle-
shanked me'. 1989.

22. R.S. beside the
front door of the
cottage at Sarn.

23. R.S. birdwatching on Anglesey towards the end of his life.

Howard Barlow

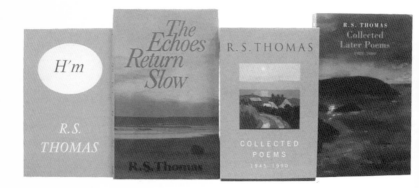

24. A selection of his later books.

through homesickness. But gradually he settled down …'
Cruel necessity, as Cromwell is said to have murmured over the
corpse of Charles I.

But Elsi, a little more honest than her husband, could in
old age still remember the postcards.

> The very first we had come from him read: 'Dear Mummy and
> Daddy, Please come to see me soon because I have a lot to tell
> you. I am not having a happy time.' But the matron Miss
> Davies with her eagle eye for seeing that all was not well had
> crossed out the 'not' so as not to encourage us to rush over
> and fetch him away.

In fact Elsi remembered it so well she did a little drawing in her
memoirs of the postcard with its large, despairing capitals.
Later, she goes on, he broke the school high-jump record. As
anyone might who dreamt of escape. But there is no mention
of any of this in Thomas's autobiographies.

Gwydion Thomas, as he puts it, felt bewildered and
abandoned. 'My mother would come and take me out some
Sundays in the appalling little grey van.' At boarding school,
cars had started to matter. 'We would go up into the little grey
hills above Llangollen. She would cook fried Spam and instant
potato on a Primus stove in the back of the van, and buy me
sherbet fountains. I think she knew if she took me home – it
was only about thirty miles – she would never get me back. At
Guy Fawkes she would buy fireworks, and we would let them
off in some God-forsaken lay-by.' And on top of the poignance
there was the odd embarrassment. Once his father came to play
football, 'I remember in red and white socks, with his white
legs running up and down ineffectively.'

But at Manafon the silence had returned.

'Going through my father's things there was one enormous gap,' said Gwydion Thomas. 'This was a man who for thirty years and more made sermons, wrote in parish magazines. Nothing of any of that had been kept, so there was this enormous gap in the dialogue between priest and poet. Half was missing.'

Not entirely. In an outhouse of the rectory in Newtown, a grand early Victorian house just about (in 2005) to be sold off to the highest bidder, with the area around it already cleared for development, was a small filing cabinet, the only thing in the whole damp upper room of the building. In this were old copies of the Cedewain Deanery magazine. The deanery then was made up of twelve parishes, the vicars of which because of paper rationing all wrote in the one monthly issue. One of these was Thomas, the first of whose contributions was dated January 1943.

What struck me was how absolutely conventional they were. Like the other vicars, he wrote about local things, gave details of confirmations, whist drives, tea parties, but this master of the English language wrote like them as well. 'A scrumptious tea in the school, and prizes given by the Headmistress were distributed by Mrs R.S. Thomas.' This may be the only time he used the word 'scrumptious'.

Then there was something odd. 'May [the New Year] see peace established amongst the nations and peace in our hearts. And may we appeal for the loyal support and faithful worship of all our parishioners.' It could be a parson's New Year's message in a time of peace, except this was in the middle of a world war, when others were praying for victory.

But when the next month a Manafon man in the RAF was killed over Germany, he was obliged to acknowledge that 'war stretches its long hand even into the smallest village of our country, and it behoves all of us to be mindful of those who suffer at this time'. When a child, aged five, died, Thomas noted only, 'Thus does God deal with us in ways we cannot understand.'

In the months which followed he chided his parishioners for poor attendance at church and for their materialism, something no vicar would dare do now ('The air of indifference prevailing in country parishes these days is painful and is in striking contrast with the keen interest evident in business matters'). He tried, and failed, to recruit a new verger, started a Wolf Cub troop and reminded his readers of the existence of Sunday School ('Parents of Manafon, for the last time I appeal to you'). In December 1944, he noted that there were just four at Sunday School, and just eleven parishioners at the Christmas service.

Often he made no contribution for months, and even when he wrote was terse. July 1944. 'There has been very little parochial news lately, but the news, from outside, has been staggering.' That was all. They must have heard about D-Day at the Rectory.

But in February 1945, there was a very otherworldly entry. 'ARMISTICE. In the event of an armistice being signed with Germany ...' The rector was giving notice that he proposed to hold a service of thanksgiving the night that happened. Except there could be no armistice, which is just a cessation of hostilities to discuss peace, not then, not ever: for two years unconditional surrender had been the publicly stated war aim of the Allies.

That duly occurred, but in August 1945, the rector of Manafon was still referring to an armistice. It was the month his cleaner retired, and to celebrate the end of the war in Europe the Wolf Cubs had an outing ('much fun was had'), then another, to the sea at Aberystwyth, to celebrate VJ Day. In *Neb* he rather grandly records that after the atom bomb was dropped on Hiroshima he was preparing to make a public protest in church the following Sunday. But Japan surrendered 'immediately', and he didn't. The only thing is, the bomb was dropped on 6 August and the Emperor did not announce Japan's surrender until 15 August, so the rector could have had his moment of drama in Manafon church.

On 17 October he recorded this: 'Baptism. October 19th. Andreas Gwydion, son of Ronald Stuart and Mildred Elsie Thomas. May God's blessing be upon the child also.' There was no mention that this was his own son.

The following year he was back to hounding his parishioners. 'A professing Church person's duty is to attend church every Sunday if possible.' Out of this may have come such lines in the poetry as 'How I have hated you for your irreverence.'

But in the spring there was a much more significant connection between the parson and the poet. This was the parson: 'February 6th, the burial of William Evans aged 49 years. Mr Evans had had a long and trying time in bed after his fatal accident.' This is the poet:

> Evans? Yes, many a time
> I came down his bare flight
> Of stairs into his gaunt kitchen
> With its wood fire, where crickets sang
> Accompaniment to the black kettle's
> Whine, and so into the cold
> Dark to smother in the thick tide
> Of night that drifted about the walls
> Of his stark farm on the hill ridge.
>
> It was not the dark filling my eyes
> And mouth appalled me; not even the drip
> Of rain like blood from the one tree
> Weather-tortured. It was the dark
> Silting the veins of that sick man
> I left stranded upon the vast
> And lonely shore of his bleak bed.

It is a very moving confession of impotence, something the parson could never make in prose.

On occasion it can be amusing to look behind the verse. That lovely poem 'Country Church' ends with the lines

It stands yet. But though soft flowers break
In delicate waves round limbs the river fashioned
With so smooth care, no friendly God has cautioned
The brimming tides of fescue for its sake.

'Fescue', not a familiar word, throws you a bit, suggesting its use is metaphorical, for surely some dreadful menace was gathering itself. Not so. Thomas, like all vicars, was simply having trouble with his old enemy, the grass. In August 1946, he wrote triumphantly, 'Helpers cut the churchyard grass in under two hours.'

But in 1947 Thomas, until then so terse, so conventional, broke ranks with the recorders of confirmations and whist drives. In June he made a long, and strident, contribution to the deanery magazine in response to a recent government measure.

Peace-time conscription is deplorable, but it shows the sinful nature of contemporary society. To us who live in Wales and are of Welsh blood it is deplorable for two main reasons. Firstly, Wales is a separate nation with its own language and traditions. It is therefore wrong to impose upon Wales a law passed by a parliament not composed of Welsh people. Secondly, Wales was the scene of one of the earliest settlements of Christianity in Britain, and Celtic Christianity established itself by peaceful and constructive means. If Christianity is to remain the religion of the people of Wales, it will only do so by those same means, and not by allying itself with a militarism that is always on the look-out for possible aggressors or rivals.

But while the logic is tangled, one thing is clear: the pacifist was becoming a nationalist as well.

The vicar at Chirk had told him, before he came to Manafon, not to reproach the farmers of cruelty towards animals, but the month after his excursion into political protest he was recommending a Humane Rabbit Trap. He was also quoting a very long letter to them on the importance of home seed production. This, by the agricultural scientist Sir George Stapledon, had appeared in the *Manchester Guardian*, which he must have been taking at the time.

These contributions may have exhausted him, for in September he was his old terse self again. 'Once the harvest is safely in, and people not so busy, I hope to get around to see you all.' Later that year he founded a youth club; he called it the Young Wales Club. Eric Jones Llwyn Copa gave a lovely glimpse of this club. 'He was all right, he did have ideas. I remember he introduced the game of musical chairs, only of course we didn't have any music. So he used to wink.' Another H.M. Bateman cartoon, 'R.S. Thomas Winks'.

'You wouldn't believe it, he was so dry and serious, but he seemed to come out of himself at the youth club,' said Glenys Bennett, who still lives in Manafon. 'He'd invent games, and people came from all over. Once a chapel minister came. And we were playing this game in which somebody called out an object, and it was the first team to get a brooch or a piece of lace, say. Anyway this time it was a button, only one team didn't have a button. And this chapel minister, he got up and there and then pulled one off his trousers. I looked at the rector, I don't think he liked anyone to see him laughing, but suddenly his whole body was shaking.'

Thomas said once that the only *Punch* cartoon that had ever made him laugh out loud was one in which a parson, preaching to a blank-faced congregation, is saying confidentially, 'Now I know what you're thinking. You're thinking that I'm being guilty of Sabellianism.' Sabellianism is a third-century heresy (the Church only kept him on, he assured his friend John Mowat, because it was useful to have someone around who could explain such things); he clearly identified with the man in the cartoon.

But his own sermons were not like that. 'Towards the end of them there'd always be a catch,' said Megan Humphries. 'Usually we'd be doing something wrong. I remember once him telling us he felt sure we'd all be much happier at home reading the *County Times*.'

In 1948 there were troubles with the help again. January: 'There is always difficulty in finding people willing to dig a grave in the event of a funeral. It is certainly not the Rector's job to run about the parish beseeching people to dig a grave.' That must have been his odd sense of humour at work. He missed three months on the trot after that, so he may have had to dig the graves himself. On his reappearance in the magazine he was worried about the church cleaner again, but then he was back among the whist drives, the baptisms, the exam successes, and not even the possible revival of the Home Guard could disturb the tenor of his contributions.

'December 1950. If the Home Guard is to be reformed let us hope that our men in this parish will not allow it to interfere with their attendance at church.' But there was a flash of the old spirit as he concluded, 'Service of the country is no substitute for religion.'

Two months later, he was forced to record, 'Instead of grumbling it is sometimes a pleasure to be able to express satisfaction, and this we do in connection with our Sunday School. It is nice to see nearly every child attending Sunday School fairly regularly and we appreciate it very much.'

In March 1951, in his last surviving parish contribution, he made an appeal to all humanity, it seems. 'The times are as bad as they can be. This may surprise people who are doing quite well, but of course we are thinking of spiritual matters … Put aside lazy and ungrateful habits, and come again to church so that the world may return to godly living.' It should be Donne or Latimer, preachers in cathedrals, men conscious of history and kings listening; instead it is a rector in the back of beyond who would have been lucky to get a congregation of eight or nine.

'He could really get up people's noses,' said Megan Humphreys. 'And at the same time he could be very kind. There was this deaf and dumb child, and he used to drive the family to different places and the doctor's. No one else had a car in the village. He used to speak Welsh to me, I was from the hills, or rather he used to try and speak it to me. His wasn't very good, he learned it when he was here, but then he had all the time in the world.

'The only thing was, he came here to be our Rector, not to learn Welsh.'

❧✝❧

This is where things get complicated. A biography of Dylan Thomas, say, is the story of one man and his talent. A biography of R.S. Thomas is not just the story of one man and his talent, it is at a fairly basic level a social and cultural history of his country, something about which most English readers know little. Dylan Thomas's story has many backcloths, of which Wales is one (his one recorded, and much-quoted, comment on Welsh nationalism consisted of three words, two of which were 'Welsh nationalism'). R.S. Thomas's story has just the one.

In 1946 the magazine *Wales* asked some of its contributors to complete a questionnaire. The first question was 'Do you consider yourself an Anglo-Welsh writer?' and the answers were varied. Most said 'Yes', though Vernon Watkins said, 'No. I am a Welshman, and an English poet. Wales is my native country, and English the native language of my imagination. I would be Anglo-Welsh only if I could write also in Welsh. I wish I could; but even then, English being the first language I learnt would remain my first language as a poet.'

R.S. Thomas replied with some vehemence. 'No! A Welsh writer. An Indian journal recently described me as a young

Welsh writer, and that pleased me as being essentially correct.'
Actually he was thirty-three. But it was what he said next that
is so curious. 'The question of a writer's language is a mere
matter of historical accident, and will seem to have little
ultimate significance.'

He would never say anything quite like that again. For in
the very same issue, Autumn 1946, he contributed a poem 'The
Old Language', which began,

> England, what have you done to make the speech
> My fathers used a stranger at my lips,
> An offence to the ear, a shackle on the tongue
> That would fit new thoughts to an abiding tune?
> Answer me now ...

In 1940 he had started taking Welsh lessons once a week in
Llangollen, driving over from his Flintshire curacy. In *Paths
Gone By* he wrote that he had done so 'in order to return to the
true Wales of my imagination', being clearly unbruised by his
failure to find the true Hebrides of his imagination. That was
written in 1972, and in Welsh.

Writing in English in *Autobiographical Essay*, he implied
learning Welsh was a shrewd career move on his part for it
meant he would have a wider choice of Welsh parishes, adding
that this would also get him out of the way of the bombers.
These, according to Gwydion Thomas, had already killed a
pheasant in the parish while his parents hid under a table and
played darts. He had, wrote R.S. Thomas, been influenced by
the poets he had read in Keidrych Rhys's magazine *Wales,* for,
though they wrote in English, they were conscious of what he
called 'their difference', and like them he too now wanted to
emphasise his. But he was about to take the process much
further.

For centuries, from the Cecils, or Seissyllts, of Tudor times
to Roy Jenkins (of whose remarkable speech it has been said

by the political columnist Alan Watkins that only one word, *situation*, betrayed his origins), Welshmen had been travelling east to reinvent themselves as Englishmen. It was the traditional route to getting on. A slight tinkering with the spelling of names (Rhys to Rees to Rice, Seissyllt to Cecil, Llywelyn to Leoline), a vagueness about geography (Roy Jenkins from the industrial valleys of South Wales informed his Oxford contemporaries, according to Lady Healey who was one, that he was from 'the Border country'), and you were away. Two or three generations, and the process was complete, though Jenkins, being ambitious, managed it in one. Thomas was equally ambitious, only in his case the other way. What he was about to do was to reinvent himself as a full-blown Welsh-speaking Welshman.

Years later, with administrative and educational jobs requiring an ability to speak Welsh, this has become more popular (it was said of one lecturer whose daughters were called Sophia, Emma and Angharad Lowri, that you could tell to the year the start of his Road to Damascus). But then it is part of the post-colonial experience to cock a snook at the registrar and change one's name (the Irish revolutionary Charles Burgess became Cathal Brugha).

Thomas's own publisher had been the bank clerk William Roland Rees until, following a mysterious incident with a shotgun in a Llandeilo bank, he became the poet Keidrych Rhys (his name, said Raymond Garlick, was the best poem he ever wrote). But Rhys, a Carmarthenshire farmer's boy, was already Welsh-speaking, and even Dylan Thomas, who made no attempt to learn Welsh, had parents from the rural West who could speak the language. It was a matter of where one was born and to whom, 'of historical accident' as R.S. Thomas, the city and port boy, noted sadly. For him it would be a long journey.

No Welshman could have been more of an outsider in his own country. He was a churchman when most of his countrymen, three-quarters of them by the end of the nineteenth century alone, were chapel (the poet David Jones in *Dai Greatcoat* said that his own forebears in Holywell were objects of suspicion simply because they attended church, regarded as an anglicising agency). More to the point, Thomas was a man whose exaggerated English accent, adopted to enrage his Welsh-speaking tormentors at Bangor, had stayed with him, and who now wanted to join 'this lot', as he had so scornfully called them. It would have astonished them.

It would also have puzzled some of his peers. Take Goronwy Rees, he of the similar ideas on personality (or lack of it). In some ways he was a mirror image of R.S. Thomas: born within a few years of each other in Wales, they both had two poems in Keidrych Rhys's anthology, both married Englishwomen, and were both fascinated by the symbolic potential of Welsh hill-farmers. In Rees's 1950 novel *Where No Wounds Were* an escaping German POW stumbles on a Iago Prytherch figure in the hills and finds his Nazi certainties crumbling before the man's far older, and unchanged, certainties.

Yet Rees, who had everything Thomas lacked, having been born to the purple into a Welsh-speaking professional family of professors and chapel ministers, could not as a young man wait to get away ('I wanted to grow up and felt I could not do so in Welsh'). He too went east.

Then he came back. In 1953 he was made Principal of Aberystwyth University, about as grand a position as a Welsh-man could aspire to in his own country, short of proclaiming himself Prince of Wales. On the eve of his return, he made a radio broadcast in which he attacked the Welsh language as a medium in which it was impossible 'to master the most advanced scientific and philosophical thought of our time', excoriated Welsh society as narrow and conventional, and spoke of his sense of liberation at having left in the first place.

He must have thought he could bring change with him. Instead after two years he got sacked, and would later describe

Aberystwyth as having been for his wife 'a Welsh ghetto [where] she [felt] as much at home as in some Patagonian settlement full of naked savages'.

This may be an extreme perspective against which to measure Thomas's decision, but there were many like-minded people who settled, in their case quietly, into the English professions, their birthrights just as quietly shelved. But in Thomas's case there was an additional problem: before he could claim his birthright he had first to find it.

Welsh in the twentieth century became for the first time a minority language. In 1911, 43.5 per cent of the population spoke it. By 1921 this had become 37.1 per cent, and the process was accelerating. In 1951 the figure was 28.9 per cent. The reasons were complex. First there was the industrial-isation of South Wales, where a new way of life, owing little or nothing to the past, meant it was Year Zero. This was followed by the migration there in great numbers of the English and Irish seeking work, then by the rise of the Labour Party, with its internationalist outlook, its priorities the defeat of recession and of Fascism (it had not helped the cause of the Welsh language that its great champion Saunders Lewis had regarded Hitler at the time of Munich as 'reasonable, and above all restrained and most suggestive ... in new ideas'). To Labour MPs from Bevan to Kinnock, Wales was a *region*. In fact it was two regions: the industrialised, and anglicised, south of the majority of the population, and the rural north and west where at the turn of the twentieth century the language held its own.

What was to happen next affected both. The main factor in the decline of the Welsh language was education in the early twentieth century, particularly in the new county schools where children were taught entirely in English. His grammar school, said the novelist Glyn Jones, 'was the most anglicising influence of my life'. R.S. Thomas in *Neb* wrote of how startled he had been to find on St David's Day in Holyhead how many of his teachers could speak Welsh; he had not known this, though these were people he saw every day. English, the key to getting on, had become the language of education, and the Welsh took to it with such enthusiasm that out of it for generations would come such strange Christian names as Handel, Haydn, and, alas, Byron.

But, though the old language had begun to shrink into the west and north, Thomas did not have to travel far to find it. At Manafon it was still there in the high hills, he had only to climb, and you can imagine the cartoon Max Beerbohm might have drawn: 'Mr R.S. Thomas in search of the Welsh', a gaunt grim figure disappearing into clouds full of worried eyes. For he could be seen as he climbed.

'When I'd spot him coming through the fields, I'd run in and warn mother,' says John Jones Penybelan. 'My mother could talk to anybody, but with him there were these long silences. Quite a fearsome-looking man, but odd. My mother used to give all the ministers boiled eggs when they called, and sometimes it'd be guinea-fowl eggs which have a very hard shell. I can remember the expression on his face now. He also had this odd way with bread and butter, he'd cut a bit off, then throw it into his mouth. As a boy I used to sit there, watching him. Once I laughed, and got sent to bed.'

Thomas would climb the hills, a copy of *Welsh Made Easy* under his arm, for his weekly lesson with H.D. Owen, minister at the Independent chapel at Penarth, the highest hill of all. Huw Derwyn Owen, minister here from 1935 to 1954, his picture still on the chapel wall, was a good-looking man with silver hair who might have made a fortune as a telegenic pastor on the religious channels of the American South. Instead he was here, at the top of the world, in Asgard, where Thomas sought him out.

'Climbing from the hollow he would look down and see the hillsides sometimes white with snow,' Thomas writes about himself in *Neb*, 'and the whole area hanging in front of him like an illusion.'

It is a lovely chapel, built in the late eighteenth century, when even chapels could be things of beauty. A hundred years later, let out at the seams to accommodate an expanding congregation, it would have been a monstrosity of painted pillars and varnish. But here there was no need, the congregation never did expand, and it is still the simple, humble meeting house it was. Yet, even though the average congregation is now just thirteen or fourteen, the chapel can seat 200. The seating is there for them, crammed into this small space, as is the huge pulpit from which a preacher could almost reach out and touch his congregation, and they him. In the chapels of Carmarthen I knew, the preacher was enthroned above them, a man above other men, but here there is an extraordinary feeling of intimacy and peace. It is the sort of place Ronald Thomas would have loved.

'The fault that he saw in Nonconformity,' he writes in *Neb*, 'was that it had started in plain but beautiful buildings ... and, after becoming respectable and beginning to win wealthier people as members, had tried to put a shine on things and finished up with grand and tasteless places.' In his 1990 *Planet* interview he was far more direct. 'How can anyone come into contact with God in the varnished, pitch-pine, mothball-smelling chapels of Wales with the worshippers, so-called, wiping a prayer off their faces before turning to take stock of who is there.' But it was to Nonconformity he turned when he set out to learn the Welsh language.

And it was in the chapel at Penarth, after two years of Welsh classes, that he gave his first public talk in the language. Today, when even the Methodists in Carmarthen have to call on Anglican priests, and, incredibly, on one occasion, a Catholic, to preach to them, this would take the form of a sermon, but in the early 1950s it was just an address. And even then the minister H.D. Owen had to ask permission of his deacons (or elders) and his congregation to hear a churchman talk: a chapel minister, Thomas wrote with some feeling, could be at the mercy of his deacons.

Thomas writes in *The Paths Gone By* that this was one of the big moments in his life, for it had taken him years to achieve this confidence.

> I remember the evening: the chapel with its oil lamps, the winds blowing outside, and some twenty local farmers and their wives assembled to listen to that oddity – an Englishman who had learned Welsh. Mr Owen introduced me, asking the audience not to laugh if I made a mistake. Then off I went for three-quarters of an hour like a ship driven in all directions by the wind. Somehow or other I reached dry land, and after a little discussion everyone went home. I myself walked home under the stars … A few days later I met someone who had been in the audience that night. 'I was impressed, honestly,' he said, referring to my performance. I went on my way, somewhat doubtful.

John Jones, that Heimdall of the hills, was also there. 'I was very bored. I was eighteen or twenty, and when H.D. had asked permission for him to come, people hadn't said "No", but not many had said "Yes" either. You know how it was then between church and chapel. His Welsh was a bit lumpy, rough you could say. I can see him now. He was just like…an object really. We had a job to understand him, people were not taking a lot in. Vicars are not like chapel ministers, they don't give much of a sermon, they just read it out. Afterwards nobody said anything.'

Thomas would climb the hills most days. 'He must have known every nook and cranny up there,' said Eric Jones Llwyn Copa. It became a talking point among his parishioners. 'Sometimes my father would see him up there, and he'd look wild,' said Megan Humphreys of Manafon.

His fitness even in old age was remarkable; in his late thirties on the hills it must have been fearsome as he paused up here to see the Wales of his imagination, the mountain Cadair Idris to the north-west, the Berwyns to the north-east, 'a prospect to raise the heart and make the blood sing', wrote the pacing vicar. His responsibilities were far below him, and from 1,000 feet seemed manageable. 'Turning to look down into the valley he would see "everything in perspective ..."' It is a significant choice of phrase, and what he saw in perspective was 'the people like ants below him, the church a small hut in the fields, and the river like a silver thread flowing down the valley' (*Neb*).

But two things still worried him. The first was that the Wales of his imagination contained that company to which he aspired, the writers in the Welsh language: would they accept him as one of their own?

That he was not sure of this must lie behind the rather mysterious parable in *Neb* which involves the Welsh-language novelist Islwyn Ffowc Elis, a chapel minister, then living some ten miles from Manafon. 'The rector called by one day to invite him to come for a walk to the moorland around Cwm Nant yr Eira, but Islwyn refused. He was too busy trying to save his own Wales. Were the two Waleses the same?' That is it, there is no more.

Then something happened. In 1951 the War Office decided to extend a British Army camp at Trawsfynydd in North Wales. Now the War Office already owned 10 per cent of the whole surface area of Wales, having requisitioned more land from a country itself one-tenth the size of England and Scotland than from the other two put together. This time some Welsh writers and nationalists decided to block the road in protest. 'The rector started first thing in the morning,' wrote Thomas in *Neb*, but what actually happened, as described by Islwyn Ffowc Elis in the Welsh-language magazine *Taliesin*, was a little different.

Whatever Ffowc Elis's aversion to moorland, Thomas had got into the habit of calling on him to practise his Welsh, also to practise his moans about Wales. 'The country's finished.

And the Nationalist Party does nothing.' Only this time the Nationalist Party was about to do something. Was he, Ffowc Elis enquired, with them?

'There was silence for some time. R.S. thought about it, then said, "But that's work for unmarried men, young men without children or family responsibilities."'

The two parted, Ffowc Elis, despite being a chapel minister and worried about breaking the law, saying dramatically, 'I shall be at Trawsfynydd, R.S., whatever you choose to do …' And on the day he and seventy others were there. He had long forgotten the conversation with Thomas, when he saw, far away, a small car like a black beetle on the road. Thomas had come.

At the time he was very worried about nuclear war. 'I remember that vividly the first time we met,' said Raymond Garlick. 'We all were, it was the time of the Korean War, but Ronald was very troubled. I remember the irony of it, he was a clergyman and ten years older than I was, and there I was, trying to cheer him up.' But Trawsfynydd was far more than an expression of his pacifism to Thomas.

When the *Montgomeryshire County Times* referred to the demonstrators as 'playboys' Thomas thundered in its letters column, 'The word is not usually applicable to clergy, ministers, professors, school-teachers and the like.' What he did not say, which had been far more important to him, was that some of them had also been the best-known writers in the Welsh language, Waldo and D.J. Williams amongst them. He named them in *Neb*, these who had accepted him as one of their own.

After Trawsfynydd, he wrote,

a new element came into his work. From trying to understand the countryman in Manafon as a man, and making him a symbol of the relationship that existed between man and the earth in the contemporary world of the machine, he turned to taking an interest in the history of Wales, her political and social problems, and his own situation as a Welshman who had to respond and write in English because of his upbringing. This was responsible for the element of bitterness in his work ...

Neb

For there was a second worry. Having achieved his heart's desire, fluency in Welsh, he had plunged himself into a crisis of his own making. He was not a young man; in his late thirties, he was approaching middle age, but he had served a long apprenticeship and was a master of the English language, a creative writer who would soon be at the peak of his powers. What was he going to do with the Welsh language, which was also in crisis?

In their anthology *Anglo-Welsh Poetry 1480–1980* (Poetry Wales Press 1984) Raymond Garlick and Roland Mathias traced Welsh poets writing in English back, as their title shows, to the late Middle Ages. But of those included up until 1900 half were Welsh-speaking, and at least a third also wrote in Welsh; for them to write in English was a matter of choice (the two languages, Welsh and English, were, one of them wrote, merely two sticks to be used when necessary). By the middle of the twentieth century for the majority that choice had gone, and a bitterness had developed between the Welsh who wrote in Welsh and their countrymen.

As Raymond Garlick recalled, 'On the Welsh side there was a feeling that those who wrote in English were less Welsh, less patriotic, less well informed, and were undermining Welsh literature.' The Welsh poet Bobi Jones, looking down from the heights of a 1500-year-old tradition, called Anglo-Welsh writing 'an interesting regional literature'. But Wyn Griffith in *The Welsh* (Pelican Books 1950) wrote, 'More than half the population of Wales does not speak the Welsh language. Does this necessarily rob it of its nationality?'

Garlick, who was to make some kind of accommodation between the two his life's work, pointedly put the quotation 'Is there no balm in Gilead?' on the title page of his magazine *Dock Leaves*, but later quietly dropped it.

In 1951 he wrote a moving editorial on the dilemma of the Anglo-Welsh. 'In some way this peculiar people, wandering in the wilderness of the modern world, cut off from the traditional culture of the nation, divorced from its language and literature, has to be reconciled to its past. It must have a past if it is to have a future.'

'It seems so long ago now,' I said.

'So long ago,' said Garlick.

For a resolution of a sort did come in the next generation. What follows was written by the poet and academic Tony Conran in *Planet* in 1989, and is a beautifully concise statement of the dilemma and of the way a younger writer like Conran coped with it in the second half of the twentieth century.

For older people, and poets among them, it had often seemed that the only thing to do with Wales was leave ... But now a new generation was coming to be aware of what we had lost. For most of us Wales was a journey into an exile we were born with. We were heirs to a richness we could only apprehend as memories of childhood. We were third-generation immigrants into our own land, easier with English people, very often, than with our own still Welsh-speaking compatriots. Threatened by both the ruling class English intelligentsia we were trained to serve, and by the native Welsh culture that we felt had the birthright, we tried to make room for ourselves. We wrote elegies for lost Wales. We proclaimed that the Dragon has two tongues. We translated Welsh poetry ...

But in the 1950s R.S. Thomas, part of an older generation, was trying to cope in his own odd way. In 1952 he wrote in Welsh about Anglo-Welsh literature in the magazine *Y Fflam*,

'The Flame', '*Gan fod yng Nghymru famiaith* ... Since there is
in Wales a thriving mother tongue, a true Welshman can
regard English only as a means of rekindling interest in Welsh
literature and of leading people back to the mother tongue.'
This was a bizarre piece of logic, the implications of which,
had they been pursued, were pointed out by the critic Randal
Jenkins in *Poetry Wales*: 'To bring about its own demise is an
extraordinary aspiration for a literature.'

What Thomas did not say was that, the year before, he had
himself contributed his first published poem in Welsh to *Y
Fflam*. He had written prose in Welsh before for the magazine,
remarkably as early as 1946, long before he was fluent in
speech, but this was different, this was verse. The poem was *Y
Gwladwr*, 'The Countryman', and is a reworking of his
Prytherch themes, but only up to a point. Nobody gobs in the
fire in *Y Gwladwr*. 'It is a very romantic poem, a bit like the
stuff the Georgian poets wrote,' said Professor Bobi Jones. The
poet is sentimental, even reverential, towards the countryman
whom he appears to see at long range, in the old way. Like all
new boys, he was being careful about what he said.

Raymond Garlick said, 'The editor, Euros Bowen, told me
he had found himself in a dilemma when it was submitted.
There were some linguistic mistakes, so what was he to do, tell
R.S. or correct them? He quietly corrected them, and Ronald
would have seen that and he would have known what it
meant. I don't think there were many poems in Welsh after.'

As Thomas told his *Planet* interviewers, he had left it too
late. Glyn Jones, who though Welsh-speaking, wrote in
English all his life, said it all turned on the language a poet
used in adolescence, 'the language of his awakening'. If so,
then Bobi Jones, whose first language was English, just made
it under the wire in time.

'I was in the first form where there was a choice between
Spanish and Welsh. The headmaster hadn't recruited enough
for Welsh, so he picked on me. "What's the Welsh for good

morning?" I just sat there. "What's the Welsh for goodnight?" Silence. "I think you'd better take Welsh, don't you?" That was the sum of my vision.' Thus Bobi Jones became one of the most famous Welsh poets of his day.

'I sympathised with R.S. He was in a quandary, tied down by his family heritage, unfulfilled, unable to write in the literature and the language he loved most. But that had been betrayed long before he could become a writer. English people, even the most liberal, sympathetic English, haven't a clue about any of this. To them it would just be whimsy on his part, they wouldn't know what the agony was about.

'He wanted to be one of us. He'd come to meetings of the Welsh section of the Welsh Academy, not the English section. And yet he wasn't one of us, he was an odd man out wherever he went. He was on the sidelines, so engaged, so involved, so deeply serious. Yet this is why he succeeded as an artist. His tension gave him a lot, gave him something to say. He was a driven man.' And then Bobi Jones said this. 'He was ... lucky.'

Thomas seemed to have acknowledged something of this himself, when, after telling his *Planet* interviewers about his failure to turn himself into a Welsh writer, he said, 'I cannot see how Welsh as it is now would have been available for the requirements I make upon language. It is a confession which gives me no joy ...' As a poet he found himself with the English language as his cellmate.

❧✛❧

In 1998, forty-four years after he had left the village and two years before his death, R.S. Thomas came back to Manafon. This was remarkable in itself. In 1976, in a letter to his Bristol friends the Mowats, he had described a car journey through mid-Wales. 'It was a lovely May day and the countryside was superb ... I collected some wild cherry between Crughywel and Talgarth, and cut through a piece of Montgomeryshire I had not visited since Manafon days, coming like a ghost to trouble joy.' When he did come back in 1998, he visited the Rectory, which had been bought from the Church a decade earlier by Lorraine Greeson-Walker, a district nurse, and her husband. 'He came in and said, "It's changed." Then after a while he said, "It's warm."'

But there was something even more remarkable about the visit. He had come to read his poems.

'I'd heard him read before,' said Dr Glyn Tegai Hughes, who was there that night. 'It was at Gregynog, and he said they would be in two sections, first the poems about Wales, then those about God. There would, he went on, be an interval. During the interval a very young girl got up and said, "What would you like to happen to Wales, Mr Thomas?" He said, "Send the English back, then concrete everything over." "But what would you have to write about then, Mr Thomas?" He said, "This is probably a good time to go on to the second part."

'But the Manafon reading, that was an unusual event, at least that is how I remember it. There was certainly a feeling among some of the people there, it wasn't just my feeling, that he owed some explanation to the people of Manafon. This wasn't expressed by him, he didn't express that sort of thing. All he did was explain something of the background to the poems. He went into this in some detail, talking about the landscape, the light on a field, or some event, the remote farm a hearse couldn't get into so the coffin had to be carried across the fields.'

Some who were there thought the reading an apology, but nobody could remember hearing the word, though the memory of the night had stayed with them all. 'Looking back, it was an extraordinary event,' said the Rev. Bill Pritchard. 'There was this man who'd been their rector and was now the greatest Anglo-Welsh poet. They hadn't realised what they'd been dealing with. The church was full, I think there were eighty-five people there, including a scholar who'd come from the States. R.S. had driven himself over from Oswestry, some twenty miles away. He had a very old man's voice, and became tired. There was a lot of emotion that evening.'

The only thing was, his audience were the children of people whose half-witted grins he had described; he had talked about the frightening vacancy of their minds, mentioned their skulls, laughed at the hill-farmers of his parish on their brand-new tractors, and shown his readers round poverty-stricken home after poverty-stricken home. Some of these poems he read.

'It was insensitive, you might say,' said Hazel Boulton. 'One of the poems he chose to read was about a man dying with his face to the wall. His people were in the church that night.'

'I think he wrote about Father once,' said Eric Jones Llwyn Copa. 'I know Father didn't like it, it was too distant somehow.'

'Well, he did have time on his hands, he only had the one church,' said Ruth Hall. 'What we didn't know then was that he was using this time to write poetry.'

Some must have done. In 1947, at 6.40 pm on 21 August, the rector was due to give a talk on BBC radio. In the script of this he referred to what he called his 'earlier work', and quoted an example (though the example had been published only a year earlier in *The Stones of the Field*). Whether he intended it or not, what followed would have been pure comedy, as Manafon families settling down to their evening meals would have heard the familiar posh voice of their rector reading.

> We who are men, how shall we know
> Earth's ecstasy, who feels the plough
> Probing her womb,
> And after, the sweet gestation
> And the year's care for her condition?
> We, who have forgotten, so long ago
> It happened, our own orgasm,

When the wind mixed with our limbs
And the sun had suck at our bosom;
We, who have affected the livery
Of the time's prudery,
How shall we quicken again
To the lust and thrust of the sun
And the seedling rain?

Unfortunately, though the village, as Ann Eldridge remembers, was waiting around its radio sets, the programme was cancelled at the last minute. Why, I have been unable to find out. So Manafon did not hear the vicar riding the surf of sexual metaphor.

He had now abandoned such work, Thomas in the BBC script airily went on, and was writing about landscapes which were localised, not general. As an example he quoted, of all things, 'The Peasant'. The west, and orgasms, were out. His parishioners, or at least the farmers on the hills who tended to be chapel, were in. He had said that Holyhead had made him a poet, but it was Manafon which made the poetry.

Thomas had been twenty-nine when he came. In *The Paths Gone By* he writes, 'It was here that I became conscious of the conflict that exists between dream and reality.' He said so himself, reminiscing in a 1972 BBC film. 'I was brought up hard against this community and I really began to learn what human nature, rural human nature, was like. And I must say that I found nothing that I'd been told or taught in theological college was of any help at all in these circumstances. It was just up to me to find my way amongst these people.'

And they, or at least their children sixty years on, recognised this. 'It must have been like walking into another country for him,' said Hazel Boulton. 'What he found here fascinated and horrified him,' said Ruth Hall.

In the 1972 BBC film he talked about muck and blood and hardness, the rain and the spittle and the phlegm of farm life.

Muck, hardness, rain, yes. But blood, spittle and phlegm? It leaves you with the impression that the Montgomeryshire hills were a vast ENT clinic. 'But, as one experienced it and saw how definitely part of their lives this was, sympathy grew in oneself, and compassion and admiration ... The strongly-charactered hardness of these Border people really did make an impression on me, as far as poetic material was concerned ...' His spiritual efforts might not have had much effect, he went on, but his experience had paid off in poetry.

The BBC film had used earlier black-and-white footage in which Thomas is shown climbing a hill, lean and fit, spring-heeled against the sky as he moves above the tree-line. He is wearing a duffel coat and a dog-collar, his usual dress in the 1950s. Fishermen's smocks came later, followed in the 1980s, after his retirement, by the tweed sports jackets and red ties.

Then in the film he is clear of the claws of the last trees, high above the farms and fields, and, at that point an old man with a thumbstick, a sack about his shoulders, pops up as though out of the rock. Whether he was there all the time, or hired from Central Casting by the BBC, is not known, but to the life it is 'That man, Prytherch, with the torn cap'.

Thomas moves awkwardly towards him like a policeman approaching a suspect, and the old man jerkily lifts his stick in salute, as you or I, or any man might, who has just seen a vicar materialise on the roof of the world, pursued by a film crew. There for a moment the two stand, ringed by sky. I would love to know what passed between them, but a Ford Cortina also materialises and accelerates, causing the two to part. Busy old place, the moor that day.

There had been such meetings.

No speech : the raised hand affirms
All that is left unsaid
By the mute tongue and the unmoistened lips.

But that might have been Thomas himself. 'Sometimes he'd say hello, sometimes he'd just pass you by,' said Jones Llwyn Copa, 'He was all right, but there were many more likeable chaps. Strange from the off, he was.'

'The farmers I met later thought him a bit of a mystery,' said the Rev. Bill Pritchard. 'Some had been farmers' sons when he came calling, and what they remembered most was that he was always on at them about not going to church.'

But it was the poems he wrote about them that first brought him to public attention. In some of these there is great compassion, as in this, 'Death of a Peasant', the poem he was to read at Manafon.

> You remember Davies? He died, you know,
> With his face to the wall, as the manner is
> Of the poor peasant in his stone croft
> On the Welsh hills. I recall the room
> Under the slates, and the smirched snow
> Of the wide bed in which he lay,
> Lonely as an ewe that is sick to lamb
> In the hard weather of mid March,
> I remember also the trapped wind
> Tearing the curtains, and the wild light's
> Frequent hysteria upon the floor,
> The bare floor without a rug
> Or mat to soften the loud tread
> Of neighbours crossing the uneasy boards
> To peer at Davies with gruff words
> Of meaningless comfort, before they turned
> Heartless away from the stale smell
> Of death in league with those dank walls.

I find that very moving, having stood in just such a room, to which relatives, let alone strangers, were only admitted in moments of extremis. I had been brought there to see my mother's brother, a huge, broken man lying in bed, and the details of the poem are as I remember them: the bare boards, the grubby sheets, the quiet, and the bewilderment of the cornered giant, whose brute strength had triumphed over everything except this. These are the things that hurt Thomas into poetry.

You can sense the shock from the way the early poems about hill-farmers in *The Stones of the Field* fall into a set pattern. There is the meeting, the wrinkling of the nose in disgust at the man's smell/joylessness/materialism, followed by the poet's recovery of his balance as he manages to see him in terms of a tree. 'a tree's/Knotted endurance', 'hands/Veined like a leaf, and tough bark of the limbs', 'Enduring like a tree', 'an old tree lightened of the snow's weight'; even this, 'An ash tree wantons with sensuous body and smooth/Provocative limbs to wanton play the whore to his youth.' The image in turn becomes the postscript that the creature is also human. 'Look, look, I am a man like you.' 'He also is human', 'Yet this is your prototype.' Poem after poem. 'A Peasant'. 'Greeting'. 'A Labourer'. 'Affinity'. Had you read these poems when *The Stones of the Field* first appeared you would have wondered where Thomas would, or could, go from here.

But amongst these poems there is the long 'The Airy Tomb'. No shock now, but a fascinated sympathy for the young man who has inherited his parents' smallholding, 'that grim house nailed to the mountain side'. He has virtually severed all connection with his own species below him in the valley, and, by doing this, with its obsession with education, love and religious faith. For him there is just the elemental round of farm life, 'With the moon for candle, and the shrill rabble of stars/Crowding his shoulders'.

His death is of a piece with this life, and is far removed from the grave into which, with horror, he saw his parents shovelled,

> and a fortnight gone
> Was the shy soul from the festering flesh and bone
> When they found him there, entombed in the lucid
>   weather.

The man whom others might consider trapped in these acres is at last part of them, and of their much older way of death. He dies as a lamb dies, his tomb the open air. In 'The Airy Tomb' R.S. Thomas seems to have broken through the limitations of his background and of his own personality: the farmer is not held here at arm's length and examined, Thomas is enthralled.

But in his second collection *An Acre of Land*, published in 1952, there is no need for nervous postscripts about a shared humanity. The farmers have acquired a grandeur in their emptying land.

> Too far, too far to see
> The set of his eyes and the slow phthisis
> Wasting his frame under the ripped coat,
> There's a man still farming at Ty'n-y-Fawnog,
> Contributing grimly to the accepted pattern,
> The embryo music dead in his throat.

Thomas's own reading of this, his voice soft in the Welsh syllables, is again very moving. Phthisis, a variant of TB, is not something you will find in most dictionaries, but the condition, or at least the word, seems to have fascinated him at this stage for he uses it again in *The Minister* ('my eyes glowed/ With a deep, inner phthisic zeal').

The poems in this collection are among the most beautiful he was to write. They include 'Death of a Peasant', the delightful lyric 'Song for Gwydion', and in 'The Evacuee' the description of the young girl waking

under a loose quilt
Of leaf patterns, woven by the light
At the small window, busy with the boughs
Of a small cherry …

And then there is the gentle comedy of this:

the knight at arms breaking the fields'
Mirror of silence, emptying the wood
Of foxes and squirrels and bright jays.
The sun comes over the tall trees
Kindling all the hedges, but not for him
Who runs his engine on a different fuel.
And all the birds are singing, bills wide in vain,
As Cynddylan passes proudly up the lane.

Thomas had seen the first tractor come to Manafon.

But, apart from Cynddylan, there are no comic characters in the poems. They were there in the pub at Manafon, a villager told me, but the rector did not do pubs. He did not do intimacy either. Given his position, this would not have been proffered (Elsi Thomas recalled a Christmas lunch to which, early on in their marriage, they were invited, when she and R.S. Thomas ate in one room, the farmer and his family in another, and she was overcome by nostalgia for the merry Eldridge Christmases she had known). But then he would not have sought intimacy. It is the hill-farmer as object that Thomas writes about: he writes about that with compassion, with disgust, with awe, but rarely with human curiosity.

There is one absence in his portraits of such men, their humour. As the poet Leslie Norris wrote in *Poetry Wales*, 1972, 'One would never know that the hill men are quick of wit and speech, tender and passionate as any other men, loyal and tolerant and helpful friends. Not all of course, and not always; but they are human. And what of their humour? Who would guess from these poems that Iago could be guilty of hilarity?'

To digress for a moment, meet Selwyn Davies. A bachelor in his seventies, Selwyn has a 117-acre hill farm in Carmarthenshire much like Iago Prytherch's: the small untidy yard, the wrecked machinery, the sheets of corrugated iron wherever there is a gap in a hedge, two broken-down vans, puppies and ducks and chickens everywhere. A plum tree in blossom in a kitchen garden. 'I've had beans from there 27 inches long. I complained about one to the man who sold me the seeds and told me they'd grow to 18 inches. I said they didn't fit into the pan. "But Mr Davies, you have to cut them."' We were drinking tea in his kitchen, which was untidy beyond belief, old plates stacked in a wash-basin, papers and letters all over the place. 'The maid left,' said Selwyn equably, who had never employed a maid in his life. And so Iago Prytherch might have talked, had the rector chosen to listen.

At the same time he could be sentimental about such men. In his essay 'The Mountains' he writes about the men in the ruined hill farms who 'spent long days … swapping *englynion* over the peat cutting'. Yes, some may have done, and one or two might have been skilled in *cynghanedd*, that intricate system of alliteration and internal rhymes in which the four-lined *englynion* were written.

An example of this in English, according to Bobi Jones, is on supermarket bags ('More reasons to shop at Morrison's'), while Glyn Jones in Soho came on 'Fifty nifty nudes'. My grandfather Philip Rogers, a smallholder, was so skilled he could talk in *cynghanedd*, though the example I treasure, but will not quote, spoken one night in the pub at Bancyfelin, has to do with farting. There was a tradition of such obscene expertise, until recently denied by Welsh scholars, dating back to the Middle Ages. Thomas does not mention this, any more than he mentions the social status of the men he met on the hills. They were not peasants, or hireling labourers; they would have owned the land, having bought their farms when the old estates were wound up.

He felt, he said in his *Planet* interview, as though he were in a vacuum in Manafon. He liked to give this impression of claustrophobia, of the lonely learned man at his papers, far from anywhere and from intelligent company. Again, it was not quite like this. The novelist Ffowc Elis was just over the hills, and Gregynog three miles down the road, the stately home where Gwen and Daisy Davies, the two sisters of Lord Davies of Llandinam, lived, and where the Thomases seem to have been frequent visitors. Elsi recalled waspishly, 'Gwen painted rather half-hearted landscapes but the room in which she worked filled one with envy, for there were shelves around the entire room with racks underneath full of unused canvases.' Servants were chosen for their singing voices, and Benjamin Britten and Peter Pears would visit to give concerts. There were paintings everywhere. 'The sisters knew little about music or painting, but had especially good advisors. Their splendid Impressionist collection, later given to the National Museum of Wales, is the best collection that exists.' When on loan to Japan in 1987 these paintings were insured for £39,000,000. And, Elsi went on, there were books, books, books, and the Gregynog Press, a grand fine-art publishing house, in the stable. It was a rum sort of vacuum that Thomas lived in in Manafon.

He also went off on his own whenever there was an opportunity. On 14 September 1944, Ruth Hall's mother noted in her diary, 'Rector went to Scotland on his holidays. Mrs Thomas here to supper. Brought jar of honey.' Towards the end of 1945, again alone, he turned up in Llanybri in South Wales at the home of Keidrych Rhys. Mrs Rhys, the poet Lynette Roberts, wrote to Robert Graves: 'A young minister and poet has been here, a gloomy sort of person – who like most intelligent ministers today doesn't believe in the church that he preaches. It is the people far more than they who have the conviction. He is R.S. Thomas and he has gone to St

David's with Keidrych with the idea of rambling and enjoying the countryside of Pembroke which he does not know.' Mrs Rhys was not much taken with Thomas or his poetry ('He is too much the vicar brooding on what he terms "the boorish farmer" ... He requires mountains to move him'). But her husband, for £60 down, published him.

In 1952, Thomas paid for a second collection of poems, *An Acre of Land*, to be published ('or rather I should say printed', sniffed his detractor Cynric Mytton-Davies). This time it was the Montgomery Printing Press at Newtown run by a Polish émigré, whose wife Elsi had met through her extramural classes. A year later the same press brought out *The Minister*, a long poem commissioned by the BBC. Thomas, though by now his poems were appearing in *Encounter*, *Poetry* (London), the *New Statesman* and the *TLS*, was still in the world of the vanity press, but this was to change quickly.

To quote Cynric Mytton-Davies again, *An Acre of Land* 'somehow caught the attention of The Critics', only he knew why. One of *The Critics*, a BBC literary discussion group, was by chance Alan Pryce-Jones, then editor of the *TLS*, whose enormous family department store at Newtown advertised regularly in the deanery magazine ('"I only wish your warehouse was in Mill Hill." Mrs JDE, Mill Hill. It makes you think, doesn't it?'; they were amazing adverts).

On air Pryce-Jones hailed a new and major voice, though Raymond Garlick, who heard the programme, remembered one of his colleagues saying that the best thing Thomas could do was to come to London and lay all this Welsh nonsense aside. In a letter to Garlick, Thomas wrote drily, 'I shall be off to London any day now to be cured of my extreme nationalism.'

There followed a moment of even more pronounced chance, a meeting at a party, and the circumstances will tell you something about the rector of Manafon's social life. James Hanley, the author of *Boy* and *Ebb and Flood*, whose 1985 *Times* obit was headlined 'Neglected Genius of the Novel', was living at the time in Montgomeryshire, having rented the gatehouse of a stately home near the village of Llanfechain, in the hills above Welshpool. The Hanleys moved between this and London, and their metropolitan friends like the MP Woodrow Wyatt and the BBC producer Leonard Cottrell often visited them at Llanfechain.

According to their son Liam Hanley, his parents' Montgomeryshire was a strange place. 'These were county people, landed gentry, squires, cotton brokers, and my mother, who was very very upper-class, got on well with them. It was an English world, of cocktail parties and gins and orange, it was rather like living in the colonies.' As for literary London, the Hanleys moved in a world of writers and publishers (Henry Miller had contributed a foreword to Hanley's novel *No Directions*). They knew everyone. This is Dorothy Hanley writing to a friend in 1953: 'It's a funny thing, when we were in London having dinner with the Rosses I sat next to a nice man, a poet called Laurie Lee.' The Rosses were the publisher and editor Alan Ross and his wife. 'He asked me where I lived and I told him. He said, "Do you know Meifod? We know some people there very well. Lady Meade, do you know her?" I said I knew of them, but we had never met. Well, when I got home with a lousy cold, Lady Meade called.' In one of her letters she mentions calling on 'the Thomases' for lunch.

'I can remember the night my father and R.S. Thomas met,' said Liam Hanley. 'My father was familiar with his work up to a point, he had read his poems in magazines like *Poetry London*, and he held this party so the two of them could meet. It was summer, and the two of them disappeared into the garden.'

They had a lot in common. Hanley, brought up in Liverpool, had also stared with longing at the mountains of North Wales. He had like Thomas's father gone to sea as a youth, and had written many books about the experience, the most famous being *Boy*; his *Times* obituarist was to single out the 'disturbingly acute, though gloomy, vision of his best books'.

He and Thomas shared an intensity in their writing, liked toffs (Hanley had married a second cousin of the Earl of Ancaster, though she had previously been married to a mechanic from Llandudno), and were fascinated by Wales and the Welsh past. 'They were both very striking men,' said Liam Hanley. 'I can see them now, walking along a beach in the wind and rain. To me, a very callow young man, Thomas was like God.'

Thomas was to retain an enthusiasm for Hanley's books, and I can remember him telling me to read them. But then he had a lot to be grateful for. He had already tried 'one or two' London publishers, and had received what he described as a cryptic note from T.S. Eliot at Faber to say that though they were not going to publish his collection, he (Eliot) hoped that someone would. This is what Hanley was now to arrange.

'My father was surprised that no one had ever published his poems, and he asked him for some and submitted these to Rupert Hart-Davis, so you could say that meeting was quite an important event. My father was very good at placing other people's work. "Send it to Mr So and So." He was the complete professional.'

It was a curious choice. Rupert Hart-Davis, an eccentric, cricket-loving Old Etonian and former Guards officer, ran a small, newly established publishing firm from what his biographer Philip Ziegler described as a ramshackle eighteenth-century house in Soho Square. His major successes to date had been *Seven Years in Tibet* and *Le Hibou et la Poussiquette*, Lear's *Owl and the Pussycat* translated into French, which sold 12,000 copies the first Christmas it was published. But he also published poetry by Charles Causley, Andrew Young and Edmund Blunden. Ironically he hated Geoffrey Hill, the only one of his poet contemporaries whom Thomas himself liked. When Hart-Davis retired as a judge of the W.H. Smith Poetry Prize he instructed his successor to resist pressure to give the prize to Hill, the favourite of Christopher Ricks, another judge, on the cheerful grounds that Hill wrote gibberish.

He would seem to be the last person to take on R.S. Thomas. Four times married, the first time to the actress Peggy Ashcroft, he lived in a flat above his offices, separated from them by another flat in which lived that mysterious actress Pamela Brown who glides through so many Powell and Pressburger films. There were books everywhere. 'What used to be my spare bedroom is now breast-high in Eng-lit.' But it was from here in 1955 that *Song at the Year's Turning* was published. Thomas dedicated it to James Hanley, which, as Hanley's biographer Chris Gostick said, was a fair indication of friendship and gratitude. The poems were a selection from his first two books, with *The Minister* printed in full. Thomas, who three years earlier had told Raymond Garlick, 'I am so hard up that I have almost ceased buying books', now wrote, 'I hope the necessity for publishing my own stuff is over.'

The book came with a foreword from John Betjeman, whom Thomas travelled to London to see. Betjeman knew his work, and had loved his version of the Welsh traditional folk verse 'The Walls of Caernarvon'; this, as he now wrote, was 'the perfect lyric'. The poet and scholar W.J. Gruffydd had published a literal translation of it in his Festival of Britain book *North Wales and the Marches*:

> One rainswept eventide I went a-walking
> On the shores of Menai in silent meditation:
> Loud was the wind and wild was the white billow,
> And the sea was hurling over the walls of Caernarvon.
>
> But on the morrow morn I went a-walking
> On the shores of Menai, and stillness was on them;
> Silent was the wind, and kindly was the sea,
> And the sun was shining on the walls of Caernarvon.

This is what Thomas made of it. He called his poem *Night and Morning*.

One night of tempest I arose and went
Along the Menai shore on dreaming bent;
The wind was strong, and savage swung the tide,
And the waves blustered on Caernarvon side.

But in the morrow, when I passed that way,
On Menai shore the hush of heaven lay;
The wind was gentle and the sea a flower,
And the sun slumbered on Caernarvon tower.

Betjeman so loved this that, as Bevis Hillier relates in the second volume of his biography, he recited it to a neighbour, a Mrs Hester Knight who, during a train strike, was driving him to London. 'Then and there I learned it off by heart by making John repeat it.' Mrs Knight, one of the Loyds of Lockinge, was one of the largest landowners in Britain. But by a freak she was also one of the Loyds of Llanwrda, whose great-great-grandfather had heeded the call, as the Welsh put it, and become a chapel minister, before heeding an even louder call to become a banker. He had gone east in the old Welsh way, and become so rich that the English were obliged, in their old way, to make his son a peer. Thus two ways of life that had diverged touched, briefly, in a car in Berkshire.

Betjeman's introduction irritated Thomas. As he wrote to Raymond Garlick on 22 February (after telling him that, after five years of correspondence, they might now start using Christian names, also that he had a new car, an Austin van), 'Betjeman's remarks ... are almost drivel, and are not a true statement of my views at all. To say that Yeats influenced me and in the same breath to say I don't believe in reading aloud is rubbish.' Betjeman had also said that Thomas was 'essentially a local poet', which must have got up his nose even more, and that 'a feeling for Dissent' (this of a church rector) gave the poetry 'a peculiar Welshness'.

But Betjeman's conclusion was graceful and heartfelt.

'This retiring poet had no wish for an introduction to be written to his poems, but his publisher believed that a "name" was needed to help sell the book. The "name" which has the honour to introduce this fine poet to a wider public will be forgotten long before that of R.S. Thomas.'

Thomas's gratitude not only extended to a poem contributed to *A Garland for the Laureate* (Celandine Press 1981), he actually turned up with all the other contributors, Kingsley Amis, Larkin, Spender, Roy Fuller, John Wain, when the book was presented to Betjeman in his Chelsea house on his seventy-fifth birthday. In a letter to James Hanley he wrote, 'I felt I had to go.' The event was filmed by Jonathan Stedall for his BBC series *Time with Betjeman* and is very funny. Larkin and Thomas climb out of the rear of a very small car, Larkin clutching a bulging briefcase.

As the news is broken to Betjeman, then in poor health, that they have all lined up in his passage, he says, 'What, old Kingers and Philip and co?' And then on cue Amis bounds in, 'Hello, mate.' Each poet in turn is presented. 'This is Ronald Thomas', and there he is, extending a hand and saying, 'Helleo', like royalty at a line-up. Even in this company his accent marks him out. 'Oh yes, great man,' says Betjeman. For this one moment Thomas is among his peers, the foremost poets of the time writing in English, and in that greeting seems the most English of them all.

But all that is far into the future. He and his publisher were to develop what the former called a pleasant personal relationship, and Hart-Davis was to publish his next 'three or four books', as Thomas put it in his grand, indefinite way. In *Rupert Hart-Davis* (Chatto and Windus 2004) Philip Ziegler tells one curious story. 'Once Rupert asked [Charles Causley, a caller at the office] whether he had passed anyone on the stairs. "No," said Causley. "That was R.S. Thomas," replied Rupert, oblivious to Causley's response. "I'm still trying to work that out," Causley wrote later.'

Meanwhile at Manafon, the distraction of their son removed, the two industrious lives went on. The seasons passed. Summer. 'Everything grew and grew, strawberries, blackcurrants, beans, sweetcorn, courgettes with michaelmas daisies all around them,' writes Elsi Thomas. Autumn. 'The trees turned to gold, and the huge ash tree at the gate by the road showered down leaves all day like golden rain.' It was, writes R.S. Thomas, 'like a golden fountain playing silently in the sun'. The image became metaphor in a poem forty years later.

> I have thought often
> of the fountain of my people
> that played beautifully here
> once in the sun's light
> like a tree undressing.

And then there was winter. 'The long room at the top of the kitchen stairs with a fire,' writes Elsi. 'Sitting in front of it meant sharing the warmth with two harvest mice who climbed onto your knee.'

But then suddenly the Manafon life was over. In 1954 Gwydion Thomas, home on holiday, was told by his mother that they were leaving the village. His father, she went on, had become more and more unhappy there, he missed the mountains and the sea, and had found a new parish on the Dovey estuary, where there were both, also more people speaking Welsh. His mother, he remembered, was crying, and then he was crying too. For though each of them had found the Garden of Eden at Manafon, R.S. Thomas was still seeking his. They were bound for Eglwys Fach, his mother told Gwydion, in the west.

FIVE

Eglwys Fach

Eglwys-fach was in a pleasant part of rural Wales. It was a village on the main road, some five miles from the sea as the crow flies, with the river Dovey flowing past it. The hill country rose immediately behind the main road, and foaming streams ran down the narrow valleys towards the few plains between sea and mountain. It was a Welsh area in its appearance, with the hills of Merionethshire rising in the north and the occasional glimpse of Cadair Idris from the high ground. After a storm, if the wind subsided, the sound of the sea could be heard from the west. And better than that, once every day the tide would come up the river and the tang of the sea could be smelt in the foam.

Neb

In short, Eglwys Fach in 1954 seemed just the ticket. But what followed was part of the black comedy never far away from the odyssey of Ronald Stuart Thomas in Wales. Each parish in turn was weighed in the balance and found wanting, Chirk too cold, though the Welsh hills were near, particularly if one had a girlfriend with a car. Hanmer on the edges of the Cheshire plain had had no hills at all, and was too English. And that was even before the bombers came.

Manafon at first had seemed perfect, but that proved an English-speaking parish, where an upturn in their economic fortunes meant his parishioners were not entirely tragic figures. 'The farmers were so worldly,' he wrote in *Neb*. And some were worse than worldly. One night, after visiting a sick man, he heard as he went away the laughter of the young people of the house, 'like the laughter of the devil himself'. When his parishioners did turn up in church, they had usually walked a mile or more to get there, and were so tired that as the 'vicar of large things/in a small parish' climbed into the pulpit, he found himself delivering his sermon to half a dozen peaceful, sleeping faces.

And though there were hills in Manafon, these were too high so there was no sunshine in the village until eleven o'clock in winter, and by two even that was gone, with terrible consequences for the rectory plumbing. Pipes freezing, pipes being unfrozen, pipes bursting, pipes … Thomas left the village, vowing he would never again live in a hollow.

In time even countries would be found wanting. Spain was fine, if hot, and France … well, he got arrested in France. But Norway in 1968, 'after a fortnight amongst monotonous pine trees, it was no sorrow for the two to head for home'.

Yet for a little while Eglwys Fach seemed so perfect you can almost see ticks on the check list. Hills: yes, they were there on his doorstep. The sea: he could smell that. The mountains: he could see them, with Cadair Idris just fifteen miles away, not so near so as to affect the plumbing. Only there was something else.

'Rather a prim small vicarage stood in a tidy small garden opposite the church, its walls covered in roses and clematis montana,' writes Elsi Thomas in her memoirs. But you can hear the small menace of the violins as she goes on, 'When we went to see it the old vicar showed me the garden, saying, "Here you can put your snapdragons, there you can put the wall-flowers …" How alarming.' At Eglwys Fach the Thomases had the feeling that they were being told what to do.

Ominously Elsi adds, 'It was a strange parish full of retired army people and retired tea-planters, a far cry from the farming community of Manafon. The army people were all arrogant, belligerent, wealthy and self-important – and the others dull.'

※✛※

It is the spring of 1960, and I am sitting in the hills above the village with R.S. Thomas. We are on one of the afternoon walks which he takes so regularly, the sight of their vicar framed against the skyline like the Last of the Mohicans has become an unnerving feature of life for his parishioners far below.

He is in his late forties, and fit as a fell runner. I am seventeen, and puffing, but these afternoons have come to mean a lot to me. They represent an escape from the University of Aberystwyth, where I am the youngest student and out of my depth amongst contemporaries many of whom, having done National Service, seem like grown-ups. It does not help that at the time I have no girlfriend. So I hitch-hike out here, pockets bulging with manuscripts to inflict my poems on him ('H'm,' says Thomas), and amongst the skulls and watercolours of the vicarage get advised on reading material (the novelist James Hanley, and, in particular, the American poet Wallace Stevens). This is not the ogre of folklore, this is someone capable of the sort of superhuman tolerance which will be recognised only by those writers who have ever been exposed to teenagers with literary ambitions.

Once he takes me to see his friend the West End dramatist Norman Hunter, now largely forgotten, but then, after his play *Waters of the Moon*, famous and successful. Hunter is then living near Machynlleth, in a large bungalow on a hillside among rhododendrons that looks as though it has been transplanted from Simla. We go for a walk above this, and I am in heaven, it is so beautiful, and I am in the company of the gods, real writers who look as real writers should look, tall, good-looking men. Only suddenly one of the gods, Thomas, turns aside and pees on the rhododendrons. *My father was a great pee-er in fields.* From then on I too, as part of a literary apprenticeship, become a great pee-er in fields.

But most of the time I listen. And on that spring afternoon above Eglwys Fach Thomas is talking about his parish. The Dovey estuary has opened like a fan beneath us, and I have said something to the effect that he is lucky to be living here (and to have so much free time, though I do not say this).

'It is going to change,' says Thomas gloomily. 'We've got a general who is about to retire, and you know what these generals are like.' I nod, who have never even met a general. 'They interfere.'

Much later I think it is odd that a man his age, and a vicar, should confide something like this in someone little more than a schoolboy. But he has clearly been brooding on it. And so at the time I say something vague, that perhaps it will not be as bad as he thinks, or that the general may not even come.

'Oh yes, he's coming, he's coming.'

I remember these words because of their resemblance to a speech Hitler made at the beginning of the war to some German midwives, of all people. Referring to the questions being asked in Britain about when, if ever, his invasion was to be expected, he said, 'Let them not worry. He is coming …' And then, a finger sweeping backwards and forwards, 'He is coming.'

And in the case of Major General Lewis Pugh, he did come. The squire, something Thomas had never encountered in his parishes, was returning to the village his family had dominated for over a century.

All his life Thomas had a knack of colliding with the bizarre, with Lorna Sage's grandfather and Beuno and the first buried cremation, but the General was off the maps. A war hero awarded the DSO three times, a man who could speak German, Urdu and Gurkhali, and had crossed the North West Frontier in disguise, he could have popped out of a Hollywood blockbuster for a breather. And astonishingly this is exactly where he returned twenty years later, to the Hollywood blockbuster *The Sea Wolves*, made in 1980, when he was played by Gregory Peck.

Of all the potential enemies he could have chosen in the world, Thomas had to pick on him: not on the sort of twitching general Richard Widmark might have acted, or one of Burt Lancaster's barking monsters, but on someone capable of being played by Gregory Peck, the Hollywood star who specialised in gentle honourable heroes, the man who played Atticus Finch in *To Kill a Mockingbird*.

The Sea Wolves tells the story of how Pugh, an Indian Army officer, recruited a bunch of boozy, retired English expats, and led them on a raid against German shipping in neutral Goa. 'My father thought the film was good, and all true, except for the lady spy who appears in it,' said Imogen Elliott, the General's daughter. 'The only thing he objected to was that Gregory Peck played him in an open shirt. I can see him stumping up and down now. "I wouldn't have gone to war without a tie on."' Except of course when he disguised himself as a Pathan tribesman.

Physically, he and Thomas were not dissimilar. They were of an age, both very tall, austere men, though Pugh had a monocle, and, according to my friend Geraint Morgan who invited him to a student function at Aberystwyth, the kinder face.

'This is Brigadier Pugh,' said Morgan, introducing him to someone.

'Major-General.'

'Does it matter, brigadier, major-general?' Morgan was a graduate of the London School of Economics.

'It matters to me,' said the General quietly.

Both he and Thomas were intelligent, complex men. Both spoke English with cut-glass accents, yet, and this is what startled Morgan, both took being Welsh very seriously. Pugh, who had spoken Welsh as a child, enrolled in his retirement at a further education class in Aberystwyth, sitting amongst the youngsters, so he could take a GCE in it: this took him four years. According to his daughter Imogen this was because he kept getting Welsh mixed up with Gurkhali. Vicar and general would have had a lot in common, were it not for one thing.

The one was a pacifist, given to agonising in print over his possible cowardice. The other was not just a soldier, he was a war hero in spades. In Manafon R.S. Thomas had met Iago Prytherch; in Eglwys Fach he met Richard Hannay.

'I mean, one can look back with amusement across fifty years, but there was a terrible battle,' said Joy Neale, the General's cousin. 'Lewis Pugh was an absolutely delightful man, and I look back on R.S. Thomas with affection. But the two didn't get on at all. I think it gave both of them a lot of pleasure. They were such very different people, Lewis a Welshman who'd become English and a general, R.S. an Englishman who'd become Welsh. He wasn't? Well, we always thought he'd come to Wales.

'What did they quarrel about? Lewis wanted a more jolly sort of sermon, not all that doom and gloom. After he went we had an ex-Army padre, which suited Lewis. He'd talk about Thomas a lot, and usually say something like "that nutter".

'And then there were all the other things.'

❧✝❧

Thomas's face is on the guidebook to Manafon church. At Aberdaron there is a permanent exhibition of his work. But at Eglwys Fach church there is nothing to indicate that he ever came and went here. Except …

'John, what would happen if you wanted to take something out of your church, or put something in?' I am talking to John Hall, vicar of Blakesley in Northamptonshire.

'I should have to apply to the Diocesan Advisory Council. You have to do that if you so much as want to put a screw in a wall.'

'John, if you heard of a vicar who'd scraped the varnish off all his pews, then painted them and his pulpit matt-black, sold off his altar cloth at a jumble sale, got rid of his brass, taken the plaques off the church wall, and was proposing to take out the stained glass, what would you do?'

'Call an ambulance.'

Thomas, looking back on his years as a vicar, wrote in *Neb*, 'He never had a house that satisfied him, and there was something missing in every church – a lack of taste or architectural deficiencies – but his wife's advice as an artist was a help in improving the situation somewhat.' His wife's advice as an artist ...

At Eglwys Fach Elsi took aesthetic exception to the old bright varnish on the pews (it looked, said their friend Penny Condry loyally, 'like treacle'). She had that removed, and replaced by a darker matt varnish, but alas, her efforts were frustrated by a Mrs Jones, who by superhuman polishing managed to get a shine back into the matt varnish.

'My mother couldn't stand a shine of any kind. She'd say of men with bald heads, "Can't they cover them?"' said Gwydion Thomas. 'I remember Mrs Jones well. She was a very small woman, smaller even than my mother, and she had all this energy.'

So Elsi Thomas, recognising she was up against an agency that was not only not of her world, but not of this world either (of Mrs Jones's house she wrote shakily that it was 'full of THINGS', every table, every chair groaning), went for broke. She had the whole lot, pews and pulpit, painted matt black.

'I remember all that. God, do I remember that. If someone were to make a musical about my father and mother I think it would be as bizarre as that thing in *The Producers* – *Springtime with Hitler*. Springtime with Ronnie and Millie.'

But fifty years on the churchgoers of Eglwys Fach are reconciled to their matt-black pews, so much so they have given them another coat. To see the church for the first time is a remarkable experience. It is not just that the interior is bare and austere, it has, because of the paint job, become dramatic, as though awaiting something to happen. 'That matt black, I know it gives you a shock when you see it, but it's very good for flower arranging,' said Margaret Mair, churchwarden. 'And much better since it had that extra coat.' We stared at the golden rod and the spray chrysanthemums exploding against the monochrome. 'If you've got a wedding, it's stunning. Mind you, we don't get many, but we had one a month ago, and it was miraculous.'

A sense of theatre was important to the vicar of Eglwys Fach. As he wrote in 1958 to Margaret Stanley-Wrench, an aspiring poet, 'Our church which is ugly looks beautiful on Christmas morning at the Communion. We have night lights and candles, and no electric lights on.'

And that was just the beginning. 'What a struggle one had to get the horrible clinging hessian − miles of it − removed from the slate aisle of Eglwys Fach,' wrote Elsi. The effect was to reveal 'huge beautiful slabs of slate', which people objected to because it reminded them of their kitchen floors. She went on, 'They so much preferred the alarming red, yellow and black tiles of the altar steps and floor.' 'Alarming' was one of Elsi Thomas's favourite adjectives.

Having heard of an English blacksmith called Alan Knight, the Thomases commissioned him to make a great wrought-iron chandelier for the church (and were to do so again at Aberdaron), also a wrought-iron crucifix and candlesticks; these they must have paid for themselves as Gwydion Thomas remembers them at Sarn. The chandelier is still at Eglwys Fach. It too is painted matt black.

But the stained glass never was taken out. It is still there above the altar, heavy Victorian stained glass, dedicated to Lewis Pugh Pugh, 1837, and to Cordera Pugh, died 1946. To the side is more stained glass, this time with the figure of St George, 'erected by Mrs Guy de Laval Landon and her daughter Charmian Rose de Laval Landon, in deepest gratitude for the peace of God during the War years'. These things R.S. Thomas would have seen every day.

'He wanted to take all our family stained glass out,' said Joy Neale. 'That had cost us thousands to install. So of course he fell out with my cousin Lewis over that. And then R.S. wrote that poem about his daughters, as though it was an offence just to be beautiful.'

The poem was written twenty years after he left Eglwys Fach, and appears in his 1988 collection *The Echoes Return Slow*. It has been described by Barbara Prys-Williams in *20th Century Autobiography* (University of Wales Press 2004) as being 'electric with malevolence'. And it is. The man who wrote this is virtually unhinged by loathing.

> And this one with his starched lip,
> his medals, his meanness,
> his ability to live cheap off dear things.
>
> And his china-eyed children,
> with their crêpe-de-Chine hair,
> product of a chill nursery,
>
> borrowing nastiness from
> each other, growing harder and thinner
> on the day's diet of yawns and smirks.
>
> His wife and his friends' wives,
> reputations congealing about their mouths'
> cutlery after the prandial remarks.
>
> What shall I say more?
> Why should I rummage
> the envy, the malice,
>
> the patched-up charm in humanity's
> wardrobe, draughty habilment
> this for the candid heart that would keep itself warm?

'Crêpe-de-Chine hair?' said Genia Conroy, Pugh's elder daughter, distractedly, having not heard the poem before. 'That means a very fine ripple, doesn't it? No, my sister and I, we both had very straight hair.'

Moreover, as Thomas himself acknowledges in the last two stanzas, he was rummaging in the past. Whatever had happened at Eglwys Fach, time had not wrought a resolution in him. Or in Elsi.

Twenty years on in her memoirs she too wrote about the General, who insisted on reading the lesson in church:

He had this expressionless voice and made rubbish of the lovelier parts of the Bible, splitting the verses up into short absurd sentences. He very much disliked RS and we very much disliked him. When Churchill died the General appeared in full dress uniform, his wife and two daughters clothed from head to foot in black. Ronald never even mentioned it in the service. 'Surely you knew he had died, it was in every paper.' Ronald said he never read a paper, at which the great General threw his hands in the air and turned to his family, saying, 'What can you do with a man like that?'

She quoted, proudly, what Pugh had said. 'The trouble with you, Thomas, is that you lack the common touch.'

'You must remember my father had grown up in the parish,' said Mrs Conroy. 'He knew everyone and they knew him. They'd call on him. "General, what do we do about this or that?" That should have been the vicar's role. Perhaps there was some jealousy on Thomas's part, I don't know. I always felt he shouldn't have been there at all. I mean, he was far too clever to have been entrusted with a small Welsh parish, and the result was a bitter, unfulfilled man. I mean why had he come to Eglwys Fach in the first place?'

'He came hoping to find Welsh speakers. And birds.'

'Well, he certainly found his birds.'

✲✠✲

The house is in the middle of a bird reserve. No cars come, no dogs are allowed, no one shoots in this place; when night falls the darkness is absolute, as the silence is absolute all the time. In a room full of bird paintings, bird engravings, bird photographs, where even the cushion covers have birds on them, Penny Condry said. 'My husband Bill wanted him to come. He thought he'd be like Gilbert White here.'

In 1953, hearing that a bird observatory had opened on Bardsey Island, Thomas had written to, and later met, its secretary, Bill Condry, the well-known Birmingham-born naturalist and *Guardian* nature columnist. William and Penny Condry lived at Eglwys Fach, the village and its salt marshes being, like Bardsey, a special place. On the flight path of many migrating species, in winter there were white-fronted geese from Greenland in the marshes, wild swans, ducks, wood sandpipers, greenshank, with peregrines and hare harriers hovering. In the spring in oak woods above the estuary there were pied flycatchers and redstart and wood warblers, mixed in with which was the odd amazing rarity like yellowlegs from North America.

'All our lives Bill and I chose somewhere to live, then we found something to work at there,' said Penny Condry. 'We were odd.'

And at Eglwys Fach, where in 1969 Bill would become the first warden of the Ynyshir Nature Reserve which he set up there for the RSPB, the Condrys had also found their Garden of Eden. To this, telling him that their vicar was retiring, they alerted R.S. Thomas, who was seeking his. A year later, having applied to the Bishop of St David's, he came.

'But what we didn't realise was that he'd have to deal with all those generals and admirals and colonels. Bill and I were pacifists, you see, we weren't part of their set. We both had a bit of a conscience that we'd ever asked him.'

It is not clear from his autobiographies when Thomas took up birdwatching, that great interest of his middle and late life, though in the BBC documentary *A Rare Bird* he said he had started to take an interest during his Hanmer years, where, he said, there was 'nothing to do really', which is a strange sort of confession for a clergyman to make. By Manafon birds were already part of the wonders of Wales. 'It was by the side of Llyn Coch-hwyad that he heard for the first time the enchanting, heartbreaking music of the golden plover.'

In his *Planet* interview Thomas said that he took up birdwatching in reaction against the encroachments of man and machine. 'The wild places are becoming domesticated. Time and distance are being annihilated by speed. So I turned to the birds.' In *Neb* he said he had found an escape from his parishioners in them. In the poem 'Swifts' he is more direct.

> The swifts winnow the air,
> It is pleasant at the end of the day
> To watch them. I have shut the mind
> On fools. The phone's frenzy
> Is over.

At Eglwys Fach he joined Bill Condry on the Committee for the Protection of the Red Kite, then an endangered species. There is a photograph of him with the Committee, standing slightly to one side of his colleagues, most of whom were English; he seems to be looking at them out of the corners of his eyes. The English, he wrote ruefully, tended to be more interested in such things, for by then, out logging the nests in the spring, he had heard his own farming countrymen deny the existence of such a bird, with one circling above them as they spoke. With Condry again, he got the local landowner Hubert Mappin, of Mappin and Webb, to declare the Ynyshir estate, over which he had been allowed to roam, a bird sanctuary. He approved of Hubert Mappin. All this gave him moments of great joy, as when he found a nest just ten yards away and stared into 'the sharp eye' of the kite as it stared back.

But mostly it was to do with beauty. At Eglwys Fach, as he painted what he considered the ugly red brick around the vicarage windows, 'his spirits were raised as he listened to the woodlark singing daily above the house. This is one of the most magical songs to be heard in Britain, and, listening to these melodious notes, there came to mind the Birds of Rhiannon and the old tale of how the listener would, on hearing them, forget time' (*Neb*). Only of course he could not forget time, or his parishioners.

At Manafon there had been a social gulf between the village rector and his parishioners, who, you remember, when they invited him to supper, did not eat in the same room, and who, according to Ruth Hall, would have found nothing strange in his English accent; they *expected* their rectors to talk like that. But at Eglwys Fach there was another human species.

Having come for the birds and the Welsh language, R.S. Thomas encountered a congregation that, having cars, did not need to walk to church and thus did not fall asleep during his sermons. There was a prep school, and a large retired element which, between bridge and sherry parties, had time on its hands. 'The smell of the farmyard was replaced by the smell of the decayed conscience,' he wrote in *The Echoes Return Slow*. In the west of Wales, where he least expected to find them, Thomas had met the English middle class.

At this point Canon Donald Allchin met him, and remembered his gloom. '"Are you good with children?" I remember his asking. "No," I replied, "not much." "Neither am I," said he, apparently rather relieved. There followed a typical R.S. Thomas remark of the kind which one doesn't forget. "My predecessor here hadn't got a brain in his head." Then, with emphasis, "*Everyone loved him.*"'

The highway ran through the parish. The main line ran through the parish. Yet there were green turnings, unecclesiastical aisles up which he could walk to the celebration of mind and nature. Otters swam in the dykes. Wild geese and wild swans came to winter in the rush-growing meadows. He hummed an air from Tchaikovsky quietly to himself. Yet on still days the air was as clerestories in which the overtones of gossiping voices would not fade.

The Echoes Return Slow

'I don't know where he'd have have heard Tchaikovsky,' said Gwydion Thomas. 'We had a hand-made stereo player by then which he used twice, I think, though I can't remember him buying a single record. But we had a radio and we'd all sit together to listen to *Round the Horne* which he didn't like, and *The Navy Lark*, which he did.

'As for the people with whom he mixed, one day I wrote down all their names. The West End playwright N.C. Hunter. Betty Vernon, whom he married at the end, and her husband: fox-hunting people. A Portuguese count. Hubert Mappin, landowner. A chap who'd been a Jewish banker and had Stanley Spencer paintings all over the house. Gentlemen of leisure. Retired colonels.'

And though, as he put it, he deliberately hid from them the fact that he could play bridge (perhaps remembering the card-sharping religious of Bangor), and twenty years on in *The Echoes Return Slow* would be contemptous of their social mores ('"How good of you to come"/(Yawning inwardly')), R.S. Thomas at the time seemed quite at home in their company.

At the National Library of Wales, having gone through the catalogues, I began to fill out order forms for those letters from Thomas which are deposited there. One of the librarians, reading the list, said, 'Doesn't seem to have known many Welsh people, does he?' Letter after letter, each on headed notepaper, which from time to time got changed. A vicar writes ...

To Miss Monica Rawlins, a Slade graduate and an English eccentric living up on the moors who called to her guinea fowl each night with a special song. 'Dear Monica, I hope that in the uproar of a luncheon party I managed to convey my thanks for the Campbell St John....' To Margaret Stanley-Wrench, poet. 'It is better to produce than to publish. I have been here three years, and in the process of settling down into a new and very difficult parish I have hardly written a thing of any worth.' Much mention of friends in common, in particular a Colonel French with whom Elsi Thomas had been to tea. Thanks for an invitation to lunch.

To Louis and Mary Behrend, benefactors to church fêtes, youth clubs, sagging church ceilings. 'We are greatly looking forward to the smile with which you will so kindly declare to the few people present that our little sale is open' (1958). 'One or two of us who are proud to call ourselves your friends would be pleased and honoured if you would spend a little of your Golden Wedding day by having lunch with us at the Wynnstay' (1960). 'Hart-Davis hopes to publish my next book of poems in the autumn. With your consent I would like to dedicate them to you. I know, and admire, your enthusiasm for "the arts" as they are called, and realise how much you have done in the past. So if this book will not be too much of a failure I would very much like to dedicate it to you...' (1961). Yours sincerely, Ronald.

Thanks for this, thanks for that, especially chocolates. Commiserations with the Behrends at Christmas, after they had moved to the Channel Islands, over 'the awful English who now fly to Jersey, dragging their turkeys and Xmas puddings with them'. Thomas seemed to have had no trouble distinguishing between the English he knew and the anonymous, threatening mass of their countrymen. When a few years later Louis Behrend died he could write, 'I shall always remember him as a cultivated English gentleman whom it was a privilege to have known.'

The Behrends had lived near them in Eglwys Fach. 'What a joy,' wrote Elsi Thomas. Having built the chapel at Burgh-clere, which they filled with the paintings of Stanley Spencer, they had moved from their large house there to one in Wales, which, being smaller, had Spencer's paintings and those of Henry Lamb hanging frame to frame. 'Louis Behrend had bought many of Stanley's paintings to prevent them reaching the public before it was ready to receive them,' wrote Elsi in a sentence which tells you something about her attitude to art, but a lot more about her. When the Behrends moved from Eglwys Fach they gave her Henry Lamb's *The Gleaners*. 'They had an ogre of a son called George who was only interested in the money value of these treasures ...'

'What people didn't realise was that my parents had squandered all their money on that mouldy chapel,' said George Behrend (author of seventeen books, four of them on railways), and from that moment on I began to warm to George. 'And then Behrend and Co. which had had rice mills in Egypt, and exported cotton seed, collapsed in 1959. People didn't know that, they assumed that if you put up chapels you could afford to do anything. They put the whole Ballet Rambert up for much of the War. Those dancers were scroungers, though not so much of one as Stanley Spencer.' His parents, said George Behrend ruefully, had been raving mad about art.

And it was a sad little echo of what Gwydion Thomas had said about his own parents. 'I think they both must have been quite lonely. But they would never admit it. So writing and painting needed to serve as dialogue and conversation and an emotional embrace ... My final impression is of two people impatient of others' daily lives and concerns, and disdainful of any activity other than Art ...' You read about the casualties of war, or of capitalism, but it is startling to encounter those who consider themselves the casualties of art.

'We were never part of that, R.S. had so many lives out-side us,' said Penny Condry. When the Thomases had come to Eglwys Fach she and her husband Bill had rejoiced, for as Bill was to say on a BBC documentary, 'He was a great success from my point of view, I had a fellow birdwatcher at last.' This was to prove a mixed blessing for Elsi Thomas. 'I remember once the two of them were going on holiday to some island to see Eleonora's falcon,' said Penny Condry. 'And she said to me piteously, "Who is this Eleonora, that I should have to go and see her falcon?"'

In 1966 Thomas and Bill Condry went on a month's holiday to Spain, when, as he put it, he was 'forced' to go abroad. It was not crime but the terms of a literary prize that made him do so (Kingsley Amis, similarly obliged to travel, gloomily referred to his prize as 'a deportation order'). 'This was intended to broaden the poet's mind, except it was left to the recipient to decide what would broaden it. R.S. used it to add to his list of birds,' said Bill Condry in a TV interview, trying very hard to keep a straight face. But then, as he said, he had never laughed so much in his life as during that month.

In France, en route, they were arrested. Having stopped Thomas's Mini estate in which they had come, they were watching a Montagu's harrier through their binoculars, oblivious to the military air base above which the bird was flying. During the day-long interrogation which followed, there was one lovely moment as the police, having established that Thomas was a priest, pounced on his reference to his son. 'How is that possible?' This of course would be the question he would ask himself in *Neb*, but he must have given the French police a less convoluted answer, for they were released.

In Spain he worried about the hazards to health posed by water and goats' cheese, and was terrified, looking for a campsite, when they approached an old cowshed and heard the loud sound of breathing in the darkness. He slept little that night, 'full of imaginings of all kinds'. Contrary to his public perception, Thomas was a nervous man.

Elfyn Pugh, a young Machynlleth policeman, accompanied him and Bill Condry one October to study the migration routes of birds on the small island of Ramsey off the Welsh coast. 'All that was to eat on the island were these huge horse mushrooms, and I couldn't face them, a frying pan full of maggots. I was starving most of the week. Bill was a vegan, he'd brought his own food, but R.S., I never saw him eat at all, though he did drink eight pints of water a day. Yet he was such a very fit man, off on his own at dawn every day, I began to wonder whether he was living off grass. I didn't ask him, we hardly had a conversation the whole time we were there, and I remember thinking, I shouldn't like to share a desert island with this guy. He stayed on after we left.'

A few days later Thomas wrote to his son from the island. 'I hope all is well, I have no news of what goes on in the corridors of power. Have been re-reading Stendhal's *Charterhouse of Parma* about human pettiness and pretensions, and am glad to be away from them. I hope you will be – one day. But you must have an interest even then. It is calm tonight. I'll see what tomorrow brings. Much love, TAD.' Alas, tomorrow brought an end to Stendhal and human pettiness.

'He had to be rescued, he'd had a nervous attack, and thought he was being attacked by red deer,' said Gwydion Thomas. 'When he came back he started being prescribed valium, which he took on and off for the rest of his life.'

But the red deer were not phantoms. They had been introduced onto Ramsey, and that October the stags were in rut; Elfyn Pugh remembered having to creep along, his back to the trees and walls. 'By the end of the week it was us who were keeping away from them,' wrote Bill Condry. But after the two left the stags seem to have closed in on Thomas, or so he thought. Some who knew him find it hard to believe in the valium, but it was to figure large in Elsi's memoirs and in her later letters to her niece. As his son said, this was a far more nervous, far more vulnerable, man than anyone realised.

'He was a mass of contradictions,' said Penny Condry. 'One minute so silent, and the next … Bill had been asked to Africa, and I was hesitating about going with him, until the day the door opened, and R.S. swept in as though he had a cloak on. "If you don't go, then Bill won't go. It's his only chance." And so I went to Africa, thinking the Lord had spoken. But it's all so long ago now.'

And there are just the voices.

I wasn't here in his time, but you hear so many stories.
They say he took out the wall plaques, but it's reputed that
Hubert Mappin, one of the big landowners, put that one
back. [The plaque, to a George Jeffreys, aged twenty-eight,
is the only one left in the nave.] I don't like his poetry
much, there's always a line like 'Life is a barrel of rotting
apples.' I'm in my seventies now, I must be really rotten.

MARGARET MAIR, churchwarden

I struggle with his poetry personally, I have to sit down and
puzzle over it. The church? I think it's very beautiful, but I
think RS did things without informing people. If you talk to
them about him it always comes back to that, to having had
the church painted black. I've never seen another black
church. The rumour is that he did it without asking for a
faculty. It's changed so much since he was here, there are
much more English people, many of them retired. You can't
blame them, it's so beautiful. I preach in English, I get
about fifteen to twenty people. I don't know when anyone
last preached in Welsh.

ADRIAN DAVIES, vicar of Eglwys Fach, but now with
two other parishes, the vicarage long sold

I used to go birdwatching with him. Though I could speak
Welsh we always used to speak English together for some
peculiar reason, possibly the birdwatching. My general
recollection is of him speaking English to everybody, and
lots of people used to comment on his accent. Where did he
come from, do you know? He used to preach these very
posh elegant sermons, all very scholarly. And gloomy. You
didn't go to church to be cheered up in his time. You got
the impression that perhaps he wasn't the happiest of men
here.

CHRISTOPHER FULLER, conservationist and parishioner

I loved him dearly. He became very friendly with us as a
family and prepared one of my girls for confirmation. Some
found him awkward, and he wasn't the easiest man you
could meet, but he'd call on us and have a sandwich, so
perhaps he found he could relax with us. I just wish he was
still around.

JOAN JONES, parishioner

Oh, very quiet man, a nice little vicar he was, never talked
anything but Welsh with him. He used to come up here
with communion for mam and dad when they got old,
carrying everything in his pocket, I think, and walking,
composing poetry all the way.

BYRON HOPKINS, farmer, talking in Welsh

I was born here in 1929. It was a very patriarchal society
then, with landowners and estates. Men either worked for
them or on the railways, things didn't change much until
the end of the Second World War, when most of the old
farms were sold, and agriculture became forestry. Our
family, the Pughs, had come in my grandfather's time,

when the old Jeffreys estate at Glandyfi Castle was being
sold up. We were a Welsh-speaking family, my grandfather
was Liberal MP for Cardiganshire, but then we got involved
in the Empire in India and became tea-planters and, in my
father's case, a Calcutta Exchange broker. But Eglwys Fach
was home.

My mother and R.S. got on very well, she played the
organ for years. When she died he rang to say how sorry he
was, and came all that way from North Wales to be with us.
Basically he was a good priest, but shy, and so very
different from the normal vicar. He was highly intelligent,
and married to a highly successful painter, it made him into
just a bit of an oddy. Of course he wasn't nearly so famous
at first, but then that changed. It is very difficult when
someone is a priest and then for many becomes a god in his
own right.

JOY NEALE, parishioner

It was at Eglwys Fach that R.S. Thomas became famous.
Nowhere in his autobiographies does he mention this. What he
does say is,

> The parishioners had heard in advance that their new vicar
> was a poet, and great were their efforts to get hold of some of
> his work to try to discover what kind of strange man it was
> who was about to descend upon them. But now, with the
> publication of the work in London, it became easy enough for
> them to buy a copy if they wished.
>
> *Neb*

That is all.

Song at the Year's Turning (Rupert Hart-Davis 1955) included
selections from his two privately printed books. 'To describe the
effect of his work it is enough to say that he often moves to tears,

and that certain lines of his impress themselves instantly, and perhaps ineradicably, on the mind. His example reduces most modern verse to footling whimsy' (Kingsley Amis, *Spectator*). 'The poems ... come cleanly off the page, sniffing of cold and ploughed earth and leafless branches' (*TLS*). 'We have had nothing quite like it: the portrait it gives is unforgettable' (*Manchester Guardian*). His old friend Raymond Garlick gave the whole of his editorial in the Winter 1955 issue of his magazine *Dock Leaves* over to a celebration of 'a body of poetry, concerned almost exclusively with Wales, which both Welsh and English critics have combined to admire and to commend'.

His countrymen had waited a long time for this. In the May 1951 issue of *Dock Leaves* the writer A.G. Prys-Jones, listing those Welsh poets who wrote in English (he named Dylan Thomas, Alun Lewis, Vernon Watkins, Henry Treece and Glyn Jones, but not R.S. Thomas), had gone on, 'We in Wales rejoice that the stream is flowing so abundantly, though some of us believe that the great interpreter of Wales in English, the acknowledged genius, will yet come from the ranks of those who are fully within the mystery of our mother tongue.' For much of their history the Welsh had waited for the Mab Darogan, the Son of Prophecy, and now such a man seemed to have come in the figure of the vicar of Eglwys Fach.

The book brought him the Heinemann award of the Royal Society of Literature, and suddenly he was moving in a different league. *Song at the Year's Turning* was dedicated to James Hanley. *Poetry for Supper* (1958) was dedicated to John Betjeman and Rupert Hart-Davis; Thomas was clearing his debts. *Tares* (1961), as he promised, was dedicated to Louis and Mary Behrend.

The famous now wrote, the Poet Laureate John Masefield amongst them, in his case to offer him the Queen's Medal for Poetry in 1964. The Medal, Masefield informed him, was 'a thing of great beauty'. Thomas in 1990 told *Planet* that this description had 'hoodwinked' him ('I would not describe what came through the post in such terms'), and, he went on, he would not now accept it. 'The Medal had not been awarded for some years, but such was the indignation at my being given it, that it became almost an annual event to mollify the geniuses that had been slighted.'

'R.S. was very grumpy about it, he wouldn't answer the phone for a long time after he got the Medal,' said Penny Condry. 'You have to look behind these clever people, they're not simple.'

Lord Tryon, Keeper of the Privy Purse, sent it to him from Buckingham Palace, asking, incongruously, for a receipt. Thomas wrote to his wife who was clearly away to tell her the news, a letter with no more greeting than 'Thank you for your last letter', and said, 'I had a letter from Masefield the other day, the Queen does so enjoy my poetry that she is going to give me a medal. Perhaps Gwydion will be able to realise a few shillings on it one day if he is hard up.' He assured his wife that he would get something cold for their supper.

His peers were writing now, Lawrence Durrell out of the blue in 1961. 'I am a fan of yours and follow your work with that pleasant nervy feeling one gets only with the poets who are scalp-raisers … [Your poems] are strong and clear and tawny as the good red wine we are drinking by an olive wood fire.' Stephen Spender writes, no, writhes. 'I have been meaning for some weeks to answer your letter of 22/4/66, in which there is a painful misunderstanding. Perhaps it was thoughtless of me to have invited you to Spoleto [to the Arts Festival] under conditions in which you are expected to pay your fare.' Thomas's response had clearly been sharp enough for Spender to go on, 'May I take this opportunity to say how much I admire your poetry.'

Thomas recorded bitchily, 'I had a letter from Ronald Bottrall in Rome, enclosing a dreadful poem for some reason. "I hardly write any poetry these days," he began. What a pity this should be one of them.'

In 1962, with Durrell and Elizabeth Jennings, he was in the first volume of the Penguin Modern Poets. In 1963 he brought out *The Bread of Truth*, in 1966 *Pieta*, in 1968, *Not That He Brought Flowers*, all published by Hart-Davis.

Because of his growing fame he now entered a kind of folklore, a process in which he sometimes participated, and which would continue for the rest of his life. Stories began to be told about him, which, as with the old heroes, became exaggerated with each telling.

'I produced a film of his poem "The Airy Tomb" which the actor Kenneth Griffith read, and Emyr Humphreys directed,' said Lord Dynevor. 'As a result the BBC decided to make a film of their own, that would be around 1962 or 1963, and came to Eglwys Fach. Anyway they wanted this scene in which Thomas came out of his church and walked down the path. Everything was set up and he appeared in a full surplice. But whether he'd become fed up, I don't know, for he suddenly raised his arms and started to run towards them, shouting, "I'm a bird, I'm a bird." It's not on film. Either the cameraman was too stunned or Thomas was running too fast.'

'My friend Julian Mitchell rang him at Eglwys Fach,' said Professor Prys Morgan. '"I'm writing an article for *Time & Tide*, would it be possible for us to talk?" Thomas said, "I'm distempering." And Julian didn't know whether this was a condition or DIY. But he turned up. "How d'you find living here?" "It's very boring." "What do you find most boring?" "The libraries, they haven't any books I want to read." "What in particular?" "Well, the van comes round, and, d'you know, they have nothing by Schopenhauer." Julian reckoned his leg was being pulled, but couldn't be quite sure. The article never appeared.'

Only it wasn't quite like that. 'Yes, I did go and see him,' said Julian Mitchell. 'It was 1962, and I'd gone to Aber to do some research. So I rang him, said I was a great admirer of his, and thought I'd write an article for the *London Magazine*.

There was a long pause. "Well if you're there you might as well come." I think he gave me a cup of tea. He started to talk about contemporary poets, but he didn't have a good word about any of them, so that very quickly dried up. What he did say was that the worst thing about living there was that the libraries were all hopeless. I didn't have the heart to mention the fact that the National Library of Wales was just ten miles away. He didn't mention Schopenhauer.'

But he might have done. Asked for some recommended reading by the Behrends, he replied, 'I haven't read anything very good this year, except Schopenhauer's *World as Will and Idea* in two volumes, which I would not press on elderly gentlefolk.' He recommended instead *The Four Voyages of Christopher Columbus*. Thomas was made for folklore.

᷒᷒᷒

But in all the books of poems which came out in the fourteen years he was at Eglwys Fach, there is an absence, and that is the village itself. He found, he says in *Neb*, no subject-matter among his parishioners (which is not quite true, for, deep underground, there was the General). There is however the odd sideways glance.

They lived in houses on the main road

Mischievously he goes on

To God, as they thought …

The main road, the A487, troubled him. 'We tried to get a 30 mph limit through the village, but the minister said that as it was dangerous everyone took care' (1964, a letter to the Behrends).

But there were always 'the green turnings', and it was

from one of these that the one specific event of his time here became a poem. The Condrys were moving out of their old cottage above the village, and on their last day there he accompanied them on a visit to a very old neighbour living even higher up in the hills. It was her ninetieth birthday, and Bill Condry recalled their visit in his autobiography.

> Mrs Jenkins was of a tough old breed. We had seen her, even in her old age, standing on top of a load of hay, high on a horse-drawn cart, piling up the grass as it was thrown up to her by Tom (her son). Isolated for years in a primeval farm-house at the end of a long, climbing track, she had the speech, the ways and the thoughts that belonged to a time much earlier than the mid-twentieth century into which she had survived ...

What follows is what Thomas made of it. What should it have been, a celebration of endurance and age, a threnody for a disappearing way of life? No.

> You go up the long track
> That will take a car, but is best walked
> On slow foot, noting the lichen
> That writes history on the page
> Of the grey rock. Trees are about you
> At first, but yield to the green bracken,
> The nightjar's house: you can hear it spin
> On warm evenings; it is still now
> In the noonday heat, only the lesser
> Voices sound, blue-fly and gnat
> And the stream's whisper. As the road climbs,
> You will pause for breath and the far sea's
> Signal will flash, till you turn again
> To the steep track, buttressed with cloud.
>
> And there at the top that old woman,

Born almost a century back
In that stone farm, awaits your coming:
Waits for the news of the lost village
She thinks she knows, a place that exists
In her memory only.
You bring her greeting
And praise for having lasted so long
With time's knife shaving the bone.
Yet no bridge joins her own
World with yours, all you can do
Is lean kindly across the abyss
To hear words that were once wise.

'Ninetieth Birthday'

The man climbing through the beauty of that hot day expects to find something memorable at the end of the long track. And he doesn't. Thomas could have made his approach sentimental, he could have made it brutal: either would have been disastrous. It is his honesty and his gentleness that make this such a fine poem. Note how delicate it is, compared to the Manafon poems: he is not using the old lady to make points as he would once have done, there are none of the insistent 'See', 'Look' interjections to draw your attention to something. This is a triumph of poise.

It is also an example of how deft his craft had become, especially in the way he could make a poem turn about its last line just by his use of a single startling word.

So two old poets,
Hunched at their beer in the low haze
Of an inn parlour, while the talk ran
Noisily by them, glib with prose.

'Poetry for Supper'

Again, my favourite, in 'The Survivors', 'the curt sand'.

At Eglwys Fach, he told Molly Price-Owen of the David Jones Society, he was 'still sort of reliving some of the Manafon experience'. Some of this was nostalgia for a time when, as he said, 'there was a dew on things'. Prytherch still came and went (twelve years after Manafon, he was still being addressed in verse), but he was a ghost now, to be summoned up in the night watches, and, once, from 'the world's roads', to be apologised to in 'Absolution', by 'One who strafed you with thin scorn/From the cheap gallery of his mind'.

The poems were more introspective now. He brooded on himself, on his marriage, his parents and the tales his father had told him, on his 'strange calling' as a priest, on his craft (there were poems about poets and the writing of poetry), on his countrymen and on the Welsh past. There was a danger, wrote Benedict Nightingale, interviewing him for the *Guardian* in 1964 (for there were journalists now), that the absence of his old subject matter might turn Thomas too far in on himself. The poems, he told Nightingale, came easily; those that required revision were usually no good. The result is that few manuscripts survive, and scarcely any drafts, something that is a source of grief to collectors, and his son.

His waste-paper basket beside him, he wrote most every day on scraps of paper, the backs of envelopes, jotting down in notebooks, amongst the details of birds, the odd phrase here and there.

'What did you do on your island, apart from watch birds?' asked Raymond Garlick.

'Well, I wrote.'

'What did you write?'

'Poems.'

When *Poetry for Supper* appeared he sent his parents a copy ('With love to my mother and father, from Ronald, 1958'). If they opened it, Tommy and Peggy Thomas would have read what their son really thought of them, for the book includes 'Ap Huw's Testament'. But all that was in verse, where Thomas could use what in a letter he called 'the old trick of using language to conceal my thoughts'. Presumably verse was a no-go area for Peggy Thomas, at least let us hope so. For later she might have read what his true, and terrible, feelings were about the priesthood she had been so keen he joined.

> We stand looking at
> Each other. I take the word 'prayer'
> And present it to them. I wait idly
> Wondering what their lips will
> Make of it. But they hand back
> Such presents. I am left alone
> With no echoes to the amen
> I dreamed of. I am saved by music
> From the emptiness of this place
> Of despair. As the melody rises
> From nothing, their mouths take up the tune,
> And the roof listens, I call on God
> In the after silence, and my shadow
> Wrestles with him upon a wall
> Of plaster, that has all the nation's
> Hardness in it. They see me thrown
> Without movement of their oblique eyes.

'Service'

That would have been Eglwys Fach, with the shadows cast by the brand-new chandelier on the plaqueless walls. As a preacher, he was, according to the Rev. Evelyn Davies, vicar of Aberdaron, given to 'waving his arms about a bit'. And the eyes of his congregation, though oblique, were open.

But there was still the Welsh past, though the present could shatter his dream.

I was going up the road and Beuno beside me
Talking in Latin and old Welsh,
When a volley of voices struck us; I turned,
But Beuno had vanished, and in his place
There stood the ladies from the council houses:
Blue eyes and Birmingham yellow
Hair, and the ritual murder of vowels.

'Border Blues'

Increasingly readers needed a degree in Welsh to understand his allusions. Talking in Latin and old Welsh? But that is
what Beuno, a seventh-century saint and his neighbour across
1,300 years at Manafon, would have spoken.

I was the king
At the church key-hole, who saw death
Loping towards me ...

'Genealogy'

This was Maelgwn the Tall, the sixth-century king who
gave the Roman fort to St Cybi at Holyhead. Hiding in a church
from the Yellow Plague of the late 540s, he, according to
legend, stooped to look out of a keyhole and saw it 'loping'
towards him.

In 'Border Blues', a poem in which he uses the collage
techniques of Eliot's *Waste Land*, Thomas quotes a ninth-
century poem and an eighteenth-century folk-song, both in
the original Welsh, and alludes to characters from an eleventh-
century prose romance. Eliot added notes to his poem, Thomas
does not. But read it. The poem sweeps you along, it is actually
very funny, as the heirs to all those riches obliviously booze,
fornicate and go to pantomimes.

'It was "The Babes" this year, all about nature.'

There had been a panto, it was *The Babes in the Wood,* and it had duly got up his nose. November 1953, to Raymond Garlick: 'Gwydion is home now. We have just endured a pantomime for him. We go all the way to Shrewsbury to imbibe these hours of English proletarian culture. However as there is no Welsh culture to put in its place – there it is. That is why we sent him to an English boarding school ...' It is an amazing piece of logic. The implication is that the boy is being deliberately kept from all things Welsh *for his own peace of mind,* else he too would become an outsider on a fruitless quest in his own country. Thomas, always an outsider, had in his journeys into the West and the hills hoped to become part of their traditions, but as he took stock of himself in Eglwys Fach he found his sense of exile had persisted amongst his own countrymen.

> What am I doing up here alone
> But paying homage to a bleak, stone
> Monument to an evicted people?

> 'Border Blues'

Even what his son called 'his push West' had been a disappointment.

> At fifty he was still trying to deceive
> Himself. He went out at night,
> Imagining the dark country
> Between the border and the coast
> Was still Wales ...

> 'A Country'

Those of his own people who had stayed were unaware of the implications of the tourism flooding their country ('an

Elsan culture/threatens us'). The others ('Bosworth blind', an allusion to those Welshmen who had followed Henry VII to London) were scurrying east ('the last hurrying feet/still seeking the English plain'). Where *was* the true Wales of his dreams?

> I have looked long at this land
> Trying to understand
> My place in it – why,
> With each fertile country
> So free of its room,
> This was the cramped womb
> At last took me in
> From the void of unbeing.

'Those Others'

It had become his own, and private, agony. Out of such feelings came that fine poem 'On Hearing a Welshman Speak' which must be incomprehensible to an Englishman, or to most Welshmen, come to that. 'Stones to the walls fly back ...' Thomas is reversing the spool of history so that everything is as it was, where the prince's house is not burned down, there are no defeats, the Bible does not get translated into Welsh, an eighteenth-century poet does not go into exile: Thomas's dream is of the old, unchanged Wales in those moments before it changed for ever. But to understand this you need to know that the poet is Goronwy Owen, the translator Bishop Morgan, the house that of Glyndwr at Sycharth.

The poem 'Sir Gelli Meurig' ('a Welsh fly/Caught in a web spun/For a hornet') is again incomprehensible unless you know that this was a squireling caught up in the Earl of Essex's treason and hanged in London (and thus another example of the 'Bosworth blind'). Thomas adds just one word of explanation for the reader, and that in parentheses, '(Elizabethan)'.

Such poems suggest a background of someone muttering to himself as he digs himself deeper and deeper into a pit of his own despair.

And yet the despair is kept from the poems being written with such beauty and economy. As Yeats put it, 'Hamlet and Lear are gay': their gaiety is the triumph of the language they use. There are two joyful poems in the poems written at this time: both are to birds. There is also the fascinated investigation, that was to last him the rest of his life, into his own marriage.

In the recklessness of extreme old age, a year before his death, Thomas talked about his marriage to Graham Turner of the *Daily Telegraph*. 'I was a loner, and my first wife was also a loner. We didn't have our meals separately or anything stupid like that, but we did sleep in separate rooms.' At Eglwys Fach her niece remembered Elsi, who was very small, sleeping on a window seat.

Their marriage fascinated the very few who got close enough to see it. 'You were very conscious, not of estrangement, but of separateness,' said John Mowat. Thomas told Turner, 'We never indulged in the effusive emotional displays other people go in for. After I'd been away for a fortnight's holiday alone, I'd open the door and just say, "Well, here we are."' The man who on his wife's death after fifty years of marriage was to write the most moving love poems written in my lifetime said that he was not a very loving person.

> To my wife all I have
> Saving only the love
> That is not mine to give ...

> 'Gifts'

But there was something in her nature that allowed her to accept this.

She goes out.
I stay in.
Now we have been
So long together
There's no need
To share silence:
The old bed
Remains made
For two: spirits
Mate apart
From the sad flesh ...

'Exchange'

Except of course that there never was a bed made for two.

Peggy Mowat heard stories of Ronald's courtship from a cousin teaching at Moreton Hall at the same time as Elsi. 'They'd come into the staff room, roaring with laughter, their arms full of the flowers they'd picked.'

Later there were the silences, and in 'Anniversary' the event that had shattered their silences.

Opening the womb
Softly to let enter
The one child
With his huge hunger.

Hunger for what? For what a child, any child, would have considered his birthright, attention, love, the reassurance of a conventional marriage? At Eglwys Fach more than one person remembered feeling sorry for the child with his huge hunger. At Eglwys Fach Gwydion Thomas became a teenager.

'For me the Eglwys Fach years were pretty grim,' he said. 'I had no friends so I became an expert at playing darts and snooker with both hands so I could play against myself. I slept a lot of the time, staying in bed all morning and listening to R.S. droning on in the kitchen below as to when I was going to get up. And then I got a girlfriend, at which point all Hell was let loose.

'I was at Bradfield by then. Fagging and flogging, Latin and Greek. And games. I'd won a scholarship which brought the fees down from £400 a year to £200. "You wouldn't be at this school if you hadn't won a scholarship," said R.S. That, it was made clear, was my contribution. I told them a great deal about what was going on in the school, but all he'd say was, "It would have been worse in Llanfair Caereinion."

'My girlfriend, from the village, was at Machynlleth sec mod, and when I was fourteen I started running away to see her. I'd catch a train, spend the night in Welshpool station by the stove, then catch the early-morning train to Glandyfi to see her. She saw me through most of Bradfield. Her fat pink letters would arrive with unceasing regularity, interspersed with the parcels of cake from my mother. Once she came to Bradfield with her father. I was miffed to see her dad, but I suppose she could hardly have come on her own aged fifteen. It was amazing she came at all. I'd already been warned off her by R.S.

'I started meeting her under the railway bridge in Glandyfi, then up in the woods and on the hills above Eglwys Fach. We'd lie against a big stone and kiss and talk from mid-morning until it got dark in the summer. Once R.S. found us and hauled me off her.'

Elsi Thomas to her brother Freddy. 'Can you have Gwydion for the holidays? He has formed this infatuation with a girl from the village. It would be terrible for the parish.'

His old girlfriend, Sue Griffiths Ph.D., by e-mail, 2004. 'What I remember of R.S. Thomas I still prefer to forget. He made a major contribution to literature, and I am sure you will be able to glean far more about him from those more eminent than I, considering the man was an insufferable snob. It is all I wish to say on the matter.'

When he was at Oxford Gwydion brought a girl home. 'The first night she walked into the silence which was normal in our house. She left the next day. "She was a real little go-getter," said my mother. I didn't go home in the holidays much to Eglwys Fach after that.'

Then two things happened. In 1965 Tommy Thomas died.

> I turned back
> To the nurses in their tugging
> At him, as he drifted
> Away on the current
> Of his breath, further and further,
> Out of hail of our love.

'Sailors' Hospital'

Then towards the end of their time in the village Elsi Thomas became ill, and a spell in hospital produced complications that were to last for the rest of her life. 'That she managed to last twenty-five years like this is astonishing,' said her son. But her personality had changed. At Eglwys Fach she had been 'Mrs Vicar' as Genia Conroy put it, someone on whom both the Pugh girls liked to call ('She was lovely, quite open, if she didn't want to see you she'd just tell you to go away'). From this point the process started that was to end in the recluse of Lleyn.

There is nothing to commemorate Thomas at Eglwys Fach. 'Bangor University wanted to put a plaque up to him, but the parochial church council refused, 'said Margaret Mair. 'Then there was a proposal to put something up in the lychgate, but we heard no more about that.'

But on the hillside above the village there is a simple stone monument. 'TO THE MEMORY OF MAJOR GENERAL LEWIS OWAIN PUGH 1907–81. SUBSCRIBED FOR BY MEMBERS OF THE MID WALES BRANCH OF THE BURMA STAR ASSOCIATION.'

SIX

Aberdaron

In 1967 we moved still further West, to Aberdaron at
the end of the Lleyn peninsula. The next move could
only be into the Irish Channel.

ELSI THOMAS, *Memoirs*

It is 2004, and I am renting a cottage almost at the end of the
Lleyn Peninsula along which R.S. Thomas said he had crawled
out as far as he could. From my window, as the mist clears, I
can see the landscape he looked out on for thirty years of his
life, the cottages and the smallholdings, the few trees and the
little fields full of stones and, almost as an afterthought, of
sheep. And, beyond all these, the huge frame of the sea.

Once families lived in this cottage, generation after
generation, part of an agricultural economy that, in the end,
failed them. The cottage is now like a space station turning in
the void, immaculate and empty, but ready at a moment's
notice to spring to life with the arrival of the next paying
visitors.

On the third day I hear a Land Rover in the lane, out of
which steps a tanned, blonde Englishwoman in a baseball cap.
She has come, she tells me, to cut my lawn, this being one of
the services provided by the agency she has been running for
the last ten years. She addresses me as Mr X, the name of the
man from whom I am renting this place. In the ten years she
has worked for him the two have never met.

For this is the Lleyn, a place of absences. On the one hand

are the cottages bought for holiday lets, and maintained by a complete service industry which never gets to meet their owners. On the other are the crumbling little farms left by Welsh families who have given up trying to wring a livelihood from these poor acres.

Looking through the letterbox of one I can tell to the month when they left, for the last magazine, delivered and unread, is February 1998. No desolation as yet, just a key turned in the door, and time stopped. But the desolation will come, as it never will to the holiday cottage just fifty yards down the track, its curtains drawn, its hedge manicured, for, whatever else it lacks, the Lleyn has sixty miles of coast, beaches and harbours.

'Some of us are surviving,' says the farmer, who can remember a family in the cottage I am renting. 'At least down here we are. Up there ...' He points to cottages higher up the mountain. 'That's where the English are.' He could have been talking about a strain of alpine goat.

'It's the view, you see. The English need a view.'

The average age of farmers in the Lleyn is now fifty-eight. Yet once this was the heartland of the Welsh people, and of their last prince: this was *pura Wallia*, the undiluted country in the West, where it was said the best Welsh was spoken, and where it was thought the national culture would make its last stand, whatever happened elsewhere. Here, in his classic account of childhood on the Lleyn, *A Place in the Mind*, Gerallt Jones, another clergyman's son who was sent away to an English boarding school, wrote that when he had been a boy there in the 1930s it had been possible to meet people who had never been beyond Pwllheli, and 'non Welsh-speaking Welshmen did not exist'.

For this was the great refuge where Beuno fled around 630, after hearing the first sounds of English in the water meadows of the Severn (his chapel survives, crouched and whitewashed inside a huge mediaeval church). Here in 1936 a university lecturer, a schoolmaster and a chapel minister, improbable arsonists, burned down some empty huts, with the result that 'the Fire in Lleyn' passed into Welsh history, and they into Wormwood Scrubs. Their action was prompted by the RAF's plan to build a bombing school there, their earlier plan to build it in Dorset having been frustrated, ironically in this context, by birdwatchers. Welsh cultural objections were ignored.

And here in 1967, R.S. Thomas came, thinking, to use his own image, to finally kiss the feet of the Welsh rainbow.

He had sought this in Manafon, and found Welsh hill-farmers at its foot. He had sought it in Eglwys Fach, and met the English middle class.

But now there was Aberdaron, the hallowed place. He was warier this time, writing even before he came to Raymond Garlick, 'I am afraid Aberdaron is very vulnerable now, and the Saints' Road to Bardsey is a thoroughfare for ice-cream vendors.' What he did not know was the scale of what was massing in the plains to the east.

'I have a parish of about 500 here. At least in winter I do. In summer I have one of 30,000.' The Rev. Evelyn Davies, the present vicar of Aberdaron.

Here Thomas met the English tourists.

❦✛❦

In August 1953, Thomas, his wife and son, had passed through Aberdaron on their way to the newly opened bird observatory on Bardsey Island. On their way over their boat was holed, and they had to bail; on their way back, a fortnight later, the boat was almost engulfed in huge waves. Thomas, as any sane man might be, was unnerved by this, perhaps even more so by the monosyllabic comments of their boatman who, when asked if it was all right for waves to be breaking over the boat, spat and said, 'It'll get worse soon.' He describes this in *Neb*.

There can be no doubt that it was a terrifying experience, for by a freak his future successor at Aberdaron was on Bardsey at the time. Christopher Armstrong, then a child, still has his mother's record of the 'startling news', as she put it. She remembered cornflakes and books floating in the water, and the boatman having to make a dash for safety.

But it was on this visit that, with an introduction from Bill Condry, Thomas called on the three Keating sisters, spinster daughters of a Nottingham architect, who between them had restored the old Jacobean mansion at Plas-yn-Rhiw. He and his family were asked to stay the night, and, as he put it, 'a relationship was established that over the years would develop into a friendship'. The Keatings were English, they were middle class, but then Ronald Thomas, as Peggy Mowat told me, always seemed so much more at home with such people than with the Welsh, and it is interesting how many events in his life turned on some English agency.

He married an Englishwoman, who was to have a great effect on his poetry; an English novelist (though of Irish descent) introduced him to mainstream publishing; an English naturalist alerted him to the living at Eglwys Fach. And now there were the Keatings. The sisters, one of whom had been at the Slade (the Thomases seemed able to sniff out Slade graduates in the oddest places), all eccentric (Thomas calls them 'remarkable'), were to give him the lifetime's lease on the cottage to which he eventually retired, and where Elsi Thomas died. This gift was not without its responsibilities.

When old, the sisters became convinced that burglars were moving at night in the woods that separated the Plas from the cottage. Thomas offered to patrol the woods for them, and one night stayed up until three in the morning, as he told the Mowats. The next day he turned up to tell them their fears were groundless. 'Oh no, last night was different. Last night they came at four.' The distinctly odd always did have walk-on parts in his life.

In *A Place in the Mind* Gerallt Jones tells the story of how, after their mother's death, his father called on the Keatings, 'to find the old lady's body propped up in a wicker basket-chair in the window, taking the sun'. He goes on, 'When they eventually buried their mother, they did so in the tiny church-yard of Llanfaelrhys, looking out to sea, under a rough boulder. When a farmer tried to build a barn between the grave and the western horizon, they instantly instructed their faithful solicitor to prevent him doing so – it interfered with the old lady's view of the sea.'

They were far more formidable than the Welsh arsonists, for they loved the Lleyn with what Gerallt Jones called an inordinate passion, though not all its inhabitants loved them ('There were many who regarded them as wrong-headed, obscurantist, even downright silly'). They bought up stretches of coastline to ensure caravan sites never came, and their refusal to sell stopped plans to build a nuclear power station, and a radar tracking station. All their energies and money, to quote Gerallt Jones again, went into keeping the Lleyn just as it had been, to the alarm of its inhabitants.

When he came to write his book he owned up to a certain guilt that as a boy he had himself shared in the prejudices against what he calls 'a sensitivity beyond the wisdom of utilitarian politics'. He goes on, 'As we walked our footpaths home from Hell's Mouth, through gorse and bracken, scaring the rabbits beneath our feet, eating the wild strawberries as we went, we might have spared a thought for the mad old ladies in Plas-yn-Rhiw. It was they who understood the basis of our summer freedom and our summer joy.'

Alas, no more. Following the collapse of the little coastal road, a highway is to tear through that gorse and bracken, and through the gardens R.S. Thomas and his wife created at their cottage. The National Trust, to which the Keating sisters willed their estate, has made no objection, and a compulsory pur-chase order has been served by Gwynedd County Council, which has, as head of planning, Dafydd Iwan, the Welsh protest singer: all this despite the protests of Gwydion Thomas who marshalled the whole conservation lobby, Friends of the Earth, the RSPB, Coed Cadw (the Welsh Woodland Trust), Butterfly Conservation, and Plantlife, against them.

For at the foot of the Welsh rainbow, as R.S. Thomas found, you do tend to find the Welsh.

❧ ✚ ❧

7 July 1969, letter to Raymond Garlick

[The people of Aberdaron] are reacting with the uneasiness and incredulity of people with a traitor in their midst. I managed to get the Post Office to put up *Y Llythyrdy* [Post Office] which my wife painted, but others such as the butcher just laugh uncomfortably at the suggestion that *High Class Family Butcher* looks a bit odd in Aberdaron. I suppose he thinks visitors confronted by a window full of sheep's carcasses might not know what it was if it had *Cigydd* painted on it.

'He'd come into the village shop and insist that they used the proper Welsh words, like *eiryn gwlanog* for peach. People just used to stare at him, they'd never heard of such a word, which, being translated, means hairy plum. At that stage he still sounded like an upper-class Englishman talking Welsh.'

Christine Evans, schoolteacher and poet, also daughter-in-law to Will Ty Pella, Will of the End House, the boatman who had taken Thomas to Bardsey.

Donald Allchin once called on a woman whose children were among those Thomas was about to take to Llandudno Zoo. She was very worried. 'I just hope he talks English to them, otherwise they won't know where they are with all his long Welsh words.' She and her children were all Welsh-speakers.

'The men who were boys when he came, they told me that he had taught them about birds, and how to keep still. For that they were eternally grateful. But he also taught them to play croquet. For that they were not.' The Rev. Evelyn Davies.

At Aberdaron, R.S. Thomas had somehow got a bee in his bonnet that the ideal activity for a youth club was croquet, that sport of English colonial afternoons. He bought many sets of the game (according to Peggy Mowat he once came all the way to Bristol to get one), so that now a generation of bemused middle-aged fishermen and builders at the end of the Lleyn look back, like Victorian curates, on a youth which, between gales, was punctuated by the clack of wooden balls on the vicarage lawn, with a gaunt figure urging them on. Could it all have been a dream?

> The house was in the sun from morning till evening, but was consequently exposed to every wind that blew. The sea was visible half a mile away, and the summit of Bardsey Island could be seen from my study window. With the wind and the sea and the strong sun and the herring gulls calling from the chimney pots, it was like a return home.

> *Autobiographical Essay*

Aberdaron had once been a large and important place, its church the wealthiest in the diocese of Bangor, being on the pilgrims' route to Bardsey, the Island of the Saints, when in the Middle Ages three pilgrimages to the island counted as one to Rome (it should now be the other way round, muttered R.S. Thomas, remembering his first boat trip). There are no streets in the village. Houses are scattered here and there as though some giant hand had rolled them down the hillside like dice, until at the bottom, at the edge of the sea, they came together in a clutch of shops, pubs and the church. The church, sinking into the sands, was actually abandoned in the nineteenth century, and a

hard Victorian barn built to replace it on the hillside, next to the
vicarage. But then the congregation changed its mind, shored
up the old church, and abandoned the new.

Here, sometimes wet through in his cassock in winter, he
pulled on the outside bell ('Bless him, there was no one else to
do it,' said Evelyn Davies), or, half asleep, gripped the lectern
in one of the two small satellite churches out in the lanes, as he
preached to a congregation of the one or two who had
interrupted their summer walks. Thomas was to minister here
for the next eleven years of his life to a community two-thirds
of whom, at Christine Evans's estimate, were chapel anyway.

When he had applied for this living at the end of the world
he had been the only one to do so. 'Luckily,' he noted. Promotion
in the church hierarchy, it would seem, was the last thing on
the minds of the priests who came to Aberdaron. When he
retired, in 1978, it was fifteen years before a successor, a former
English monk, Christopher Armstrong, was appointed. When
Mr Armstrong left five years later, it was two years before
Evelyn Davies came, a vicar's widow and a psychologist who in
middle age had herself taken holy orders. Mrs Davies had lived
on Tristan da Cunha, where she survived on albatross ('like
goose, except it tasted of kippers'), and where the winds blew
planted vegetables out of the ground: Aberdaron to her was a
summer meadow.

'I'd been visiting the place for twenty-one years, and I'd
always felt that I was in a strange land. But then I started
having this recurring dream in which I sat in an Aberdaron
church which had become so dirty and unkempt, in the end I
rang the archdeacon. Ten minutes later the Bishop was on the
phone.' Mrs Davies put on a sepulchral voice. '"*Evelyn, come
to Aberdaron.*" I think R.S. would turn in his grave if he knew
a woman priest was here.'

In the *Oldie*, asked about what special effects he might
require at his funeral, Thomas, tongue in cheek, replied, 'A
cortege of women priests in gaiters.'

After he retired, the large vicarage with its twelve chimneys was sold to two doctors, who then came so rarely that the garden Elsi created has run wild, and grass now covers the drive. When Evelyn Davies arrived ('on a half stipend'), she was obliged to take a mortgage out on a small bungalow, and even then that required a lot of work done.

'This chimney needed a cowl, so I made a deal with a builder. He was getting married, so in return for the ceremony he agreed to put it on. The day came, he turned up at the church with the cowl, and after his marriage he climbed up on my roof. And that was how I got my cowl.

'I was told I was not to think of myself as being in the shadow of R.S. Thomas, not that that was hard. I had to do a lot of healing here. There were those he'd walked past in the road, and ignored. I told them he was on a different planet. Then there were those who hadn't liked his nationalism and his aggressive attitude to holidaymakers. And then there were those who hadn't understood his poetry but had understood his references to them in his autobiographies, and hadn't liked these.

'You hear such stories. Someone would have come miles to knock on his door. This would open a crack. "What do you want?" "I should like to talk to you about your poetry. There's something I don't understand." "Well, if you don't understand it, there's very little I can add." Bang. But I think he used to blame that on the wind.'

He had a case there. He wrote in *Neb*, 'The wind was the main feature of the place, with its boisterous music filling the vicarage almost every day. It would blow from the north-west for days sometimes, whistling under the front door and making it very unpleasant to open this to whoever came by. The walls of the house were clad in slate, an attempt to keep out the driving rain, but one morning there rose a strong wind from the south-east snatching slate after slate from off the house like cards. This was the sort of weather that R.S. had been used to in Holyhead, but it was somewhat grievous for a delicate person like his wife.'

Elsi had developed a thyroid condition in Eglwys Fach. In 1970 she was operated on for this, but contracted a bug whilst in hospital. Treated with cortisone, she blew up like a balloon, with the result that, not liking to be seen, she became a recluse, 'a person who scuttled into the back of the church at the last possible minute', said Evelyn Davies, 'and was first out again'. Eventually it was rectified, but there were further complications which produced a fluttering at the edge of her eyes, and made painting difficult. Increasingly she hid from their few visitors, from pilgrim academics and, with her husband's growing fame, from television crews. It must also have increased the separateness within her marriage.

'They lived one at each end of the vicarage,' said Evelyn Davies. 'They shared the kitchen, but they lived solitary lives. I think they were quite unhappy. And then after her death he wrote those poems, I think he realised how much was missing.

'I am very fond of him, I admire his honesty. Most priests don't have that, they pretend they have faith, but in the poems he admits to the absence of God. I admire him intensely for that, for his faithfulness in a lonely calling, and for the fact that he stuck fast to his principles. But I don't know whether I'd have been fond of him when he was alive.

'I met him once, in the 1950s. My husband's uncle was archdeacon of Montgomery, and gave a garden party to which Thomas came. What was he like? Oh, just like any clergyman of that time, untidy, ascetic, treated women like, you know ...

'But I understand him a bit. I've lived in those huge vicarages, known the poverty of the Welsh clergy. A good harvest offering, and we'd have vegetables for supper, and once my husband and I, we had to cut a tree down in the morning just to have a fire that night. Thomas wasn't much of a pastoral priest, he did very little here, but he was good with the old and sick. The old ladies liked him, he brought them bread he'd made. He was good at making bread.' Of the people I talked to in Aberdaron the person who seemed to have liked him least was the baker.

'There was no parochial church council in his time, and no parish records, he just didn't see the point of those. All we have is the odd letter turning up at the bottom of a box.'

Aberdaron Vicarage, 26-10-67.
The Clerk, Lleyn RDC.
Sir,

I received your notice of condemnation of [a church cottage], as being unfit for human habitation on October 14th, 1967, and write to say that the churchwarden and myself will not re-let this property without doing the improvements necessary to meet your requirements.

At the same time may I say that it would be a help to us to know what those requirements are.

I remain, yours truly ...

In *Neb* Thomas suggests that in terms of geography Aberdaron was his journey's end. 'He had reached the destination of his own personal pilgrimage. Standing on the summit of Mynydd Mawr on a fine day, he could see Holyhead in the north and imagine himself as a child forty years before, playing on the beach there.' Actually it would have been nearer fifty years, but never mind.

'Forty years distant in time, and only forty miles the distance. If one took a map of Wales, it would be easy enough to trace his geographical journey from being a child in Anglesey to being an old man in the Lleyn Peninsula. It formed a kind of oval.'

In *Autobiographical Essay* he writes that it was also journey's end in terms of his own cultural pilgrimage.

As a member of the so-called Anglo-Welsh school I had indulged in a certain amount of attitudinizing, a kind of beating the breast and declaring, 'I'm Welsh, see.' But after reaching Aberdaron I found myself among a simple but kindly people, who had never spoken anything but Welsh, until the English visitors began arriving. In moving amongst them and speaking Welsh daily, I gradually lost any need to emphasize my Welshness, but settled down to be what I had always wished to be: a Welsh-speaking Welshman in a thoroughly Welsh environment.

But these are his public statements. 'I can't see how he could make them,' said Gwydion Thomas. 'I mean, this is a man who daily spoke English to my mother, and to me when I was there, and would daily have written poetry in English.' But set that aside for a moment. A push westward to the Wales of his dreams had occupied most of his adult life. First there had been the hills, but he had not found his dreams there, so he had crossed them, smelt the sea in the salt meadows, and now the covered waggon, or at least the minivan, was, as Elsi Thomas wryly put it, at the sea itself. It was over.

In a film it would be the last scene, Thomas standing on the beach at Aberdaron, ringed with the setting sun, as the sound track swelled with a baritone belting out some hymn - only he disliked hymns intensely, so perhaps with a voice-over intoning the last two lines of the poem written by a twelfth-century Welsh poet on his deathbed.

Creawdr a'm crewys a'm cynnwys i
Ymlith plwyf gwirin gwerin Enlli.

'The Creator who made me will welcome me/Into the parish of the faithful of Bardsey.' Except....

Aberdaron Vicarage, Pwllheli.
November 21, 1968.
Dear Warden ...

'Thomas is writing to the old warden of his student hostel, the 'somewhat effeminate' Dr Glyn Simon.

It was good to hear from you. I had meant to write and say I was glad that you had been elected Archbishop, but titles embarrass me as they probably do you ... It is wonderful out here, yet very sad. I begin innumerable poems about Bardsey, but never finish them. There is an unresolved problem. I don't know whether it is in the place, the times or in me.

That was one year on.

A few months after he arrived in Aberdaron he was already writing, 'It is the most servile to the English area I have come across. The effect of tourism and low employment. What would we do without the English? ... My respect for Welsh intelligence grows less every year ... However the area is superb.' That was to Raymond Garlick, to whom all the following letters are addressed.

1968: 'It's good to be by the sea at Christmas, the real sea, though the idea of Christianity I am in touch with in this area is a long way from the 20th century, with the altar among the hoi polloi.' 1969: 'It is socially very lonely here. I don't suffer from loneliness as I am always content to be alone in nature like the Celtic saints. But complete mental conformism among one's neighbours can produce another kind of loneliness ...' 1970: 'This part of Wales is a dead loss to Welsh nationalism, yet they speak Welsh as their first language.' 1972, April: 'Aberdaron is almost entirely without national consciousness. It seems to live by singing a few outmoded hymns in the winter, whilst waiting for summer to bring the English money.' 1972, Christmas: 'It is so much better here in winter, wild and undomesticated by the English, with their dogs and children. Still it is an unenviable record that Wales has a greater proportion of television sets than the rest of Britain. So Aberdaron keeps in touch with the English until they return in strength.'

In 1973 Peggy Thomas died, and Thomas wrote about 'the strange workings of the female mind, if mind is the right word for it. However mine became more tractable towards the end, and there was compassion.' He was concerned by the endless forms he had had to fill in in English ('because that is the easiest and quickest way').

1974: 'Here I float over the foundering British Empire, wondering what fragments I can shoar against my own ruin – unChristmas-like thoughts wrought partly by the WNW gale that rages. However we expect the Sunday School party here today, a handful of kids who will enjoy themselves in Welsh to my satisfaction. In dulce jubilo.'

1976: 'A birding friend of mine was a manic depressive of sorts. When he was discharged from hospital last year his wife greeted him with the news that she was leaving him.' 1977: 'I shall be 65 next March so I shall perhaps not have so long in the Church, which seems to me to be taking the wrong turning. I was asked to go and bury [the English poet] Thomas Blackburn earlier this month. He had a cottage at Croesor. As I went up Cwm Croesor on a smiling August day I was more than ever convinced that the world has taken a wrong turning too.'

And, later that year: 'I am retiring at Easter. I am glad to go from a Church I no longer believe in, sycophantic to the Queen, iconoclastic with language, changing for the sake of change, regardless of beauty. The Christian structure is a meaningful structure, but in the hands of theologians or the common people it is a poor thing ...'

Thomas did not keep a diary, so these letters, more than

poems intended for publication, are the only record of his day-to-day broodings in Aberdaron. Luckily there is another record, that of the people who met him there.

My name is Mary Roberts, I am the organist at Aberdaron. When did I come to the village? If I tell you that I tell you my age. Which is seventy. A round woman, Mr Justin Wintle described me, that's me. [Actually he described her as 'round, gentle, infinitely polite' but it is the first adjective that stuck.]

I remember five vicars. Most were middle-aged, nearing retirement. They took the services, and went round the parish. And then there was him. I played the organ at his induction, he was very good-looking. Wore a duffel coat, a camel one, then a nice grey one. Always a red tie, I used to wonder how many he had. Didn't see much of his wife. Very thin and pale, she was.

I liked him very much. Full of humour if he came to call. But always looked cross. Or down in the mouth. Wouldn't waste time talking about the weather if he met you, especially if he met you in the town. I think he was shy. Perhaps he should have stopped more to talk to people, it's a small village after all. Always walked fast, always thinking about something. But I remember he wanted things to start on time, especially weddings. He married me.

He would visit the sick. My brother thought the world of him. When he was poorly, R.S. came to our house every day. If he took his coat off in the doorway, you knew he was stopping. Did people like him? Some did and some didn't. Same with all vicars, but perhaps not so strongly as with R.S. He baked cakes, you know. Didn't have TV, but went to someone else's house to watch rugby matches. I always thought I could confide in him. He used to say, 'Anyone who wants help can come to me ...'

No, there were no harangues about Welsh nationalism.

He never talked about poetry either. Talked a lot about birds. Did a charity thing once, got people to sponsor him at 20p a bird. Only he then went and saw a hundred, which took everyone aback.

I was sorry to see him go.

My name is Christine Evans. I taught English at Pwllheli Grammar School. I am also the daughter-in-law of the island boatman, so R.S. Thomas used to call at our house quite often. He'd sit by our fire and tell jokes, he was very good at accents. I remember him doing a New York taxi-driver.

He was this odd mixture. He was quite capable of leaving grieving families at the graveside, and vaulting the wall to go home. Yet he had a tender side to him. He called once, and my small son asked if he wanted some whisky. He poured out some squash and R.S. very gravely took the plastic beaker.

There was a landslide on the approach to the beach, and the young men said, 'Leave it, a JCB will come.' But my father-in-law went down with a spade, and instead of laughing R.S. got a spade and worked with him. Of course the next day a JCB came.

The last time he came to our house he had a CND petition. He'd got very involved with that. Anyway this petition, I think he'd written it himself, was very fanatical, I think it wanted to ban *all* weapons, and Ernest, my husband, said, 'I can't sign this.' And R.S. got very huffy, so I said, 'I'll sign it.' But he took it away, saying, 'I'll never come to this house again.' And he never did.

But before that I asked him once if he'd come and talk to my A-level pupils. He agreed, but only on condition that I wasn't present, and that I didn't quiz them after. He then asked me if I wrote myself. I said I did, I wrote poetry. So he said, would I like him to read the poems, and that was how it started. On February 17, 1972, he wrote me a letter.

It was a gentle letter, but uncompromising. I was twenty-six remember.

Dear Christine,

These aren't bad. I'm not being patronising. It is a way of saying there is no need to despair or give up. The technique is on the whole competent, but there are many reservations. I see the sincerity of some of them, but here again you have a problem. You have an attachment to this area and Bardsey; no wonder. And in so far as you can put down some of the feelings it arouses in you, that's fine; they are sincere, and give you relief. But – they are to a large extent private. Only the few of us, who know this area, really understand.

And to make private and personal and dear things universal is one of the great tasks in which only a few poets succeed. This is made more difficult by the times. The rocks at Braich-y-Pwll are some 600 million years old. The main human reverberations here are from vanished hermits and pilgrims, and nameless peasant farmers and fishermen. How do we reconcile these with television aerials and the cheap bric-a-brac of Aberdaron tourism and write about it in verse which is contemporary?

I sense the uneasiness in places in your poems, where a cheap colloquialism jars with more traditional description, and does not come off.

You are at a disadvantage in submitting your poems because some of them are rather long. Editors tend not to like long poems unless by well known writers. Have you tried condensing? I find some of these rather discursive. If you are going to ramble on at some length, there should be the odd jewel here and there; sun piercing the cloud now and then on a grey day. Try retaining some of your more successful lines and leaving others out.

Some of the things you write about are what many

others write about, and it is difficult to say original things about hackneyed subjects. Young ladies tend to have much the same feelings when pondering on certain subjects!

Have you tried suggesting, rather than putting things patiently down? Try a course of Wallace Stevens. Words are so important, as you know. It is words from which poetry springs, yet we will keep trying to describe our mental states and emotions, thinking that that will be poetry. But it is words that are creative, arousing strange thoughts and emotions in us. Rhythm, too, is important.

I'm afraid, as I said the other afternoon, that as a teacher you are short of the time necessary to make endless attempts and experiments. Still these convince me that it is worth your keeping at it.

Yours sincerely,

Ronald Thomas.

Young ladies ... I didn't write a poem for seven years after that. When I did I wrote about the letter in a poem I called 'Bonanza'. It ended,

I was silent for a long time.
Then, in between
Washing some nappies and kneading the bread
And lambing a speckle-faced ewe,
I stumbled over one, and now they spring up
Haphazard as mushrooms after August rain,
Glistening, and jostling to be picked.

That became the first poem in my first book, *Looking Inland*.

The last time I saw R.S. I was doing a poetry reading at Portmeirion. I looked up and there he was in the audience. I felt very intimidated, but as I went to sit down he grasped my hand as I went past.

My name is Ann Vaughan. I used to go birdwatching with
R.S. Thomas, he was one of the best friends I ever had. We
met when I was teaching at Aberdaron school, and he'd
come and talk to the children on the first morning of every
term. I used to take the children on nature walks so he
knew I was interested in birds and flowers. One day he said,
'Oh Ann, next Saturday we're going to see the red kite.'
They were very rare, I'd never seen one. So we drove and
drove, and at Tal-y-Llyn he stopped the car, and we got
out. 'What's that?' There was a bird above us. 'That's a red
kite.'

Mrs Thomas, she didn't mind at all him going off, she
used to give me posters I could put up for the children, she
was a lovely person. But he never spoke English to me, not
even in front of her. But then you don't have much time to
talk when you're birdwatching. We went to Anglesey, we
went to all sorts of places. We saw a grey-back shrike, and
once a golden oriole killed by a falcon on Bardsey.

When my mother was ill at the end, and I was having to
go and see her in hospital at Bangor, he said, 'Right, I'm
coming with you.' Not 'do you mind' or anything like that.
It was a horrible night, the mist came down, but I don't
remember the coming or going, he was such good company,
he talked all the time. God never came up once, or poetry. I
can't even imagine the cold side that people talked about.
When we got back, he gave me some money, 'for the
petrol'.

I saw him just before he died. I'd married and was living
on a farm, so I hadn't seen much of him. I wanted him to
sign a book for me, and he was laughing away,
remembering the times we'd gone out. He was the same
old friend I'd had years before. A fortnight later he was
dead.

My name is Jon Gower, I am BBC Wales's Arts
Correspondent. I met him when I was sixteen. I was going
through a very rebellious phase, and, wanting to leave
school, I'd got a job as a bird warden on Bardsey. My
parents drove me all the way from South Wales, but when
we got to Aberdaron there was no sign of a boat. Or of
people either. Apart from this one wild-looking man.

So we asked him about the boat, and he said I might
have to wait a few days because of the weather. My parents
asked where could I stay, and he said, 'He can stay with
me.' Then he said who he was, so my parents must have felt
it was all right. And that was how I got to stay with R.S.
Thomas. I was there for three or four days.

What do I remember? We ate a lot of bread and cheese, I
remember that. And there was a candle burning in a skull.
Oh yes, and to my shame I remember asking him, 'They say
Wordsworth was a pantheist, do you know what that
means?' But most of the time we talked about birds. The
birds he'd seen … He'd seen the first goshawk nesting in
Wales, and the first ring-billed gull. A cynic might say he'd
gone from parish to parish because of birds, and the birds
must have improved.

I remember once, birdwatching with him, and this guy
came up and said he'd seen the gulls 'pruning' themselves.
What he meant was 'preening'. Thomas just burst out
laughing. I remember laughing a lot myself during these
three or four days. I've met three funny men in my life. One
was Lenny Bruce, one was Ken Dodd. The third was R.S.
Thomas.

He was quite avuncular, it was he who got me to go back
and do my A-levels. I used to see him about once a year,
either birdwatching or at the Eisteddfod.

In Aberdaron Thomas published six volumes of poetry. In all these, few, perhaps one or two, living human beings figure, outside his immediate family. One is the gentle poem 'Marged' about a simple-minded unmarried daughter of the sort you sometimes get on Welsh farms, kept behind to help with the work. Yet this was a man whose early poetry was a gallery of portraits. So where did all the people go? In *Autobiographical Essay* Thomas tries to explain, and it is another moment of black comedy. Away from the pulpit of his verse, Thomas, like many poets, was curiously vulnerable.

> In my first two parishes I felt a certain bitterness at the failure of the people to be worthy either of the beauty of their surroundings or of the Bible insights. In Aberdaron, with the growth of nuclear rivalry between the major powers and the increasing power of the multinationals, there was a growing feeling that the few inhabitants of the peninsula could hardly be blamed for the world situation.

In other words he was unable to bring charges against any of them, so a redundant public prosecutor goes on, 'Apart from the need to preach Sunday sermons, therefore, the tendency was for me to become more absorbed with my own spiritual and intellectual problems and to see what poetry could be made from them.' From these came some of the finest poems he was to write.

In Eglwys Fach, he says in *Neb*, he wrote poems which were of an occasional nature, 'rather than poems which arose from a more specific point of view'. Aberdaron gave him that point of view. He may have run out of land, but it was not journey's end, as he had thought: his journey was only just beginning, and it would be into terror. Before him was the sea ('Beneath that smiling surface, what horrors! And as if conscious of the grotesques within it, the sea would sometimes become wildly agitated'). And above him in those winter night skies, and even more terrifying, were the stars: his was to be a journey of the imagination into infinity. Like all his journeys it was a quest.

Christopher Hill, in his biography of Cromwell *God's Englishman*, has a remarkable last sentence in his penultimate chapter: 'God, who had been so close to Oliver Cromwell, withdrew into the vast recesses of Newtonian space.' R.S. Thomas, who had always felt Nonconformist ministers a bit forward in their approach to the Almighty ('When they prayed, too often it was as though they thought God was eavesdropping outside the door'), now prepared to follow Him.

> For me now
> there is only the God-space
> into which I send out
> my probes. I had looked forward
> to old age as a time
> of quietness, a time to draw
> my horizons about me,
> to watch memories ripening
> in the sunlight of a walled garden.
> But there is the void
> over my head and the distance
> within that the tireless signals
> come from. And astronaut
> on impossible journeys
> to the far side of the self
> I return with messages
> I cannot decipher …

'The New Mariner'

His imagery now reminds me of the covers of the magazine *Astounding Science Fiction* I once read.

the thin dribble
Of his poetry dries on the rocks
Of a harsh landscape under an ailing sun.

'He'

From the poem 'Earth':

It is such a small thing,
Easily overlooked in the multitude
Of the worlds.

He probably would not have read Arthur C. Clarke, but in
Night Sky he seems to come close to Clarke's fantasy of the
Overmind, the ultimate stage in evolution, when matter has
fallen away like discarded technology.

They have gone on from the human;
that shining is a reflection
of their intelligence. Godhead
is the colonisation by mind

of untenanted space …

But if the skies over the headland forced one perspective
on him, there was another that required a different journey,
and not in space.

[At Aberdaron] I became aware of a much older time scale. It
was, of course, satisfying to think of those early Christians,
and to look at the Romanesque arch over the church door and
the pre-Reformation water stoup. But out at the end of
Bardsey there were Pre-Cambrian rocks, which were anything
up to a thousand million years old. The mind reeled.

Autobiographical Essay

Man leaves his footprints
Momentarily on a vast shore.

All he can do is throw out grappling irons to the security
of familiar things, to the smell of hay coming in through the car
window in 'The Earth Does Its Best for Him', and to his own
fireside.

In front of the fire
With you, the folk song
Of the wind in the chimney and the sparks'
Embroidery of the soot – eternity
Is here in this small room,
In intervals that our love
Widens; and outside
Us is time …

'The Hearth'

The love poems he wrote to his wife at this time are
poignant because of her illness and because of the imperatives
forced upon him by his new perspectives.

because time
is always too short, you must go by
now without mention, as unknown
to the future as to
the past, with one man's
eyes resting on you
in the interval of his concern.

'Marriage'

In 'Seventieth Birthday' he moves from laboratory to
emotion, and it must be one of the strangest, and most moving,
openings to any love poem.

Made of tissue and H₂0,
and activated by cells
firing – Ah, heart, the legend
of your person! Did I invent
it, and is it in being still?

The familiar themes of his earlier work are jettisoned. In
'He Agrees with Henry Ford', 'I have drawn the curtains/on the
raw sky where our history/bleeds ...' And with that the Welsh
past dwindles, and with it the hill-farmers he once wrote about.

Will they say on some future
occasion, looking over the flogged acres
of ploughland: This was Prytherch country?

                                       'Gone?'

For he has gone back beyond agriculture and nationality,
beyond even recorded speech and time. In 'Probing' he comes on
an indentation in the land, probably that of some neolithic grave.

Would it help us to learn
what you were called in your forgotten
language? Are not our jaws
frail for the sustaining of the consonants'
weight? Yet they were balanced
on tongues like ours, echoed
in the ears' passages, in intervals when
the volcano was silent. How
tenderly did the woman handle
them, as she leaned her haired body
to yours? Where are the instruments
of your music, the pipe of hazel, the
bull's horn, the interpreters
of your loneliness on this
ferocious planet?

This is imaginative writing of a high order.

But such perspectives exact a price from a priest. In 'Pre-Cambrian' he looks back on gods long put away, like toys children have outgrown, and, with them, the great minds of pagan mankind. All dwindle beside the reality of the sea in front of him, and its horrors.

> What I need
> now is a faith to enable me to out-stare
> the grinning faces of the inmates of its asylum,
> the failed experiments God put away.

But what is this God, and where? Neither science, nor 'the incense of the Hebrews/at their altars' can call him up. Tapes, cameras, record no presence, no more than worship can. But these are ideas. This is how Thomas transforms them into poetry:

> They laid this stone trap
> for him, enticing him with candles,
> as though he would come like some huge moth
> out of the darkness to beat there.
> Ah, he had burned himself
> before in the human flame
> and escaped, leaving the reason
> torn. He will not come any more
>
> to our lure. Why, then, do I kneel still
> striking my prayers on a stone
> heart? Is it in hope one
> of them will ignite yet and throw
> on its illumined walls the shadow
> of someone greater than I can understand?

'The Empty Church'

Two words recur in these poems about God. One is 'lonely', the other is 'absence'. 'In looking back over some of the poetry I've realised that God was there from quite early times,' he rather charmingly told Molly Price-Owen of the David Jones Society, '… even in Manafon.' Yet the waiting priest at his prayers, this dweller in silence, now adds God to his dramatis personae. He tries picturing him, and his God is a remote scientist, indifferent to the individual dramas of his creation.

> I think he sits at that strange table
> of Eddington's, that is not a table
> at all, but nodes and molecules
> pushing against molecules
> and nodes; and he writes there
> in invisible handwriting the instructions
> the genes follow, I imagine his
> face that is more the face
> of a clock ….

'At It'

He compares him to a wild beast pacing inside its cage, totally without interest in the watching humans, sometimes as much of a victim as his creation. For God, too, seems powerless before the advance of the Machine, Thomas's composite for the overwhelming forces of science, technology and capitalism, for which man is responsible and before which he dwindles and is brutalised. Yet God is capable of vindictive delight.

> And God said, I will build a church here
> And cause this people to worship me,
> And inflict them with poverty and sickness
> In return for centuries of hard work
> And patience. And its walls shall be hard as
> Their hearts, and its windows let in the light

Grudgingly, as their minds do, and the priest's words
    be drowned
By the wind's caterwauling. All this I will do,

Said God, and watch the bitterness in their eyes
Grow, and their lips suppurate with
Their prayers. And their women shall bring forth
On my altars, and I will choose the best
Of them to be thrown back into the sea.

And that was only on one island.

'The Island'

Bobi Jones, you will remember, is convinced that in that last line Thomas was sending himself up. It is quite possible, for there is humour in these poems. It is there, grimly, in the way, with Prytherch and his historical Welsh figures gone, God has been recruited into his thinning repertory company, and not as a hero. It is there in this poem to a little girl.

And if you ask her
She has no name;
But her eyes say,
Water is cold.

She is three years old
And willing to kiss;
But her lips say,
Apples are sour.

'Madam'

But there was something else, which Thomas felt obliged to address in *Autobiographical Essay*. Because of his new subject-matter, he writes, 'my poetry underwent a change of style. I broke up the lines and introduced more scientific or technological terms into my verse. It appeared that many of my readers, accustomed to thinking of me as a Welsh country poet, were unable to adjust to the new work.'

One of them was Kingsley Amis, who had given him such a rave review twenty years earlier. Writing in the *Observer* in 1974 about which poets qualified 'under the night owl test', the perfect accompaniment to the final Scotch of the day, he was careful to specify 'the early R.S. Thomas'. Thomas himself preferred his own later work (when at the end of his life he compiled his *Selected Poems* for Penguin Modern Classics four-fifths of them date from Aberdaron on), and it irritated him when others disagreed. But it was not just an argument over subject-matter.

In 1993 he wrote to Raymond Garlick, 'I see some people are still nit-picking about my so-called lack of form. I wish they'd catch up. John Wain, one of the Movement bunch, seems to have begun it, and Donald Davie, another Movement fan, agrees, carrying on about enjambement etc, as if that mattered any more.' Enjambement is when the syntax, unbroken by punctuation, is carried on into the next line of a poem: in other words, the run-overs.

Wain, in a lecture as Professor of Poetry at Oxford, had said, 'there was a time when the depressing nature of what Mr Thomas conveyed was irradiated and made bearable by his beautiful sense of rhythm and sound. The poems in *H'm* offer no such consolation.' As an example he cited the poem 'Via Negativa'. Donald Davie cited the same poem, but narrowed his objections to the run-overs, which he said jarred on the reader's ear when he read it aloud. This is the poem.

Why no! I never thought other than
That God is that great absence
In our lives, the empty silence
Within, the place where we go
Seeking, not to hope to

Arrive or find. He keeps the interstices
In our knowledge, the darkness
Between stars. His are the echoes
We follow, the footprints he has just
Left. We put our hands in
His side hoping to find
It warm. We look at people
And places as though he had looked
At them, too; but miss the reflection.

I have just been listening to Thomas reading that. He read poetry as Yeats did, casting his voice in a chanting monotone, much like the old Nonconformist ministers. Such a technique should emphasise the jarring Davie complained about (he took exception to the run-overs between the third and fourth lines, between the four and fifth, fifth and sixth, seventh and eighth, and in particular, that between the ninth and tenth: it is quite a catalogue). The curious thing is that no jarring occurs in that very old voice (he made the recording not long before his death). Try it for yourselves.

Davie considers the run-overs an irritating mannerism. But see how they allow you to emphasise the words *Within* (would you expect the silence to be within?), *Seeking*, *Arrive*, *Between*, *Left*: they begin to have the dramatic effects that preachers aimed at.

Thomas tried to explain what he was about when he was interviewed by two Cambridge undergraduates, the poets Gwyneth Lewis and Peter Robinson, for a feature later published in a university magazine. 'When I write, I'm listening with an inner ear to the way it sounds. I build the poem up like that. And if there's a word too many, it goes into the next line. But the thing is that I never really wrote them to be read out loud. There's a contradiction here: they may look artificial on the page, but they must sound right ...'

The autobiographical element in these poems is slight. In

'Relations' he broods on his mislaid relatives ('An ordinary lot'), dull and respectable in terraced houses, but is brought up short in his sense of superiority by the memory of one of them, with rescue impossible, smoking his pipe as his ship foundered. It is a nice twist.

> And he
> Was of their company; his tobacco
> Stings my eyes, who am ordinary too.

Gwydion makes one appearance, invested with the startled bemusement Thomas in the poems reserved for his son, and for the responsibilities the boy brought into his life.

> It was your mother wanted you;
> you were already half-formed
> when I entered. But can I deny
> the hunger, the loneliness bringing me in
> from myself?

'The Son'

'In Memory' records the occasion when, following the death in 1973 of Peggy Thomas, he put a stone on his parents' grave in Holyhead. Thomas, who disapproved of so much, of Christmas cards and hymns and wallpaper and the sound Hoovers made, disapproved of gravestones as well, but put this one up

> in memory of those afternoons
> when they slept, when happiness descended
> an invisible staircase
> of air.

In other words, when a strange little boy was left to his own devices.

When Thomas writes about Peggy's old age in his Welsh-language autobiography he merely states the facts. 'He knew that his mother expected to be allowed to come and live with them, but he was unwilling to have her. She was a difficult person to live with and it would not be fair to his wife.' This is a normal family experience, a dilemma many only children face and have to resolve in their own way. But how many of us can think about such an experience with any kind of honesty, let alone write about it?

In *The Echoes Return Slow*, published three years later, Thomas looked back on those years when 'we made her live/on, not out of our affection/for her, but from a dislike of death'. In the end, hearing that she could no longer look after herself, he took her in, but only for a few days.

> The ambulance came
> to rescue us from the issues
> of her body; she was delivered
> from the incompetence of
> our conscience into the hospital's
> cleaner care. Yet I took her hand
> there and made a tight-rope
> of our fingers for the misshapen
> feelings to keep their balance upon.

Read that again, taking out the 'Yet' in the sixth line. Do you notice how much more tender the poem has become? The action is then instinctive and human: amends are being made, and what is dramatic is the way the adjective 'misshapen' is transposed from what you expect it to refer to, the fingers of the old hand he is taking, to 'feelings'. But now replace the 'Yet'. A sense of distance comes, and the emotion drains. But this is how it must have been for him, there is something chilling in that 'Yet'.

My wife, meeting him for the first time in his old age,

when he came to supper, said afterwards, 'They should never have let that man become a vicar.' In her case it was because our young daughter had been there, at that time a golden child. The Welsh are usually fascinated by children, especially when they are beautiful, but Thomas showed no more interest in her than in a household ornament. What he could, and did, respond to, as Christine Evans said, was pain. She had seen his expression, and his voice, change as he talked about one of the nuns on Bardsey. 'Oh, the pain in that woman's face.'

Yet, again a yet, this could still surprise people who knew him as well as anyone. 'It was obvious to everyone who knew him at all that R.S. Thomas was not what you would call a *natural* parish priest,' wrote Canon Donald Allchin in *The David Jones Journal* 2001:

An almost total lack of small-talk, a lack of that kind of superficial cheerfulness and interest in the details of other people's lives, which can ease the beginnings of a conversation, these were obvious disadvantages. He could be angular and critical. He could seem distant and aloof. At Aberdaron there were some who thought that he was so busy hurrying up to the headland to greet the latest flock of birds from Ireland, that he failed to recognise his own parishioners when he passed them on the bridge.

But Allchin then went on to tell this story.

Having spoken of him briefly at a meeting in Kent, an old friend of mine, a retired police officer, a foursquare and eminently sensible-looking person, surprised me by saying that she had once had a long conversation with R.S. 'I didn't know that you'd ever met him,' I said. 'Ah, you see it was a telephone conversation.' What makes this so remarkable is that Thomas hardly ever made a phone call. The woman went on, 'One day I had a call which said, "I am a clergyman ringing you from Wales, you won't have heard of me, my name is R.S. Thomas." I replied, "Oh, I do know you, you're the poet."'

From there the conversation went on in a way my friend had hardly expected. R.S. insisted that she sat down because he wanted to talk for some time, and she said, 'I sat there for ten or fifteen minutes, listening to this wonderful and compassionate voice speaking of the spiritual and psychological turmoils of a young man I had been trying to help and who had gone to visit R.S. when he was in Wales. It was a revelation of his understanding and insight into the problems of another person.'

Donald Allchin was so taken aback he could only add, 'How often Ronald's gifts as a counsellor were used I do not know. But it is clear that they were there and were sometimes brought into play.'

The Rev. Evelyn Davies, when she came to Aberdaron, was puzzled to find a lobster pot in the church. This was Thomas's doing, when his efforts to help a fisherman in a state of deep distress failed, and the man committed suicide. Thomas put the lobster pot there so he could see it every time he came into his church, and remember.

> I take their hands,
> Hard hands. There is no love
> For such, only a willed
> Gentleness. Negligible men
> From the village, from the small
> Holdings, they bring their grief
> Sullenly to my back door,
> And are speechless ...

'They'

At Easter 1978, he resigned as vicar of Aberdaron. As he says in *Autobiographical Essay*, he had hoped to stay on in the vicarage, and, knowing that the clergy would not be queuing up to succeed him, he wrote to the Bishop to say that in return he would be prepared to do voluntary work. The reply, he says, was 'inconclusive', so on his sixty-fifth birthday he resigned, retiring to his cottage burrow at Sarn, and, ever the actor, as his son said, he burned his cassock on the beach beneath. No one saw him do this.

The Church, which he had assured me would look after him, had failed to do so.

SEVEN

Sarn, and Beyond

I don't know what the Social Services would have
done had they come on the set-up at Sarn. Sectioned
my parents for a start.

GWYDION THOMAS

OLD COUPLE FOUND 'LIVING HAPPILY
IN DEEP FREEZE' SHOCK

Startled Pwllheli magistrates were told yesterday that the
temperature in the house of a local couple, both in their late
seventies, was one degree above freezing. 'And that was in
their kitchen with the fire lit,' said a social worker. 'The rest
of the house was a deep freeze with windows.' When social
workers pointed out that temperatures like this were not
even reached in igloos they were shown the door by the
couple.

Only the social workers never called. Had they done so, on 1
January 1987, they would have found that the temperature in
the kitchen of the cottage to which R.S. Thomas and his wife
had retired nine years earlier was 33 degrees Fahrenheit, 1.8
degrees Celsius, with the fire lit. Elsi Thomas, recording this in
her memoirs, amazingly made no comment beyond saying that
the wind that day was from the north-east. Age Concern
declares that at anything below 60 degrees F, 16 C, there is a
danger of hypothermia, and their neighbour Gareth Williams,
calling on them one day, found he afterwards had to stand for

half an hour in front of his Aga before he regained the power of speech.

It was also a house so damp that when Thomas sat writing at his desk on a winter day his son saw mould on his shoulders. The fact that the two of them in old age managed to survive here one must count as one of the triumphs of the human spirit.

When it turned out they could no longer go on living in the 'large, roomy, if draughty' vicarage at Aberdaron, Thomas wrote, airily, in *Autobiographical Essay* that he had 'of course, been making some sort of contingency plans'. But what contingency plans, and where? 'The only house that would have satisfied my father would have had turrets and peacocks,' said Gwydion Thomas.

The one home the two had ever owned in the course of their long married life was a cottage at Nantmor, near Beddgelert in Snowdonia, bought in the late 1940s by Elsi for £200, when they were still at Manafon, the money coming from her father. It is curious to record that R.S. Thomas, that campaigner against holiday homes, once had one himself. But that had been sold in 1962 at the insistence of the Keating sisters as a pre-condition of giving them the lease on the cottage called Sarn, which he and his wife then used as a sort of retreat, or, as he sometimes referred to it, their 'holiday home'. The £2,000 they got for their cottage went towards its renovation.

Here, above the bay which, because of the wrecks of sailing ships blown here long ago, was called Hell's Mouth (he was retired, the poet informed one startled journalist, and living at the mouth of Hell), in this seventeenth-century cottage he had the perfect stage set for his last role, the Ogre of Wales peering over his half-door for photographers. The coast road that runs past it has now collapsed and ends in air. This is Sarn.

R.S. Thomas, who had so often told his son, 'My inclination to seek out Welsh parishes meant I couldn't provide your mother with a decent vicarage', brought her here, ageing and ailing, as part of his contingency plans. And it was here, with the lights on all day, its interior sunk in shadow, that she was to paint, her eyesight failing, for the next thirteen years, her feet in a cardboard box (until she put an electric fire in as well, and was badly burned). And here, carrying her in, that he brought her home from the hospital to die. She had loved Sarn.

The house is built into a wooded hillside, the contours of which it follows so completely it could be a natural feature in the land until you notice a building there among the stones and the trees. Only this is a building out of recorded time, this is neolithic (or 'positively Mycenaean in size', wrote his friend John Mowat, a classicist), the boulders in its walls four feet wide, three feet thick, some of them, estimated Thomas, weighing a ton. How it ever got built, what species of mankind was able to lift the stones into place, is a mystery.

With one bedroom, reached by ladder, one hall 'with a huge stone hearth and enormous chimney rising up which most effectively takes all the heat of the fire up to the heavens', as John Mowat drily put it, and one kitchen, the house is small, hunched and huge at the same time, a dwelling for trolls. However many old cottages you have seen, you will have seen nothing like this. Imagine a long barrow from which someone had managed to scrape away the earth, throw out the dead, then fit tiny windows and a door, and you have Sarn. Outside it is a ruined pig pen and a goose pen.

Gwydion Thomas likes to tell the story of when, after inheriting the tenancy from his father, he rented it out, only to have his wily subtenant call the social services in to inspect the conditions under which he was living. Within weeks the man was snug in a council house.

The walls are so uneven no painting can hang on them, so Elsi's paintings which had lined the walls, frame to frame, in all the rectories, had to be sold, stored or given away. Most of the furniture went, and over half of their 3,000 books, so in moving here they had the shock of being parted from their belongings; if there was contingency planning it was that of a shipwreck.

But Thomas, at a cost of £17,000, had a room added at right angles to the cottage, a study bedroom, an odd feature of which is that no door opens from it into the main house. It has its own bathroom and cupboard space, with an attic above. Light and airy, this would have been a perfect studio for Elsi, instead he claimed it. 'A gentleman's dressing room, some-thing he'd always wanted,' said Gwydion. Elsi would write of her joy in working there ('light, light, white walls') when he was away, which he often was, but, again, makes no complaint beyond saying that in her own crouched room she was lucky for the odd wandering ray of sunshine.

The last bit of contingency planning was extraordinary. Somehow they had had central heating installed, though God knows how this was got through the walls, but then, when they moved in for good, Elsi found the radiators and the piping so unappealing she insisted on the lot being ripped out. Comfort was never an option.

All her watercolours, she wrote, were put into black polythene council rubbish bags 'as being the only way I can think of to keep them moderately dry here in my room, which is very damp'. But again, no comment, just a statement of fact. 'Endless things to do, chaircovers, cushion covers, mouse-eaten mattress to cover. Things can be camouflaged if rooms huge and light, but, if small and dark, one is right on top of them all the time.' Gwydion Thomas is bitter about the conditions in which his mother lived at Sarn, blaming his father, but it seems not to have occurred to either of his parents that people did not live like this in Britain at the end of the twentieth century.

Like many retired clergymen, Thomas probably could not have afforded to buy a house. They had little money (it was only in the 1990s that he began to earn royalties of £12,000 a year from his books), but their attitudes to it were very different. To him it was something he simply did not understand, which worried him ('You are a *debt-or*,' he had told his son in horror, having discovered he was overdrawn at Oxford). To Elsi, it was something other people had, but which for her, when accumulated, could be given away, usually to her son and grandson, which she enjoyed doing. And then there was Gwydion, who was in the habit, Thomas told Peggy Mowat, of ringing up to ask cheerfully, 'Anything in the kitty?' The Thomases were not readers of *Money Mail*.

'We live very simply,' Elsi wrote in 1986. 'R.S. has a church and a national pension, and a bit from his books, so we live on that and I keep all my pension, which is lovely because I can give away whatever I like.' Her old age pension (she was four years older than he was) was a source of wonder and delight, a weekly supply of fairy gold which materialised in Pwllheli Post Office. He felt like scattering it on the pavements, Thomas told Peggy Mowat.

In 1987 the cliff road collapsed, that had run past the house. Elsi wrote in her memoirs, 'The contractors have put up traffic lights which they have to plug in to Sarn electricity. They pay £2 a day, and use 60p worth. Astonishing payment. Cheque for £90. Profit will go to tickets for *Wizard of Oz* at the Barbican for Gwydion.' Wistfully she added, 'With a bit of luck the lights might come again.'

So Ronald and Elsi Thomas, in the different wings of their tiny house, grew old together.

> I look out over the timeless sea
> over the head of one, calendar
> to time's passing, who is now open
> at the last month, her hair wintry.
>
> Am I catalyst of her mettle that,
> at my approach, her grimace of pain
> turns to a smile? What it is saying is
> 'Over love's depths only the surface is wrinkled.'

The Echoes Return Slow

That was how he saw her. How she saw him is in the letters she wrote to her niece Ann Moorey in the late 1980s. 'Miss Eldridge', as he sometimes referred to her in public, was slowing perceptibly while he was in energetic health, driving across Britain to give poetry readings.

He was by now a famous man, but at home he was an object of fascination and fun, and occasionally of irritation, to a wife who never seemed to know what he would get up to next. Her letters to her niece, dating from 1985 to 1990, are affectionate, if bemused. They are also very funny. They offer a unique glimpse of what life was like at home for the Thomases.

> [He] still has his mania for consuming large quantities of raw garlic. Terribly good for him, I believe, but rather alarming in a small house … He used never to move further than the nearest good spot for watching birds, but now covers hundreds of miles.

'I invited him to give a poetry reading at Ipswich, he was in his eighties then,' said the author Ronald Blythe. 'And he drove all the way across Wales and England. During that evening someone asked, "Can you read a little louder?" He said, "No, sir", and went on just as before.' Blythe dedicated his latest book *Borderland* to him.

And then there were the pilgrims, the graduate students and the TV crews, for whom she, increasingly reclusive ('I am inclined to bolt up into the wood, and have to be very firm with myself, for it is always an American or a student looking for Ronald to talk and talk and talk'), had to make tea, and, in the case of the TV crews, tidy up. Only at the very end was there a small rebellion. 'I've decided it is no good trying to keep Sarn clean and tidy,' she wrote in 1990, a year before her death.

31 January 1984: 'Ronald is roaring around making bread. Such a palaver, it takes him from lunch to supper time, and the

result is three whole loaves which he adores and is terribly proud of. I don't eat bread luckily, for he eats it at top speed.'

In 1985 Elsi sent her niece a cartoon of herself hobbling on a stick ('hump-backed, gone in the middle, spindle-shanked'). In 1990 she wrote, 'I wish I was a dull old spinster and could just grow more decrepit without being watched.'

Oh, she was tough. In her later years, with what she described as 'extreme pain in eyes at night', and she was not given to exaggeration, she reflected on a hospital interview at which R.S. Thomas had been present. 'Giving him all the details which one knew only too well, and had kept to oneself for years and years. Most tiresome. Far better for no one else to know, makes personal relationships much easier ...'

Doctors she disliked. Of one eye specialist, treating her for cataracts, she wrote, 'The arrogant and vicious young man was not interested in what I had to do with my eyes, but only whether I could see or not. Suggested I should have an implant lens in both eyes. Not likely. Cannot think of anything more unnatural than a lump of plastic in each eye.' The implant lenses, like the central heating and the Hoover, stood no chance, being part of the unreal modern world in which she found herself.

> The old methods and cures were often so much better. A carrot poultice will remove pain from most infected areas, even leg ulcers. The ingredients of the cure for skin cancer which the old man had in the shop near Aberdaron were entirely made from plants in his own garden.

But Ronald was always a source of amusement, even of awe. To her niece she listed the three months' itinerary of a man of seventy-four, and just out of hospital.

> Tomorrow he goes to the National Eisteddfod where he addresses the anti-nuclear section, and is leading a protest

march through Portmadog – so – he must be completely recovered, and greatly looking forward to three months' birdwatching, ending up with a fortnight in Norfolk and Northumberland, after that, the Scilly Isles.

'My aunt mothered him a great deal, and admired his talent,' said Ann Moorey. 'She put up with all his fads.' There were food fads.

It had to be this morning that Ronald thought up a two-day fast on vegetable juices every hour – so I found myself rushing round grabbing handfuls of nettles, dandelion leaves, the odd carrot and fennel and potato juice – I'm not sure what mixture I ended up with, but he still seems to be alive this evening. (1985)

March 1990:

Strangely I have turned to hotter and hotter food, and masses of sauce and gravy – all things which R.S. makes, and only now realise how much I hated his cold and dry meal affairs. Saving grace is that he will eat masses of cake and tarts and jellies. Informed me last week he wished he could live on chocolate and sherry ... [He] is always made happy by a bar of chocolate of any kind.

Then there was the Welsh language. 'Ronald has decided he will only speak Welsh, and has given me a "Learn Welsh" book. I struggle – had it for a year – reached p. 48 – 312 to go! How many years does that make?'

But they were well suited. Christmas, 1986. 'We were feeling particularly alone – from choice. I adore being alone, and Ronald adores being alone, so we decided to be alone together, but felt a bit guilty about being so indulgent.'

The great man is watched fondly, if from a distance.

Ronald has had what we call a moss attack. When he is not feeling very well he rushes round the garden, pulling all the moss off the grey stone and hacking down the alarming ivy from the trees. I always know that it is the time to persuade him to take a few valium before he does something really wild. Today he is sitting quietly in his chair, eating 'Medici bounty' chocolates, so I imagine he has taken one on the quiet – would rather die than do as urged to do and say so.

The 'Medici bounty' was payment from the Medici Society for paintings she had done.

The memoirs, written in her large, clear hand, are part flashbacks, part gardening diary, part a journal of one year, 1987, at Sarn. The white azalea Thomas had sent to Bart's when she was hospitalised there sixteen years earlier dies in the winter from lack of light. 'Everything seems to be disappearing around me.' But that is the one moment of anything approaching self-pity. She dreams of painting in oils again, but somehow never does. Instead she paints, in watercolour, ducklings, robins, mice, small creatures, for Medici Society cards.

She remembers the odd joke. A young woman books into a French inn, and finds no mattress on her bed. '*M'sieu, il n'y a pas de matelot sur mon lit.*' The innkeeper is stunned. '*En Angleterre, nous avons toujours un matelot sur le lit.*' The man turns to his wife, '*Ah, c'est vraiment un pays maritime.*' There are moments of mischief, as when the Gregynog Press's *The Mountains of Wales* comes, a book of essays to which Thomas had contributed. Edited by Ioan Bowen Rees, it had a biographical note on the editor ('Wandered the mountains of Wales for forty years, climbed the Alps, Rockies and Himalayas, came to rest at last as chief executive of Gwynedd County Council. Tra-la-la').

Old lines surface ('Cover her face; mine eyes dazzle, she died young'), and old memories. She is at the RCA again, then Gwydion is a small child, trying to catch the sunlight during a service at Manafon church. She listens to concerts on the radio, and to a tape of Shakespearean sonnets her son has brought her; she tries to restrict herself to a sonnet at night, but fails. And then, suddenly, there is the note, 'Thank God for my bed, and for peace to lie in it.'

Thomas brings her skulls, and flowers, from his walks; she gardens. So it has been for half a century, but occasionally he can surprise her.

> I showed him a painting. 'How awful,' he said. In what way? 'Such sentimental faces.' Realised I had not even looked at the faces, but at all the details of colour placing, light and dark contrast, and the shape of bodies. A perfect example it would seem of what a person sees or looks for if they are not painters, a face being the most important part to them of a human being. Gave me a jolt, I must say.

She feels so strongly about this she dismisses out of hand his series of poems about particular paintings in *Between Here and Now*. 'The quality of a painting is paint. It cannot be expressed in any other medium.' Bang. Why, he had never even seen the originals ('What a tangle'). This is the one recorded disagreement between them, and in Thomas's later comments on the poems in the magazine *Planet* he acknowledges that the painters involved would have found his efforts 'reprehensible'.

But elsewhere Elsi quotes him with reverence.

> Talking about a broadcast of Gavin Ewart telling everyone what a good poet he is, R.S. fell to talking about never having succeeded in putting over the one thing that is really good poetry – the suggestion, the elusive something that is found, or rather not found, in beauty, in life, in God – that miraculous suggestion which gives a thrill of the unknown almost.

The year turns. The flower catalogues come. And then it is summer, with Thomas whitewashing the front of Sarn ('at £16 a can'). Summer brings a remarkable rarity, guests. 'R.S. had the Mowats. Fed them royally. Ham, new potatoes, strawberries. While here poked around all over the house.'

Elsi used to tell her son that Ronald had chased all her friends away; he maintained they had never had any. 'You see, we are not so nice as you,' he told the Mowats, who were as close as anyone got. Bristol academics, they had met Thomas at a poetry reading in the 1960s; he often stayed with them when he came to England, they visited him and Elsi at Aberdaron and at Sarn. After each meeting Peggy Mowat wrote it up, and what follows is her account of the day she poked around all over the house.

> July 16, 1987. Elsie on the phone said that Ronald had been 'gallivanting about in London', having a hernia operation done. It turned out that he had had a horrid time, three anaesthetics. He came round from the first one to find that he'd had nothing done, the surgeon not having the right instruments! He'd then been swapped from the Fitzroy Square (C of E clergy hospital) to Guy's, where the correct instruments were available. But he *had* had lunch with A.E. Dyson, editor of the *Critical Quarterly*. This was about the only 'gallivanting' that we could discover.
>
> The steep approach up the cobbly path was splendid with the lesser spotted orchid (28 of them, Elsie said, which they had seeded from the bank above). We stood in the mediaeval hall house feeling our way into knowing each other again (no handshakes, kisses etc.) ...

The afternoon which followed was typical of their meetings: the 'exquisite lunch', then the afternoon walk with Thomas along the cliffs (on an earlier one he had told them helpfully, 'Don't slip, or you'll gather momentum until you hit the sea').

Before his hernia, he, at seventy-four, had skipped like a billy goat over the rocks, but Elsi, who had broken her thigh a year earlier, rarely accompanied them. Peggy Mowat wrote that this time she could no longer see to draw, but went on, 'Now that the troubles of old age have really come upon them, they appear remarkably more cheerful and indeed healthier.' And then there was 'one of Elsie's superb teas'. Homemade scones, angel cakes, iced coffee cakes, shortbread. The recluses of Sarn lived well.

Through all this is threaded R.S. Thomas's table-talk. There was his young grandson Rhodri, born in 1980, who as a boy seemed to horrify and fascinate him at the same time, and spent his days watching videos of *The Incredible Hulk*. Then the Welsh, another source of fascination and horror, who filed past his CND stall at Pwllheli market without stopping. Finally, his peers, who did not seem to fascinate him at all.

He told them about a local church key used to marry people who could not afford a ring.

> 'Must have had a jolly big finger,' said Ronald. I said imagine clanking around with that for the rest of your life, and he thought that quite funny. He told the story of 'I had a great uncle who fell at Waterloo.' 'Oh, which platform?' And the capping of this with a third man missing the joke. 'As though it mattered which platform.' Very pleased with the final version.

His father's jokes, said Gwydion Thomas, were one of the disadvantages of coming home, though usually it was only his family who heard them.

Thomas's friendship with the Mowats across thirty years was an unlikely one. They had had a holiday cottage near Abergavenny, at which he also stayed. Out of this came the poem 'Strangers'.

We don't like your white cottage.
We don't like the way you live.
Their sins are venial, the folk
With green blouses you displace.
They have gone proudly away,
Leaving only the dry bed
Of footsteps where there was grass.

But the truth was that Thomas did like the way they lived. He liked the reserve and the formality of the English upper-middle class. Later they had a caravan near Harlech, and he visited them there too, this man who once sent them a postcard showing a foreshore bristling with caravans near Pwllheli ('Thought you'd like to see where the Welsh oracle hangs out – something the Delphic one did not foresee'). When Elsi Thomas died Peggy Mowat sent him a letter of condolence in which she wrote, 'Much of her quality lives so long as man can breathe or eyes can see in your poetry, and, thank goodness, you write it in English.' Had anyone else said that, the poet would have been enraged. But they seemed at ease with each other.

He amused her.

Talked about Aberdaron. In the middle of his services he can hear Merseysiders calling 'Coo-ee, coo-ee' ... Has perfect ear, and can imitate any accent. 'Coom on down 'ere, mother. Coom on, it won't hurt yer' in the middle of his sermon. Story of Scots minister who prayed for rain and got a downpour. 'Lorrd. Lorrd, this is pairfectly reediculous.'

For he could be funny in spite of himself.

I told him Idris Williams (Welsh farmer and owner of the caravan park) said that as a policeman, when he had to deal with young men, he had asked them three questions. One, what had they done on Sunday morning? Two, did they read their Bible? Three, did they support the local eisteddfod? In those three things, Idris said, lay Welsh culture.

'I don't like Welsh policemen,' said RST.

They talked about language.

I said I thought the different strains in English add to its richness – kingly, royal, regal. RST said there were five or six words in Welsh all meaning 'bowels'. However the Welsh themselves used the word 'bowels'.

They walked.

Looking down on two bays, one pebbly, one sandy, he said, 'God said now we'll make a stony one for them, now we'll give them some sand. He's a jolly fellow.' He seems to have it in for God.

She took him to Bristol Zoo. 'Walked past the bird cages with his eyes shut. Fascinated by the tigers' gait, in particular that of a white male tiger.' This became the poem.

It was beautiful as God
must be beautiful; glacial
eyes that had looked on
violence and come to terms

with it; a body too huge
and majestic for the cage in which
it had been put ...

'The White Tiger'

It was in the zoo that she made the mistake of quoting one of his own poems to him, when she said of the antelopes 'arranged romantically in the usual fashion'. Thomas, she recorded, 'looked quite blank'.

There was always the need to be careful.

> Feel I know RST very well now, but I would be really frightened to intrude upon his personal life by trying to make more explicit what is said, so beautifully distanced – not impersonalised – in his poems. Sometimes not even distanced, as in 'Careers'. How can one say, what does your wife think about this?

But once, greatly daring, she wrote to ask him what he had meant in the poem 'Aubade'.

> I awoke. There was dew,
> and the voice of time singing:
> It is too late to begin,
> you are there already.
>
> I went to the window
> As to a peep show: There she was
> All fly-wheels and pistons;
> Her smile invisible
>
> As a laser. And, 'No.'
> I cried, 'No' turning away
> Into the computed darkness
> Where she was waiting
>
> For me, with art's stone
> Rolled aside from her belly
> To reveal the place poetry had lain
> With the silicon angels in attendance.

I quote his reply in full, for it is the comparatively rare, in his case unique, example of a poet explaining his poem.

How irksome to have to explain my poem when I don't know what it means either. This is the trouble with analysis in search of a prose meaning for what is not prose.

I imagine I had Larkin's *Aubade* in mind. The standing ruefully at the window at dawn. The 'she' is the Machine, that which time makes it impossible to escape. I remember also the story of the peepshow where there was one hole giving on the Venus de Milo. But nobody looked because she was beautiful.

The 'No' is the rejection of the Machine. The computed darkness means there is no escape, even in nature. The end is, of course, ironic. Playing on the idea of the empty tomb we find that, whether resurrected or not, poetry is no longer there, and that even the angels have become technological.

Eheu, fugaces !

Ronald. 24.ii.89.

He seemed happiest in the shooting gallery of his contemporaries. Peggy Mowat records his comments about the poet Charles Tomlinson ('I said there was a good poem about his wife coming home after a journey. He said, "He's lucky to have a wife who does come home"'). Walter de la Mare ('A nice man, but he wrote some dreadful poetry. Educated his son on the strength of *The Listeners*'). Dylan Thomas ('now being exploded, but "Fern Hill" he thought a great poem, would like to have written it himself'). Dylan he thought a disastrous influence on his contemporaries, but in 1954, having heard *Under Milk Wood* on the radio, he wrote to Raymond Garlick that it was 'excellent'.

Ted Hughes, he thought, had more power and passion than he had (he considered his own poems 'much of a muchness'), but Sylvia Plath was 'an example of female hysteria'. Disliked the idea of meeting other poets. 'So awkward having to say you don't like their poetry.'

The stars in his firmament were Yeats, Eliot and Wallace

Stevens, but his favourite English poets Shakespeare and Blake ('They are capable of lines that give you gooseflesh.' Quoted as examples, 'Pah, it smells of mortality' and 'He is at dinner. Not where he eats, but where he is eaten'). 'Then nightly sings the staring owl' he thought a perfect arrangement of vowels.

'He has been offered facilities at some place on the coast of California, where an American millionaire has provided a sort of artists' study centre, with views of the sea. He has written back, saying he already had a good view of the sea.' And then there were the soufflés and coutardes and poulet blanc, also Muscatel and Beaune de Venise, the sweet white wines he loved, and every year his hands shook more and more as he poured them.

❦

At Sarn the years were also passing in Elsi Thomas's memoirs. There is mention of just one jaunt together, when he drives her to the Plas to see the magnolia in the gardens, but this is how she wanted her life to be. 'I think I would like to have been part of a family involved in different aspects of the same occupation – definitely alone. Each section of the work must be done entirely working in solitude. One must be alone.'

Housebound in Sarn, unable to drive because of her eyesight, she mentions one absence (he was off to hospital again), '[He] cut the grass and hedge perfectly, as well as leaving me enough food to feed the whole village.' That was the time of his 'gallivanting', and on his return, she writes grumpily, 'It all sounds awful, but he was so well and did not have any pain and was so spoiled by all the nurses, and has just completed six weeks complete rest, not even lifting a typewriter, and is now anxious to get into Duc de Berry haycock making as he disapproves of the way I am doing it.' For the high artistic life extended into gardening: the haycocks in this style were something they had seen in the Duc de Berry's mediaeval *Book of Hours*. As a lady who had called on them at Aberdaron told me, 'A stranger couple it would be hard to find outside of fiction.'

But there was one part of his life in old age in which Elsi played no part.

An ex-vicar writes. From Sarn to his old friend Raymond Garlick, 'to give you the address of a retired Christian'. These letters to Garlick convey his restlessness during the later years, when Thomas was up and running from the moment of his retirement.

On 28 October 1978, on his return from Ireland after 'three months birdwatching and counting whales', as his wife put it, he called at Llanpumsaint in Carmarthenshire,

> to see the east window Elsi did years ago. The church was locked, it was like a village of the dead. Then suddenly a herd of cows appeared with four men and dogs. The cows stampeded, the dogs barked, the men shouted in Welsh, and a resurrection of a sort occurred. I called on Geraint Bowen too, but he was out.

There is a nice Pooteresque touch to that last sentence.

Thomas was in the habit of writing to Garlick at Christmas time ('I don't like hilarious Santas and over-red robins to speak for me'). 'Our stationer in Pwllheli has a special box marked Religious Xmas cards, which is a nice thought' (19.12.78). He recommends a book of poems by Geoffrey Hill ('The best now writing in English. I wish I wrote with his economy and intelligence. And he is only 46'). Garlick recalled, 'I struggled with it.' Like Rupert Hart-Davis, he did not like Geoffrey Hill.

'The Church is imperfect, God knows, but it has the Scriptures and sacraments, if it only will have the grace to let those who prefer the old forms continue to enjoy them. So I shall go along on Christmas morning. Perhaps you will?' (13.12.79). 'The apathy and Philistinism of Lleyn are beyond imagining' (16.12.80).

His contemporaries are savaged in passing. 'English criticism is a morass, and is made worse by certain dons who should know better, who delight in saying stupid things in public, like the Merton Professor of English at Oxford [John Carey]. 'Everybody knows by now that Seamus Heaney is a great poet. Etc ad nauseam.' (26.1.82) Like Larkin, who thought the future Nobel Laureate had 'a cloth ear', Thomas had little time for Heaney.

'I shall be a septuagenarian next March, so Macmillan are bringing out a selection of later poems to balance the earlier selection. I wish they were in Welsh. Awake at night, I try to get back to sleep by composing *englynion*. I generally get back to sleep, but without the *englyn*. I don't know how. *Yr hen iaith Saesneg diawledig yn yr isymwybod.*' 'The old devilish English language in the subconscious'. (16.12.82)

On the eve of his birthday he writes on 27 March 1983, reviewing his own career as a poet,

There is certainly no feeling of achievement at all, but rather of falling short of what I would have wished to achieve. The sort of yardsticks I have used have been 'Le Bateau Ivre', 'Le Cimetière Marin', 'Sailing to Byzantium' etc. And when one falls short of those one knows one hasn't been chosen.

I am writing this while still in my sixties! Tuesday is the fatal day. Cofion, Ronald.

But two years earlier, in 1981, there had been a social breakthrough: Thomas had begun to meet his neighbours.

With costs rising I have been falling back on this area and cultivating Welsh contacts, although my age is against me. We have formed the Dwyfor branch of Yr Ymgyrch Gwrth Nuclear CND. The apathy and willed ignorance of this area are extreme, but are *beginning to* crack here and there ... I am having to push my way in here and there locally, and it is heartening to find pockets of 'good' Welsh people, and to tune my ear to Lleyn Welsh.

And, beyond his neighbours, there were political and social causes. The 1980s were his public years.

> I served on a dozen committees,
> talked hard, said little, shared the applause
> at the end. Picking over
> the remains later, we agreed power
> was not ours, launched our invective
> at others, the anonymous wielders
> of such. Life became small, grey,
> the smell of interiors ...

'That Place'

He was a seventy-year-old louring public man now, regional secretary of CND, secretary of Cyfeillion Lleyn, the Friends of Lleyn, a local pressure group he himself had founded ('as an effort to save something of Lleyn Welshness. New English families arrive here monthly, with kids to cancel the Welsh majority in the primary schools. It rains and rains'). He was on the committee behind a new local community Welsh newspaper, and, briefly, was the chairman of the Bardsey Trust Council. It was during this time that he, this most private of individuals, became the most notorious man in Wales.

In Eglwys Fach he had joined the Committee for the Protection of the Red Kite (the other members, he noted gloomily, were English). Then in 1978, following a successful public appeal to buy Bardsey, he had seemed the perfect choice to be appointed the first chairman of the Island Trust Council, though he seemed to have had misgivings from the start. In a letter to Garlick, dated 15 June 1978, he said things were being held up by the lack of a Welsh-speaking secretary, though 'a competent Anglo-Welshman is eager and ready'. For to him Bardsey was not just a potential nature reserve: it was the old place, with a spiritual significance in the Welsh past. Thomas resigned in March 1979.

Christopher Armstrong, his successor as vicar of Aber-daron, said this was because of the acceptance of a £200,000 grant from the British Nature Conservancy Council, which Thomas regarded as English money *(David Jones Journal* 2001). It may sound a lunatic objection, the money was needed for maintenance, but Thomas had this dream that if the Welsh were to survive it should be by their own efforts, so the naturalist and patriot in him were pulling in different directions. According to Justin Wintle, quoting a local man, there was also the matter of siting a beacon on the island for yachts and pleasure craft, which Thomas thought would merely encourage tourism. The beacon went up, but a storm blew it away, and it has not been replaced. It was again a matter of black comedy.

Then there was CND. 'Silly old man sitting down in roads, he'll catch his death of cold,' Elsi Thomas told her niece. On 16 November 1983, he writes to Raymond Garlick, 'The Lleyn and Eifionydd CND are going by bus to Caerdydd [Cardiff] on December 3rd, but as we have to leave at 4.30 am, I don't know whether I shall be awake enough to walk in procession.' A month later, he writes ruefully, 'Because of lack of numbers we went in private cars.'

'[Ronald] is absurdly well,' wrote Elsi Thomas to her niece in 1984, 'rushing all over the peninsula after birds, and also collecting members for his newly formed branch of CND. He tells me I must keep a large bottle of Paracetamol in case of nuclear attack, but that sounds a bit extravagant.' She had a nice line in irony. The jar of paracetamol was presumably so she could commit suicide.

In May 1986, he drove twice to Carmarthen to protest over the council's new nuclear bunker, built just in time for the ending of the Cold War. Like Thomas, Carmarthen District

Council had come late to the threat of nuclear war, and at first had tried to pass its bunker off as a hospitality suite for its chairman. But then someone looked at the planning application and found that the chairman would have been dispensing hospitality sixty feet below ground.

It was at this time that, campaigning for CND, he called on an old lady, gave her a quick briefing on the cost of Britain's nuclear defences, and was stunned by her response. 'Mr Thomas, they have to spend their money on *something.*' Later he would quote that against himself, but argument was something new for a man who in the pulpit, or in poetry, had never been interrupted.

And then there was Wales. 'I heard him speak against the proposed Pwllheli marina,' said Angharad Tomos, novelist and chairman of the Welsh Language Society. 'He was heckled, and I felt very embarrassed.' Dafydd Lewis, also there, said, 'He was under a great deal of pressure. Half of them were shouting, "If you feel so strongly about the Welsh language, why don't you write in it?" He was quite nervous, but determined. He carried on.'

The marina was intended to encourage tourism, and that is the dilemma peculiar to Wales. Its most beautiful areas are also its poorest, so tourism would seem to be the answer, but while tourism in English highland areas might replace one economy with another, in Wales it replaces a national identity. For these areas are also the heartland of the Welsh language. And in them, in the late twentieth century, the second, holiday, home, occupied for perhaps a few weeks at most, had now begun to proliferate.

In the late twentieth century rising property prices in England meant the native population could be outbid for anything that came on the market in Wales. 'In the early 1980s, with 40,000 English people migrating to Wales each year, the fear arose that Welsh-speaking rural communities would be utterly swamped' (John Davies, *A History of Wales,*

Allen Lane, 1993). The fear was well founded, as every winter under the mountains and in the little ports the lights began to come on in half the houses, or less. What made it worse was that the people who bought these were unaware of the effect they, and their actions, were having. 'You can pick one up for next to nothing,' said an Englishwoman to me blithely at a wedding lunch, having mistaken my accent for Hungarian. The Welsh, and in particular Welsh intellectuals, were only too well aware. In 1979 the empty holiday cottages began to burn in Wales.

Over the next ten years 130, perhaps 140, as well as the offices of some estate agents, were torched, the estimates vary, for which a secret organisation calling itself Meibion Glyndwr, the Sons of Glyndwr, claimed responsibility. And it was now that R.S. Thomas the public man became notorious. It started with a radio interview.

On 7 June 1988, he writes to Raymond Garlick:

> The morning after the latest extension of the campaign to warn England and to draw attention to an injustice by pushing a few more devices through the letter boxes of estate agents, I was telephoned for my reaction [by a news reporter]. It was news to me, but I said, as you know, that these people, if caught, will be subjected to very heavy sentences by the bought judiciary, that I admired their courage. I don't see a close connection between this and your long condemnation of violence against the person.

There was nothing new in his remarks. Three months earlier he had appeared on the TV programme *Byd ar Bedwar*, as he told Garlick. 'I hear from other friends that my two main points were omitted as "inflammatory". They were 1) that property is of far less value than life, and 2) that even if one Englishman got killed, what is that compared to the killing of our nation?'

What was new was that now these remarks, and in particular the second, got translated into English. Enter Tony Heath, *Guardian* stringer in North Wales, and R.S. Thomas's Nemesis in the national press.

May 10 1988:

POLICE CHIEF CONDEMNS POET'S BACKING
FOR WELSH ARSONISTS

A senior police officer yesterday rebuked the Rev. R.S. Thomas, Wales's leading poet, for supporting the holiday home arsonists who have attacked more than 140 properties and several estate agents in England and Wales in the past eight years.

Mr Thomas praised the fire raisers, claiming they had the courage to stand up for Welsh values. In an interview he said, 'What is one death against the death of the whole Welsh nation?'

Curiously, nowhere in this news story does a senior police officer rebuke, let alone condemn, R.S. Thomas, or, come to that, anyone else by name. Tony Heath mentions a John Owen, assistant chief constable of North Wales, but in the quote attributed to him Mr Owen says only that there had been too little condemnation of the arsonists from the churches and the community leaders.

Undeterred, Mr Heath embarked on a piece of escalation two days later. 12 May 1988:

A potentially lethal clash of culture and politics is threatening the stability of rural Wales. The fuse was lit in December 1979 with the start of an arson campaign against second homes. More than 130 fires later ... [The number has shrunk, 140 to 130] and with the arsonists still at large, the Rev. R.S. Thomas, Wales's leading poet, has supplied the detonator with a ringing declaration of support for the terrorists who,

284

he declares, are the only true defenders of the Welsh language and culture.

Well, he hadn't quite, but never mind. Anyway, with a fuse already spluttering, why bother with a detonator? Mr Heath had a reckless way with metaphor. But whatever R.S. Thomas had said, those who might be considered his sympathisers felt a need to distance themselves. 'He could say it and be damned,' said Angharad Tomos of the Welsh Language Society, and an activist much admired by him. 'We had to be careful. If the press phoned us we said we stuck to our non-violent principles.' Thomas's intervention appalled my mother, it startled Professor Bobi Jones, so there was a moment of isolation for this new public figure. The irony is that Thomas was rescued by someone who had no intention of rescuing him, who now came forward with a can of petrol himself.

Tony Heath went on,

The poet was described yesterday by the leader of Plaid Cymru, Mr Dafydd Elis Thomas MP, as a Celtic copy of Jean-Marie Le Pen. 'The attitude of blaming immigrants for economic, social and cultural changes is reminiscent of much of the obnoxious talk of the European Right,' the MP declared.

What worries constitutional nationalists is that the Rev Thomas's advance towards racism may encourage others misguided enough to believe in the dual politics of the incendiary and the ballot box.

Small wonder that Mr Dafydd Wigley, the Plaid MP for Caernarfon, feels apprehensive: 'If we don't get it sorted out we're going down the road to Northern Ireland.'

Mr Heath ended his article in an implosion of metaphor. 'Caernarfon is still a long way from Crossmaglen, but the warning signs are beginning to crystallise.'

Dafydd Elis Thomas had never had much time for the poet's political ideas. In the 1972 *Poetry Wales* celebration of R.S. Thomas's work the politician had materialised like the Wicked Fairy to castigate his namesake's 'despair-laden view of Wales generated by a historically motivated nationalism ...'. But this time he had gone too far, and suddenly people felt the need to distance themselves from Dafydd (now Lord) Elis Thomas, then the leader of a party with three seats in Parliament and about to fight its first European election.

The sociologist Glyn Williams wrote in the Welsh magazine *Barn*, 'Plaid Cymru's patriotism, if not its nationalism, has collapsed. Now it is apparent that the best thing that could happen to the nationalism of Wales would be for Plaid Cymru to lose its three seats.' The university lecturer Ned Thomas wrote in *Planet*,

> In expressing admiration for the house-burners [R.S. Thomas] was not advocating a policy but saluting an act of resistance which dramatises a situation. One might have expected some radical historian of the Rebecca Riots to seize upon an analogy in the arson campaign, but it took a poet to see its symbolic charge, and it took a politician – Dafydd Elis Thomas – to tell us that a nation should never listen to its poets.

But it had been a close thing. Gwydion Thomas remembers staying at Sarn at this time, when one night there was the sound of feet outside the door. When he opened it there was no one there, just a neat parcel, inside which there was a T-shirt with the inscription 'Meibion Glyndwr'. He remembers the stunned silence, and then next morning the fire in the garden as his father burned the T-shirt.

Later that year he was able to write mischievously to Raymond Garlick:

An enforced pacifist, I would be no good in a scuffle any more, so I go round in the dark, burning English cottages! A tiny cottage near Botwnnog, that was partially burned a few years ago, has had a new, larger bungalow built on the site, which is on offer by the English owner at £85,000. Is it any wonder that the young people of Lleyn live in caravans?

But there was one last passage of arms. On 17 September 1990, Mr Heath was at it again in the *Guardian*, this time in a short news story which he wrote with Angella Johnson.

The poet and novelist [novelist? Thomas had never written a novel, and no fiction apart from *Gwenno the Goat*] and retired clergyman, the Rev. R.S. Thomas yesterday called for a campaign of 'non-violent night attacks' against the homes of English people in Welsh-speaking areas.

Addressing a rally of the breakaway nationalist group The Covenanters of the Free Welsh at Machynlleth, Powys, Mr Thomas said posters should be put up on English homes and all English name signs pulled down. 'This must be done at night so the authorities are prevented from finding out the extent of the opposition to the incomers,' he said.

This time Thomas replied. In the December issue of *Planet* 1990, he wrote,

The burden of my talk was that, since to adopt the methods of Owain Glyndwr was out of the question, how could we meet the English threat to our identity non-violently. I did not express hatred of the English, nor did I urge attacks on their property. Afterwards I gave a short interview in Welsh, and in reply to the ritual question about the burning of cottages in Wales, I replied, as usual, that I was not prepared to incite others to do what I was not prepared to do myself.

The reporting of his remarks, he went on, was characterised by 'hysteria, over-reaction, libel, vilification, abuse, and so on'.

As if to make amends, the *Guardian,* by now clearly fascinated by R.S. Thomas, sent a retired senior reporter, Gareth Parry, to interview him on his eightieth birthday and the day his *Collected Poems* were published, 29 March 1993. It was also, coincidentally, three days after the end of the only trial with possible links to the arson campaign. Three men had been charged at Caernarfon with conspiracy to cause explosions, of whom two were acquitted, and a third gaoled for twelve years for possessing explosives and sending letter bombs to leading personalities. Before and during the trial Thomas had set up a fund to help their families.

'When I rang him he said, "You do realise I only do interviews in the Welsh language." He was a bit startled to find I could speak it,' said Mr Parry, who, like Thomas, came from Anglesey.

'The only thing was, after seven or eight minutes we were both struggling a bit, and I was delighted when he said, "Let's switch to English." I have to admit, I'd gone along hoping for some radical outbursts, but there were none. There was just this calm, considered intelligence. I ended up liking the man very much.'

Mr Parry was almost as surprised by Thomas's appearance in tweed and flannels (the 'look of an English gentleman of the Shires, not a Welsh dragon'), and felt obliged to write, 'Photographs have always shown him in the Fifties poet's uniform of duffel-coats, smocks and so on, his wild white hair cleverly back lit to suggest a figure of malevolence, even madness.' Only the *Guardian* then used a photograph of Thomas in a duffel coat, his wild white hair cleverly back lit by the limewashed walls of Sarn.

The two went over some old ground. Yes, he had said that the death of one Englishman would be worth the saving of the Welsh language. That remark he would never retract. In

October 1995, in the *Oldie*, asked by Naim Attallah whether he still stood by it, Thomas said, very simply, 'Yes, indeed.' But he was a pacifist, Thomas told Parry, and had never encouraged or condoned violence. What the English needed to know was the context in which he had said it.

'The issue of homes for the Welsh, as apart from holiday homes, is a cause worth fighting. Many young people in Wales cannot afford their first home, never mind a second. How can four walls and two windows built for £90 be worth £45,000?' But it was too easy to blame the English, he went on. 'Wales is such a beautiful place with its share of damn fools who are prepared to be overriden. I love Wales more than its people.'

See him there for a moment, bitter and baffled and old, no longer a figure of controversy, just someone who knew there was absolutely nothing he could do about it ('I wish that I could have helped alleviate some of that pain, and comforted and helped').

But there was always the small stage of the Lleyn. He contributed articles to the community newspaper he had helped found, which no national stringers would ever read, articles on nuclear waste and the nuclear winter, on the use of the Welsh language in business, and on the Bardsey Island boatman; he also helped organise its various fund-raising activities, like mackerel-fishing competitions. The result has been an unqualified success: the paper, which has never received a grant, now has a circulation of 2,500 and is a lively production with its own sports pages.

More to the point, it is self-supporting, and it is a measure of its self-confidence, and that of the businesses underwriting it, that even their advertisements are in Welsh. Thomas, who used to say that English loan words in Welsh were like bluebottles buzzing in his ear, would have been delighted by that, also amused by a local beauty parlour's heroic attempts to display its wares in perfect Welsh. *Triniaeth cwyr*, that is waxing (though of unspecified areas). *Tyluno'r corff*, body massage. But *triniaeth galfanio* took some working out. Galvanising treatment has more to do with the building trade than beauty, until I made a guess and came up with electrolysis. Hair removal. Thomas, who wanted to purify the Welsh language, would have been stumped by that one. The beauty parlour, though, is called Raffles.

The late 1980s were also the years of the Friends of Lleyn, whose secretary he had become in 1985, and they were years of agitation to get reopened those local shops and petrol stations which had closed, an uphill job, for as one man said, 'You can't *make* people buy anything.' Thomas he remembered as being very quiet in committee, but it was on him that the job devolved of writing letters. It had its advantages, having a great poet on the committee.

As Tony Brown wrote in his monograph on Thomas in the *Writers of Wales* series,

> Here we see a Thomas who is willing, week after week, month after month, to expend time and energy in the often thankless task of engaging in correspondence with public bodies, with the Welsh Office and the Welsh Language Board, with officials at local councils and with MPs, doggedly pressing at an issue and infrequently achieving a positive outcome.

Though Thomas, when he writes to Garlick, says only, 'I have written scores of letters and attended dozens of protests, without much visible effect. And yet it is better that we exist, rather than not.' Letters about the building of holiday homes, about the proposed dumping of nuclear waste, about the use of English-only material by the Post Office, the Red Cross and the British Legion. In March 1992, the deputy keeper of the Ashmolean Museum, Oxford, must have been surprised to get a letter from one of the foremost living English poets, even more so when he found this contained the sentence, 'I write in English for your convenience only.'

'That was something to do with me,' said Gareth Williams, a retired surveyor and smallholder.

In 1895 my grandfather had dug up some stones, reputedly a memorial to a fifth-century Welsh saint. I knew they'd been taken to the Ashmolean, but when I called in 1989 they were nowhere to be seen. It was then a curator told me they were stored away in the basement, they were surplus to requirements or something. So I got Thomas as Secretary of the Friends of Lleyn to write, and we got them back, they are in an art gallery in Llanbedrog now.

He was my neighbour, I sold him eggs. He'd call every Friday evening about nine. It was always half a dozen eggs.

I met him first when he was vicar of Aberdaron. Tall man, stood out in a crowd. It was when the school at Rhiw had closed, and there was a local effort to use the building for some kind of employment, which in the end we got. It became a carpenters' workshop. But it was when he retired here that I began to see a lot of him. I've read lots of stuff about him, some of it miles from the man I knew. He was very funny, he had this dry wit, he could be great company.

I'd read the early poetry, and that had made me uneasy. I didn't know what he was trying to say, or whether he was sympathetic to the people he was writing about. It was meeting him that put my mind at ease. This was a man who, when he called for the eggs, would often stay talking by the Aga until midnight, or who'd pass in his car and say, 'I'm off to Caernarfon, want to come?' I never thought of him as anything but a neighbour. If he called, he never bothered to phone first.

He'd bring figs from his fig tree for my children, and

when my wife was seriously ill and confined to her bed he used to sit with her for hours, talking about when he was a boy or about Montgomeryshire, where she was born. He told us about the time there, out walking in the hills, when he met and tried talking in Welsh to some farmers, one of whom after a while asked, 'Excuse me, are you a German prisoner of war?'

Of course you were aware that he was a bit different. He'd talk about the time he'd been invited to Ireland. 'And d'you know they sent a car for me. Terrible driver. Went everywhere at 100 mph.' And once we met when he had some people with him from Oxford or somewhere. He knew I wrote poetry in Welsh, the only thing was he introduced me as the finest poet in Wales. But I did see the other side of him once. We'd met some walkers with an Ordnance Survey map, who asked after Hell's Mouth. 'Never heard of it,' he said.

He had his odd ways. I called on him once, a cold November day, he was on his own by then, and he was sitting huddled by this huge open chimney. The chimney wasn't pulling. He said, very drily, 'I'm sure you don't want to take your coat off.'

But at the end of the day he was as normal as any neighbour could be. I could tell you stories about the others, but nobody asks. They're all incomers now. Oh yes, they farm, they have horses. But they're from away.

And then Gareth Williams said something that didn't register until I was going through my notes. 'He was part of a community which disappeared.'

The man who had seen the Wales of his dreams from a train window, who had sought it in the hills, and then in the West, who had learned its language, had finally achieved his heart's desire. At long last he was part of a community. It had disappeared, but he had *belonged*.

... the traveller gets down
onto a midnight platform
and knows from the rustle
of unseen water-
falls he has come home ...

'Afallon'

The letters to Garlick still got written. In September 1989, having received a postcard from him in Greece, he replies, 'I wonder what the original Troy was like? And Helen? Llywelyn's castle at Dolwyddelan is such a small affair.' But the strain of looking after Elsi is beginning to tell. He suffers from panic attacks, from claustrophobia and uncontrollable shivering, followed by extreme depression, brought on, he thinks, by a vegetarian diet.

At the end of 1990 he writes, 'So the Christmases pass, and I begin to have the feeling I have stayed too long. But I must not go yet, because Elsi is in poor shape and needs help.'

On 16 March 1991, there was this letter. 'I have the sad news that Elsi passed away from the world last Sunday, March 10th ... Mercifully the end came quickly and she died peacefully. Gwydion came at once and was a great help over the worst few days.'

He had brought her home from the hospital at Caernarfon, carrying her up the steps himself as he might a bride, even though he was recovering from a hernia operation at the time, 'when he shouldn't have been lifting so much as an apple'. It is such a vivid phrase. Justin Wintle, who recorded it, had talked to his nearest neighbour, Megan Williams, in the farm a hundred yards away, who saw this. She said that Thomas had not sought help ('It was always like that between them'). He was seventy-eight then, his wife eighty-one. Elsi Thomas died four days later.

He buried her ashes in the bleak little graveyard above the

cliffs at Llanfaelrhys, once one of the churches in his care, and
the most remote, lost in endless tiny lanes. Near the graves of
the Keatings, there is a piece of slate in the ground which reads
'Mildred Elsi Thomas, 1909–1991'. Nothing about her being an
artist or anyone's 'beloved wife', just that, and a small cross in
the top left hand corner.

> Her name
> echoes the silence
> she and her brush kept.

To the right of her lies a man from Worcestershire, to the
left Thomas Jones Pierce, once Professor of Welsh History at
Aberystwyth, whose lecture on the death of Llywelyn each
year reduced his students to tears. There was one pink
campion when I was there, flowering against a stone behind
her grave, and a tiny lavender bush in front.

> Others
> will come to this stone
> where, so timeless
> the lichen, so delicate
> the brush strokes,
> it is as though
> with all windows wide
> in her ashen studio
> she is at work forever.

'In Memoriam: M.E.E.'

Late in the autumn of 2005 as I walked in the garden of
Sarn, I saw something I had not noticed before. The house was
empty, with Gwydion Thomas away, but in the tiny window
of the attic which Elsi Thomas had crammed with things I saw
a small white hand. I stared for a moment, until I remembered

this was her hand that she had sculpted, which Ronald Thomas, in a rare moment of house cleaning, had shattered, and which she had reassembled.

But in that moment, before I realised what it was, it appeared to be waving.

✤

The relationship between Ronald and Elsi Thomas even puzzled Elsi's own mother, said Ann Moorey. Neither Mrs Moorey nor Gwydion Thomas ever saw the two touch, the most being the hand on the shoulder. In the few photographs, even on their wedding day, they stand apart.

It may be the fact that we are dealing with another generation. I never once saw my father take my mother's hand, and the only time he ever saw his father kiss his mother, said an old friend, was when the ambulance came to take him to hospital for the operation on a terminal cancer. But in Thomas's case there are the poems.

Thomas wrote poems to his wife throughout, and after, their long married life together. In terms of biography it would be much easier had he not done so, for then a biographer would not pry into this most secret part of their lives. But the poems exist, and are of such an intimacy and detail, that he has to acknowledge them. Were they to be collected in one volume, and at the time of writing it was intended they should be, it would be an anatomy of a marriage across five decades. Some, but by no means all, are love poems.

In 'The Way of It', published in 1977 in Elsi's lifetime, Thomas, brooding on the early years of their marriage, suggests there was a lack of romantic love, at least on her part.

I saw her,
when young, and spread the panoply

of my feathers instinctively
to engage her. She was not deceived,
but accepted me as a girl
will under a thin moon
in love's absence as someone
she could build a home with
for her imagined child.

Which, you will remember, is more or less what she herself says in her memoirs. 'R.S. and I were on the moor at Bwlch
y Fedwen, the wind blowing across the bleached grass, and the
golden plover calling, when we decided that we could live
together.' But she had remembered the time and the place.

The collection *Mass for Hard Times* was published after
her death, and has the inscription, 'To the memory of My Wife
M.E. Eldridge, 1909–1991'. She had loved the poem which
gave the collection its name ('a good poem and a very original
idea'), and had copied it out in full in her memoirs after it had
been published in 1987 in the *Poetry Review*. But the collection
also contains the poem 'Nuptials'.

Did she listen
to him, plaiting the basket
from which he would take
bread? Once the whole loaf:
flesh white, breasts risen
to his first kneading;
a slice after, the appetite
whetted for the more
not to be; the fast
upon fast to be broken
only in love's absence
by the crumb of a kiss.

This is oblique (Elsi approvingly quotes her husband's
dictum that poetry should state obliquely, not directly), but,

its metaphors decoded, it has to do with the fading of sexual relations within a marriage. This was something no one ever told her would happen, Kathleen Tynan wrote rather endearingly in her biography of her own husband. It is tempting to forget metaphor and ground the poem in domestic detail (Thomas, as his wife records, was an enthusiastic baker; she herself did not eat bread), but the poem turns on metaphor, and it is a strange thing for an elderly widower to write.

'Golden Wedding' suggests there was a resolution:

Cold hands meeting,
the eyes aside
as vows are contracted
in the tongue's absence.

Gradually
over fifty long years
of held breath
the heart has become warm.

And then, after this, the love poems pour out, all of them poems of absence.

She left me. What voice
colder than the wind
out of the grave said:
'It is over'? Impalpable,
invisible, she comes
to me still, as she would
do, and I at my reading.
There is a tremor
of light, as of a bird crossing
the sun's path, and I look
up in recognition
of a presence in absence.
Not a word, not a sound,

as she goes her way,
but a scent lingering
which is that of time immolating
itself in love's fire.

'No Time'

Absence he could respond to, and understand, having
had such a long experience of this with his God. The love
poems he now wrote in old age were the most lyrical he was
ever to write, one of them as lovely and delicate as anything in
the English language.

We met
under a shower
of bird-notes.
Fifty years passed,
Love's moment
in a world in
servitude to time.
She was young;
I kissed with my eyes
closed and opened
them on her wrinkles.
'Come' said death,
choosing her as his
partner for
the last dance. And she,
who in life
had done everything
with a bird's grace,
opened her bill now
for the shedding
of one sigh no
heavier than a feather.

The *Sunday Telegraph* printed that in full when in 1995 I wrote an article about his being nominated for the Nobel Prize. He was then living with, but not yet married to, his second wife. 'Better not put that in,' he said breezily, and, I thought, a little proudly. He was eighty-two, but, like T.H. White's Merlin, was living life backwards: the things other people did in youth, political protest, living in sin, travel, he was doing in old age.

Then the matter of his fee came up, for the poem had been printed in full. I got him £100 (he had never had an agent), and wrote to tell him. I have his letter here. 'Any chance of making it payable to [his lady]. I promised her she should have it as compensation.' I cannot imagine Hardy, who in old age and a second marriage also wrote great love poetry to his first wife, ever saying that. An unlikely comedy was always lurking somewhere, just as these late love poems lurk, bursts of rock flowers amongst the overwhelming granite of the religious poetry on which for some his reputation will turn.

❦✛❦

Thomas, since the end of his relationship with Rupert Hart-Davis, had never been happy with his new publishers, his relationship with whom coincided with a slump in his popularity. *H'm*, brought out by Macmillan in 1972, was the nadir, being a hard-cover edition of 500 copies, which, naturally, has made it extremely collectable. In spite of this Macmillan went on publishing him (*Between Here and Now* (1981); *Later Poems 1972–1982*; *Experimenting with an Amen* (1986); *The Echoes Return Slow* (1988)), without much enthusiasm on his part, or, he suspected, on theirs.

What changed everything was the approach in 1986 by Gwydion Thomas, then acting as his father's agent, to the Newcastle poetry publishers *Bloodaxe*. Thomas's *Selected Poems 1946–68*, published in 1973, had never gone into paperback. Bloodaxe now secured the rights and sold an astonishing 20,000 copies, at which point they became Thomas's main publisher, bringing out his last four collections, and, after his death, the *Later Collected Poems*. All these, said Neil Astley of Bloodaxe, averaged upwards of 9,000 copies, where publishers usually counted themselves lucky to shift a thousand copies of any book of poetry.

In 1999, nine months before his death and already suffering from the heart trouble which meant, as he said, he could no longer climb a hill, he who had climbed them all his life, Thomas was interviewed by Graham Turner of the *Daily Telegraph*. Turner was startled by the eighty-six-year-old poet, 'a man of stark honesty and the most unexpected opinions'. For in the course of it, being more used to interviewing captains of industry and politicians, he had rather engagingly asked him the direct question, why did the Almighty make such frequent appearances in his verse? No messing about. Bang.

Thomas looked dumbfounded. 'I believe in God,' he said baldly, as if there was nothing more to be said …

Very well, but what sort of God? 'He's a poet who sang creation,' replied Thomas, 'and He's also an intellect with an ultra-mathematical mind, who formed the entire universe in it. The answer is in a chapter of Augustine's *Confessions* where it says, "They all cried out with one voice, He made us."'

Many interviewers would have given up then, but Turner, and I warm to him at this point, pressed beadily on.

But did he also love God? 'I've been much influenced,' said Thomas, 'by the American poet Robinson Jeffers, who says somewhere, "the people who talk of God in human terms, think of that!" George Herbert, the seventeenth-century divine and poet, must have been a dear man, but when he speaks of the touch of the Lord pressing against his soul, I simply can't conceive of God in that way. As for Gerard Manley Hopkins and the sort of endearments he uses, it's almost as if he had a sexual relationship with God. No, loving God is too much of a human construct. What there must be is awe.

'I feel much more at home with Wordsworth's vision of Snowdon in *The Prelude*, where he says, "It seemed to me the type of a majestic intelligence ... the emblem of a mind that feeds upon infinity."'

As I discovered, Thomas often shies away from the idea of love, human or divine ...

In what to him was his second vocation, that of a clergyman, R.S. Thomas did not regard himself as anything other than an orthodox working priest of the Church in Wales, and said so more than once. 'I never felt I was employed by the Church to preach my own beliefs and doubts and questionings' (*Autobiographical Essay*). He liked in later life to say he had found some of his duties amusing, as when he told me, mischievously, 'I could never have coped with a town parish. I was asked to stand in for a vicar in Aberystwyth once, and had to read the week's notices. A Mothers' Union meeting here, a coffee morning there. I found myself reading this stuff out and I just burst out laughing in church.'

But if you read through his Manafon parish notes you will find that he did not shirk such pastoral duties as whist drives and the youth clubs, one of which he actually founded, and went on to inflict croquet on the young of Eglwys Fach and Aberdaron. The man did try. He may have refused to conduct the hymn singing on the beach that has become popular with some seaside clergy, but that probably had more to do with his aversion to hymns ('the silly twaddle that there is').

For there was always the matter of his first vocation, poetry. 'I'm obviously not orthodox,' he told Molly Price-

Owen of the David Jones Society in her interview with him a
year before his death, 'I don't know how many real poets have
ever been orthodox.' The only thing was, had he confined his
lack of orthodoxy to his verse there would have been no
problem (poetry, as Auden wrote, 'survives in the valley of its
saying/Where executives would never want to tamper'), but
as he became more famous there were interviewers who
wanted to know what these beliefs and doubts and questionings were. And he, an honest man, told them, no longer

> Saving his face
> in verse from the humiliations prose
> forced on him.

'A Life'

One such humiliation occurred in 1972, when, still at
Aberdaron, he was interviewed by John Ormond for the BBC
TV film *R.S. Thomas, Priest and Poet*. Until then, as he told
Molly Price-Owen, he had been, as he put it, lucky ('obviously
I would have been for the chop in earlier days. The Inquisition
would have rooted me out; even in the nineteenth century I
would probably have been had up by a bishop and asked to
change my views, or to keep them to myself'). But then on the
TV film he said this:

'The message of the New Testament is poetry. Christ was a
poet, the New Testament is a metaphor, the Resurrection is a
metaphor; and I feel perfectly within my rights in approaching my whole vocation as priest and preacher as one who is
to present poetry; and when I preach poetry I am preaching
Christianity, and when one discusses Christianity one is
discussing poetry in its imaginative aspects. The core of both
are imagination as far as I'm concerned, so that I'm not
personally worried about this at all.'

JOHN ORMOND: 'You are saying that the notion of Christ's Resurrection is a metaphor?'

'I consider that the Resurrection is a metaphorical use of language, as is the Incarnation. We are not so hag-ridden today by heresy hunters as they were in the early centuries of the church.'

He seems to have had misgivings about this later, for as he was ruefully to tell Molly Price-Owen three decades later,

I said the resurrection is a metaphor and I was taken up by this and I like to kid myself that I hadn't put it like that, that I really meant to say the Resurrection is metaphor, not *a* metaphor, but they were able to produce tapes to show that I had said 'a metaphor' but I don't quite mean it like that. I mean that I say 'resurrection is metaphor' because we are the slaves of language.

He elaborated on this:

These so-called disciples, 2,000 years ago, they experienced something. I don't think you can deny this, they experienced something, whether it was Jesus rising from the dead, the empty tomb, all these sorts of things, but they were then forced to tell other people and certainly to convey it by means of manuscripts, or whatever they used, in language. And we have to take their account in language, but there are aspects of language which are most successfully conveyed by metaphor, and the risen Christ, the resurrection, to me, as I said, is metaphor. It's an attempt to convey an experience of a kind of new life, an eruption of the deity into ordinary life, a lifting up of ordinary life into a higher level ...

The effect of this is to present a man who at the end of his life had distanced himself from orthodox Christianity, or at least from the orthodox Christian narrative. He told his *Planet* interviewers that he found it difficult to believe in a super-natural Christ ('At times his divinity, in its unique sense, seems to me a product of the mythopoeic imagination'), and pointedly used the past tense when discussing him. He told Mollie Price-Owen that he had problems with the idea of Christ as saviour, and with convictions about an afterlife.

These interviews, with their qualifying phrases, their careful punctuation, where the nature of belief can turn on an indefinite article, are not of our time at all. They read like a court report of the Inquisition, or that of Sir John Oldcastle before his judges. Thomas was old and reckless, but honest, when he phrased his replies.

A retired priest asked me just one question. 'Did he ever say such things in the pulpit?' And the answer would seem to be 'No.' There is no record of any outrage in any of his parishioners, apart from General Pugh, whose outrage was secular anyway, and R.S. Thomas, who preached weekly for forty years, never published his sermons.

Yet this was a man who all his working life portrayed such things as objective truth. What strain was he under, week after week, year after year, in what would in one sense have been a double life? In whom could he have confided, after those morn-ings spent reading Kierkegaard and Schopenhauer? Probably in no one. For Thomas, unlike some of his colleagues, these were the agonies of the study, not of the pulpit. And for him there was always one safety outlet.

Read out this poem. The loneliness it conveys seems unbear-able, and the terror in it. The poem is called 'Balance', though a more accurate title would have been 'Vertigo'. After you have read it, think what its effect transposed to a sermon would have been on the six or eight people listening in the pews beneath him.

No piracy, but there is a plank
to walk over seventy thousand fathoms,

as Kierkegaard would say, and far out
from the land. I have abandoned
my theories, the easier certainties
of belief. There are no handrails to
grasp. I stand and on either side
there is the haggard gallery
of the dead, those who in their day
walked here and fell. Above and
beyond there is the galaxies'
violence, the meaningless wastage
of force, the chaos the blond
hero's leap over my head
brings him nearer to.
Is there a place
here for the spirit? Is there time
on this brief platform for anything
other than mind's failure to explain itself?

Language was always his safety outlet.

He told Mollie Price-Owen that he could not rise to great acts of faith. But he was fascinated by those who could, and when he writes about them wistfulness creeps in, as in the poem 'The Chapel'. It is such an ugly little chapel, the traffic passes it by, and no tourist stops,

But here once on an evening like this,
in the darkness that was about
his hearers, a preacher caught fire
and burned steadily before them ...

And then there is Ann Griffiths, the young eighteenth-century hymn writer, who saw Christ waiting for her among the myrtles, '*Wele'n sefyll rhwng y myrtwydd*', an opening as throw-away, and as astonishing, as Vaughan's 'I saw eternity the other night'. Thomas writes about her in his beautiful

'Fugue for Ann Griffiths', and the impression the poem leaves is of an awestruck child, its nose pressed against a toy-shop window.

> She listened to him.
> We listen to her.
> She was in time
> chosen ...

That was written by a man who knew he himself had not been chosen, and for whom there had been no moment among the myrtles.

> I have waited for him
> under the tree of science,
> and he has not come.

The Echoes Return Slow

But there was a moment, and it was among trees.

It made such an impression on him that he wrote about it twice, once, greatly daring, in prose. 'A Thicket in Lleyn' appeared in 1984, being one of eleven pieces by various authors in *Britain: A World by Itself* (Aurum). Ted Hughes wrote about a Devon river, Jan Morris about the Black Mountains; but R.S. Thomas wrote about the one mystical experience of his life. On an October day he has come upon a clump of bare trees, walking so quietly his approach has gone unnoticed. Then he steps inside.

it was alive with goldcrests. The air purred with their small wings. To look up was to see the twigs re-leafed with their small bodies. Everywhere their needle-sharp cries stitched at the silence. Was I invisible? Their seed-bright eyes regarded me from three feet off. Had I put forth an arm, they might have perched on it. I became a tree, part of that bare spinney where silently the light was splintered, and for a timeless moment the birds thronged me, filigreeing me with shadow, moving to an immemorial rhythm on their way south.

Then suddenly they were gone, leaving other realities to return: the rustle of the making tide, the tick of the moisture, the blinking of the pool's eye as the air flicked it, and lastly myself. Where had I been? Who was I? What did it all mean? When it was happening, I was not. Now that the birds had gone, here I was once again ...

That was what happened. What follows is what he thought happened.

In *Biographia Literaria* Coleridge discussed the nature of imagination as part of the creative experience. 'The primary MAGINATION [*sic*] I hold to be the living Power and prime Agent of all human Perception, and as a repetition in the finite mind of the eternal act of creation in the infinite I AM.' That is all, for Coleridge then went on to discuss the secondary imagination which to him was an echo of the first, but which can coexist, as he put it, 'with the conscious will'. In other words when the creative artist is aware at the same time of being S.T. Coleridge, which by implication he was not when he experienced the former. This fascinated R.S. Thomas. He quotes it in his introduction to the *Penguin Book of Religious Verse*, and adds, 'The nearest we can approach to God, he appears to say, is as creative beings.'

Something of this sort, he suggests in 'A Thicket in Lleyn', had happened to him.

While the experience lasted, I was absent or in abeyance. It was when I returned to myself that I realised that I was other, more than the experience, able to stand back and comprehend it by means of the imagination, and so by this act of creation to recognise myself not as lived by, but as part of the infinite I AM.

In the poem of the same name he misquotes Coleridge to underline what he thinks happened to him:

'A repetition in time of the eternal
I AM.' Say it. Don't be shy.
Escape from your mortal cage
in thought. Your migrations will never
be over …

For a moment he had had a whiff, not just of infinity, but of eternity. And not in the terrifying chaos of space, but among the goldcrests in a clump of bare trees. The probes could be dismantled.

The Echoes Return Slow, published in 1988, has this, which, copied on slate, is in the church at Aberdaron:

There are nights that are so still
that I can hear the small owl calling
far off, and a fox barking
miles away. It is then that I lie
in the lean hours awake, listening
to the swell born somewhere in the Atlantic
rising and falling, rising and falling
wave on wave on the long shore
by the village, that is without light
and companionless. And the thought comes
of that other being who is awake, too,
letting our prayers break on him
not like this for a few hours,
but for days, years, for eternity.

R.S. Thomas had become tender towards his God.

Amongst these poems there is tenderness, too, in the poem with the phrase which gives the collection its name. The background to it is a lifetime of sick visiting.

> They keep me sober,
> the old ladies
> stiff in their beds,
> mostly with pale eyes
> wintering me.
> Some are like blonde dolls
> their joints twisted;
> life in its brief play
> was a bit rough.
> Some fumble
> with thick tongue for words,
> and are deaf;
> shouting their faint names
> I listen;
> they are far off,
> the echoes return slow.
>
> But without them,
> without the subdued light
> their smiles kindle,
> I would have gone wild,
> drinking earth's huge draughts
> of joy and woe.

Life in its brief play was a bit rough.

In 1999, after many hours, Molly Price-Owen reluctantly drew her interview with the poet to a close. 'You do realise, Ronald, we haven't done love yet.'

He said, 'Love will have to wait until next time.'

R.S. Thomas, who in 1990 had told Raymond Garlick that he had the feeling he had stayed too long, wrote again in 1996 to say 'I am hoping to retire from air travel now, but who knows?' He was halfway through the last, and most remarkable, decade of his life, in which the recluse of Rhiw became a world traveller and socialite. On 8 November 1996, after a long diatribe against his biographer Justin Wintle, he ended a letter to Garlick, 'I remarried in August, someone I have known for many years, so here we are, two octogenarians trying to ignore the fact. Best wishes, Ronald.' Just that.

She was Betty Vernon, who had been one of his parish-ioners at Eglwys Fach. 'A smoking, swearing, drinking/fox-hunting female,' he marvels to himself in an unpublished poem, and, short of a colonelcy in the WRAC or a consultancy to the nuclear power industry, a more unlikely inventory it would be impossible to contrive. They married on her eightieth birthday. 'We had lived in sin, and it was wonderful, then we got respectable,' said the second Mrs Thomas. 'My Ronnie', or 'Ronnie boy', as she referred to him, was her fourth husband ('I like husbands'). Born in Ireland, of a family which migrated to Canada, she was the daughter of a vicar ('I can't get away from bloody vicars').

'How did we meet? I guess it was when we went to church. He was a marvellous preacher, short and snappy, and don't forget, I've been stuck with parsons all my life. And he was such a good-looking man, really sexy. We caught each other's eyes as soon as I saw him in the pulpit. He was a man full of *fun*.

'My then husband was Richard Vernon, typical English gentleman, liked to go to church every Sunday. What did he do? Sweet fanny adams. He was wealthy. Didn't so much as squeeze his bloody toothpaste himself. He lived for hunting, he was a sporting squire. We lived in a house with forty rooms.'

She and Thomas had some happy years together, but there were never forty rooms again. Instead, Betty Thomas being, like most people, unable to put up with 'that bloody Sarn place', the two octogenarians moved around North Wales from rented property to rented property like a teenage couple. At one point they lived in the Bell Tower at Portmeirion.

And then there were the travels: to Alaska (to see whales), to Dubai (for the birds), on top of which there were the literary conferences. Breezily he wrote to Raymond Garlick, 'In Greece we pursued God up Olympus, but he vanished, as always, into thin air. Perhaps God is a monkey after all. They like to urinate at strangers.' People noticed a change in the grim figure, which seemed to require a response. 'What shall I call you?' asked the poet Gwyneth Lewis at a writers' conference in Barcelona. 'Call me Ronaldo,' said R.S. Thomas.

There was much socialising. Henry Jones-Davies, the publisher of *Cambria* magazine, was introduced to Thomas by Dafydd Iwan at a party. But Thomas, whose fame turned on his mastery of the English language, refused to speak it, and with Jones-Davies unable to speak Welsh, Dafydd Iwan, whose fame turned on his Welsh songs, had to interpret between the two, one of whom already knew what the other was saying. Jones-Davies felt he had walked through the looking-glass with Alice, but then Betty Thomas turned up. 'Do help yourself to a gin and tonic, darling,' said R.S. Thomas.

I called on him at this time, at a rented house in Anglesey with excellent views of a nuclear power station. 'Ironic, that.' He was immaculately dressed, in what his son called his 'retired brigadier mode', sports coat, flannels, brogues, red tie, but his hair, which his first wife used to cut, was now sparse in the front, and long and wild at the back: he looked like a brooding mediaeval mystic in fancy dress. The two were not married at this stage, and Thomas explained what he called his 'domestic circumstances' as we went for a walk. It was a long walk, and I was eager to get away, but as we got back to the house he told me, like an anthropologist explaining a new tribal custom to a colleague, 'You'll be lucky to escape without a cup of tea.'

My wife and I had them to supper some years later, and they were amusing company. No silences now, in fact quite the opposite. The Hay Literary Festival came up, and I said I had never been. 'Hah, probably never been asked,' said R.S. Thomas, showing off in front of his new girl. He had told me that her eyesight was poor ('Her doctor tells me she could probably drive, but that he wouldn't want to be in the car if she did'), and as they left I saw him take her hand as this very old couple walked into the night, and it was moving.

In one of his unpublished poems he writes:

> What is anguish? It
> is the love of an old couple
> for one another's
> pain mitigated
> by being spared their reflections:
> the cracked smile, the toothless
> euphoria, each of them pardoning
> the other's credentials.

Some days later they invited us out to supper at a nearby hotel, at which they were regular customers, and I remember Thomas, a veteran of homemade elderflower sherry, scrutinising the wine list. 'Côtes de Rhône [*sic*], that's a good one.' At one point Mrs Thomas began to talk about Welsh history, and mentioned 'all those Druids fighting the Vikings'. I looked at Thomas, who had read all there was to be read about Welsh history, for there was something like a thousand years between the Druids and the Vikings, but his face was quite blank.

This last Thomas was a bit of a shock to those who knew him, and now saw him and his wife queuing for lottery tickets at Tesco's. Old friends like the Mowats, hearing him addressed as 'darling heart', also found themselves staring at that blank face. It was also a shock even to those who had never met him before. This was Graham Turner's experience in 1999:

When I arrived at the cottage, Thomas was out seeing the doctor after a spot of heart trouble. They couldn't receive me in the sitting room, apologised his second wife Betty, a lively Canadian related to Lord Longford: it was a disaster area of damp patches and displaced furniture, so it would have to be the dining room. She offered me tea and poured a generous slug of brandy into her own. 'I'm completely unlike the wife I should be for my husband,' she said, lighting up a king-size Raffles. 'Our views are often poles apart. For example, he's strongly against war, whereas I'm all for it.'

When Thomas himself returned, muttering about tablets, he reported that the doctor had asked whether he was under any strain. 'Yes,' he'd replied, 'my wife', and a ripple of mischievous amusement flitted across the hawk-like face.

But one part of the old routine was still rigidly observed. In the mornings he read and wrote, as he had always done. 'He used to sit there, and there was this awful silence, I wasn't even allowed to answer the phone,' said Betty Thomas. For even now the poems poured out, and there were four collections just from the last ten years of his life.

In the summer of 2000 the Mowats, coming north for their annual holiday, wrote to him, and got a reply dated 15 August. The old wild handwriting has become spidery, and the lines straggle across the page, but even in extremis he is as brief and to the point as he always was.

It was good to hear from you. I have become a moron, able only to struggle from room to room and find that I cannot write a cogent sentence, much less a poem. Betty is a little spriter [sic] but gets minor strokes, 'incidents' they call them. My heart is the trouble, among other things. I am on so much medication that I fall asleep as soon as I sit down. We have given up receiving visitors, even good friends, as no one wants to listen to self pity. I hope your family flourish.

With love, Ronald.

He died in a hospice on 25 September 2000, the two having found themselves no longer able to cope. His ashes are buried in the parish church at Porthmadog, a bleak Victorian Gothic building on a hill, where the small plaque bearing his name and dates is hard to find.

'I burned three bags of poems after he died,' said Betty Thomas. 'I thought they were lousy poems, he did write some very bad poems. Why not? Why didn't he burn them himself, you mean? He was dead, for Chrissakes. We had a very close understanding, and I can judge poems. He just churned them out.'

Which did create a bit of a problem, as R.S. Thomas had appointed a literary executor for his unpublished work. Professor Meurig Wynn Thomas of Swansea University had been summoned north for an interview that had left him feeling stunned.

'He told me he was making me responsible for deciding whether anything he left was worthy of publication. It was amazing. I told him, "Only you know that. You're entrusting your poems to me, I'll make mistakes." And he said, "Don't worry, there won't be any poems left."'

Only there were. When Professsor Wynn Thomas went north again there were shoe-boxes full. A few months later more surfaced, and, at intervals, two more caches again. Like the wreckage from a submarine, they kept coming up. Even the man who had bought R.S. Thomas's car after there had been too many bumps, and he had been forced to give up driving, found one in the glove compartment, where usually only forgotten tubes of boiled sweets and tapes are found. Out of all these came the collection *Residues* (Bloodaxe, 2002); another collection, of ninety-five pages, has yet to be published.

A tribute was held to him at Westminster Abbey, when Seamus Heaney and the Poet Laureate Andrew Motion read his poems, and Motion realised something that had not occurred to him before. 'I had been aware that some of the poems were similar, and that night I realised why this was. They were all fragments of a Masterwork.'

There was another tribute at Portmeirion. The poet and singer Twm Morris, son of Jan Morris, was there, and wrote to Gwydion Thomas:

> But here's a strange thing. During the lectures we all heard a loud tapping noise coming from somewhere, I couldn't for the life of me work it out. It seemed to come from behind Hercules in the plaster ceiling. But then I saw from where I was in the front row that there was a blue tit pecking furiously at the window pane. Blue tit in Welsh is *Titw Tomos Las*. It must have been your father.

When he looked again the bird had gone.

❧ BIBLIOGRAPHY ❧

✠

Poetry by R.S. Thomas

The Stones of the Field (Druid Press 1946)
An Acre of Land (Montgomeryshire Printing Company 1952)
The Minister (Montgomeryshire Printing Company 1953)
Song at the Year's Turning (Hart-Davis 1955)
Poetry for Supper (Hart-Davis 1958)
Tares (Hart-Davis 1961)
The Bread of Truth (Hart-Davis 1963)
Pieta (Hart-Davis 1966)
Not That He Brought Flowers (Hart-Davis 1968)
H'm (Macmillan 1972)
Young and Old (Chatto and Windus 1972)
Selected Poems 1946–68 (Hart-Davis, MacGibbon 1973)
What is a Welshman? (Christopher Davies 1974)
Laboratories of the Spirit (Macmillan 1975)
The Way of It (Ceolfrith Press 1977)
Frequencies (Macmillan 1978)
Between Here and Now (Macmillan 1981)
Later Poems 1972–1983 (Macmillan 1983)
Ingrowing Thoughts (Poetry Wales Press 1985)
Experimenting with an Amen (Macmillan 1986)
Welsh Airs (Poetry Wales Press 1987)
The Echoes Return Slow (Macmillan 1988)
Counterpoint (Bloodaxe 1990)
Mass for Hard Times (Bloodaxe 1992)
Collected Poems 1945–1990 (Dent 1993)
No Truce with the Furies (Bloodaxe 1995)
Residues, ed. M. Wynn Thomas (Bloodaxe 2002)
Selected Poems (Penguin Modern Classics 2004)
Collected Later Poems 1988–2000 (Bloodaxe 2004)

Prose by R.S. Thomas
Selected Prose, ed. Sandra Anstey (Poetry Wales Press 1983, revised edition Seren 1995)
Neb (Gwasg Gwynedd 1985)
Blwyddyn yn Llyn (Gwasg Gwynedd 1990)
Autobiographies, trans. Jason Walford Davies (Dent 1997)

Books edited by R.S. Thomas
The Batsford Book of Country Verse (Batsford 1961)
The Penguin Book of Religious Verse (Penguin 1963)
Selected Poems of Edward Thomas (Faber 1964)
A Choice of George Herbert's Verse (Faber 1967)
A Choice of Wordsworth's Verse (Faber 1971)

R.S. Thomas's readings of his work
R.S. Thomas Reading the Poems (Sain, Caernarfon, SCD 2209)

Books and essays on R.S. Thomas (a selection)
Agenda, R.S. Thomas special issue (1998)
Anstey, Sandra, ed. *Critical Writings on R.S. Thomas* (Poetry Wales Press 1982)
Bohata, Kirsti. *Postcolonialism Revisited* (University of Wales Press 2004)
Brown, Tony, *R.S. Thomas*, Writers of Wales series (University of Wales Press 2006)
David Jones Journal, R.S. Thomas special issue (2001)
Davies, Damian Walford, ed. *Echoes to the Amen: Essays after R.S. Thomas* (University of Wales Press 2003)
Dyson, A.E., *Yeats, Eliot and R.S. Thomas* (Macmillan 1981)
Poetry Wales, R.S. Thomas issue, 1972
Prys-Williams, Barbara, *Twentieth Century Autobiography* (University of Wales Press 2004)
Taliesin, R.S. Thomas special issue (Welsh language, spring 2001)
Thomas, M. Wynn, *Internal Difference: Twentieth-Century Writing in Wales* (University of Wales Press 1992)
Thomas, Ned and John Barnie, *An Interview with R.S. Thomas, Planet* (April/May 1990)
Wintle, Justin, *Furious Interiors: Wales, R.S. Thomas and God* (Harper Collins 1996)

INDEX

Abbott and Holder, 111
Aberdaron, 4, 6–7, 37, 93, 196, 227, 231–2, 301, 307; Thomas at, 257, 258–9; Thomas insists on Welsh-language signs, 230; Thomas on, 236, 237–8, 247, 273
Abergavenny, 272
Aberystwyth, 5, 35, 40, 153, 301
Aberystwyth University, 161–2, 191, 293
Ackroyd, Peter, 19
Africa, 207
Alaska, 310
All Blacks, 100
All Souls College, 95
Allchin, Rev. Donald, 145, 201, 230, 257–8
American Civil War, 101
Amis, Kingsley, 6, 75, 187, 205, 210, 253
Aneirin, 89
Anglesey, 59, 62
Anglo-Welsh Poetry 1480–1980 (Raymond Garlick and Roland Mathias), 168
Arkansas, University of, 21, 85
Armstrong, Christopher, 228, 232, 281
Arney, Gill, 113, 148
Arnold, Matthew, 103
Arts and Crafts Movement, 42, 117
Arts Council, 93
Ashcroft, Peggy, 185
Ashmolean Museum, 290
Astley, Neil, 299
Athill, Philip, 111, 112–13
Atlantis, 103
Attallah, Naim, 289
Aubade (Philip Larkin), 276
Auden, W.H., 301
Augustine, St, 300

Bad Blood (Lorna Sage), 119–20
Bala, 106, 119
Ballet Rambert, 204
Bangor, 231
Bangor University, 38; Thomas at, 1, 7, 9, 72, 84; Thomas revisits, 89; Thomas uses initials, 1, 7, 9, 38, 72, 84, 89, 224
Barchester Towers (Anthony Trollope), 75
Bardsey Island, 4, 289; birdwatching, 117, 199, 227–8; pilgrimages, 231; sold, 10, 280, 289
Bateman, H.M., 11, 99, 156
Battle of Britain, 119
BBC, 182, 212
BBC Wales, 243
Beaumont Hamel, Battle of, 50
Beaux Art Gallery, 106, 111
Beddgelert, 262
Beerbohm, Max, 22, 163
Behrend, George, 204
Behrend, Louis, 203–4, 210
Behrend, Mary, 203–4, 210
Belloc, Hilaire, 42, 106
Bennett, Alan, 20
Bennett, Glenys, 156
Berenson, Bernard, 137
Berriew, 132
Berwyn mountains, 166
Bethesda, 97
Betjeman, John, 6, 185, 186–7, 210
Beuno, 132, 218, 226
Bevan, Aneurin, 162
Bible, 38, 220
Biographia Literaria (Samuel Taylor Coleridge), 307
Black Mountains, 306
Blackburn, Thomas, 238
Blaenau Ffestiniog, 71
Blake, William, 276
Bloodaxe, 299
Blunden, Edmund, 184
Blythe, Ronald, 266
Bonham's, 112
Book of Hours (Duc de Berry), 277
Borderland (Ronald Blythe), 266
Borrow, George, 127
Bosworth, Battle of, 220
Bottrall, Ronald, 211
Boulton, Hazel, 75, 131, 148, 173, 174
Bowen, E.G., 63
Bowen, Euros, 170
Bowen, Geraint, 278
Box Hill, 109
Boy (James Hanley), 182
Bradfield College, 223
Bradman, Donald, 67

Brahms, Johannes, 144
Braich-y-Pwll, 241
Brancusi, Constantin, 111
Bristol Zoo, 274
Britain: A World by Itself (various), 306
British Nature Conservancy Council, 280
Britten, Benjamin, 181
Brompton Cemetery, 132
Brown, Pamela, 185
Brown, Tony, 38, 290
Browning, Robert, 19
Bruce, Lenny, 22, 244
Brummell, Beau, 22
'Bryn Awel', 80
Bryn Coed, 105, 117, 119
Bubbles (John Everett Millais), 71
Bundle of Sensations, A (Goronwy Rees), 95
Burgess, Charles, 160
Burghclere, 204
Burma Star, 224
Burton, Richard (actor), 147
Burton, Richard (explorer), 75
Bwlch-y-Fedwen, 75, 118
Byd ar Bedwar (BBC Wales), 283
Byron, Robert, 75

Cadair Idris, 166, 189, 190
Caergybi *see* Holyhead
Caernarfon, 285, 287, 293
Calcutta Exchange, 209
California, 276
Camberley, 76
Cambria, 311
Cameron, Ian (cousin), 65, 66, 67, 76, 87, 102
Campbell, Colin, 81
Campbell, Len, 81
Campbell, Roy, 128
Canna, 116
Cardiff, 64, 99, 100, 281
Carey, John, 278
Carmarthen, 125, 281
Carter, Ray, 76
Caruso, Enrico, 126
Causley, Charles, 184, 187–8
Cecil, Lord David, 75
Ceiriog, 12
Ceiriog Valley, 69
Cemaes, 62
Channel Islands, 203
Charles I, 151
Charterhouse of Parma (Stendhal), 206
Chatwin, Bruce, 75
Chesterton, G. K., 42, 106
Chirk, 21, 101, 102, 106, 189
Church of Wales, 87
Churchill, Winston, 198
'Circus Animals' Desertion, The' (W.B. Yeats), 20
Clarke, Arthur C., 247

Cledwyn, Lord, 59, 76
CND, 279–81
Coleridge, Samuel Taylor, 307
Committee for the Protection of the Red Kite, 200, 280
Condry, Bill, 143, 199, 200, 205–6, 214, 228
Condry, Penny, 199, 204–5, 206, 211
Confessions (St Augustine), 300
Connolly, Cyril, 122
Conquest, Robert, 146
Conran, Tony, 169
Conroy, Genia, 198, 224
Corot, Jean Baptiste, 146
Cottrell, Leonard, 183
Covenanters of the Free Welsh, The, 286
Cowdray, Lord, 10
Cox, Professor C.B., 6
Crimean War, 125
Critical Quarterly, 271
Crompton, Richmal, 53
Cromwell, Oliver, 151, 245–6
Crookenden, Henry, 132
Cwm Croesor, 238
Cybi, 60
Cyfeiliog, Owain, 122
Cyfeillion Lleyn, 280, 289, 290

Dai Greatcoat (David Jones), 161
Dance of Life, The (Elsi Thomas), 140–1
Darling, Frank Fraser, 54–5, 117
David Jones Journal 257, 280
David Jones Society, 215–16, 251
Davie, Donald, 253–4
Davies, Adrian, 207
Davies, Daisy, 181
Davies, David, 65
Davies, Rev. Evelyn, 107, 217, 227, 231–4, 258
Davies, Glyn, 92
Davies, Gwen, 181
Davies, John, 134, 282
Davies, Paul, 89
Davies, Professor Walford, 32
Davies, Selwyn, 180
D-Day, 72
de la Mare, Walter, 276
de Walden, Lord Howard, 102
Devon, 306
Dictionary of National Biography, 92
Diocesan Advisory Council, 194
Dock Leaves (Raymond Garlick), 169, 210
Dodd, Ken, 22, 244
Dolwyddelan, 292
Dorset, 227
'Dover Beach' (Matthew Arnold), 96
Dovey, River, 189, 192
Dr Faustus (Richard Burton), 147
Druid Press, 125
Dublin, 63, 118
Dublin Magazine, 69

Durrell, Lawrence, 211
Dwyfor, 279
Dynevor, Lord, 212
Dyson, A.E., 271

Earp, Tommy, 106
Ebb and Flood (James Hanley), 182
Eglwys Fach, 5, 7, 33–5, 43, 145, 146,
    189–91, 194, 228, 301; BBC at, 212;
    birdwatching, 198–200; Elsi at, 190–1,
    195; Gwydion at, 43, 45, 222–4; meets
    second wife, 309; poetry from, 213,
    245; Thomas becomes famous, 209;
    Thomas Love Peacock and, 42;
    Thomas's friends at, 37; vacuum
    cleaner, 39; varnishing the pews,
    195–6
Eldridge, Ann, 107
Eldridge, Elsi *see* Thomas, Elsi
Eliot, T.S., 19, 75, 184, 218, 276
Elis Thomas, Dafydd, 285
Evans, Christine, 230, 232, 240–1
Ewart, Gavin, 270

Faber and Faber, 127, 138, 184
Fascism, 162
Fern Hill (Dylan Thomas), 276
Fflam, Y, 170
Ffowc Elis, Islwyn, 37, 166, 181
Fishguard, 63
Fitzroy Square, 271
Fong, Gisela Chan Man, 133
Forsaken Merman (Matthew Arnold), 103
Four Voyages of Christopher Columbus, The
    (Christopher Columbus), 213
Franco-Prussian War, 109
French, Colonel, 203
Friends of Lleyn, 280, 289, 290
Fuller, Christopher, 208
Fuller, Roy, 187

Garland for the Laureate, A (various), 187
Garlick, Raymond: on the Anglo-Welsh,
    168–70; *Dock Leaves* editorial on
    Thomas, 210; Eglwys Fach, 33; first
    meeting, 167; friendship blossoms, 71;
    quoted, 19; a reason for Thomas using
    initials, 1; Thomas writing to, 59, 61,
    182, 186, 219, 230, 237–8, 253, 278–83,
    286, 310
Gildas, 60–1
Gill, Eric, 42
Glandyfi Castle, 208, 223
Gleaners, The (Henry Lamb), 204
Glyndwr, Owain, 101, 121

Gobowen Orthopaedic Hospital, 112, 140,
    144
God and the New Physics (Paul Davies), 89
God's Englishman (Christopher Hill), 245

Gostick, Chris, 185
Gower, Jon, 22, 131, 243
Graves, Robert, 181
Greeson-Walker, Lorraine, 172
Gregynog, 131, 172
Gregynog Press, 52, 181, 269
Griffith, Kenneth, 212
Griffith, Wyn, 169
Griffiths, Ann, 305
Griffiths, Susan, 45, 223
Gruffydd, W. J., 23, 185
Guinness, Alec, 75
Gurkhali, 192, 194
Guy's Hospital, 271
Gwynedd County Council, 229, 269

Hackney, 147
Hall, David, 133–4
Hall, John, 194
Hall, Ruth, 173, 174, 181, 201
Halton, 101
Hamlet (William Shakespeare), 221
Hanley, Dorothy, 183
Hanley, James, 182–4, 185, 191, 210
Hanley, Liam, 183
Hanmer, 119–21, 189
Hardy, Thomas, 20–1, 25, 298
Hart-Davis, Rupert, 52, 184–5, 187–8, 203,
    210, 278, 299
Hart-Davis MacGibbon, 4
Hawarden, 88
Hay Literary Festival, 311
Haydon, Benjamin, 140
Healey, Lady, 160
Heaney, Seamus, 30, 278, 315
Heath, Tony, 284–5, 286
Helen of Troy, 123, 292
Hell's Mouth, 262, 291
Hennel, Tom, 108
Henry, Thomas, 53
Henry V (William Shakespeare), 130
Henry VII, 220
Herbert, George, 5, 300–1
Herrick, Robert, 5
Hibou et la Poussiquette, Le (Edward Lear,
    trans.), 184
Hill, Christopher, 246
Hill, Geoffrey, 44, 184–5, 278
Hillier, Bevis, 186
Hiroshima, 153
History of Wales, A (John Davies), 134, 282
Hitler, Adolf, 54, 119, 162, 192
Holy Island, 59, 60, 80
Holyhead: Maelgwn, 218; parents' grave,
    255; Thomas in, 59–63, 76, 80, 83–4,
    90, 174, 235
Holyhead School Magazine, 86
Home for Miss Fieldmouse, A (Dorothy
    Richards), 138
Home Guard, 157

Hopkins, Byron, 208
Hopkins, Gerard Manley, 300
Hore-Belisha, Leslie, 54
Horizon (Cyril Connolly), 122
Hughes, Glyn Tegai, 131, 133, 172
Hughes, Lloyd, 59, 62
Hughes, T.J., 92
Hughes, Ted, 13, 44, 306
Humphreys, Emyr, 1, 212
Humphreys, Megan, 133, 157, 158, 165
Hunter, N.C., 145, 191, 202

Iolo Goch, 89, 128
Industrial Revolution, 130
Irish Sea, 63
Island Trust Council (Bardsey), 280
I Tatti, 137
Iwan, Dafydd, 230, 310

James, M. R., 82
Jarrell, Randall, 44
Jarrow, 62
Jeffers, Robinson, 89, 300
Jeffreys, George, 207
Jenkins, Randal, 170
Jenkins, Roy, 75, 160
Jennings, Elizabeth, 211
Jersey, 203
Johnson, Angella, 287
Johnson, Hewlett, 103
Jones, Bobi, 145, 168, 170, 171, 284
Jones, Cassie, 86–7
Jones, David, 161
Jones, Eric, 132–3, 138, 149, 156, 165, 173, 176
Jones, Gerallt, 226, 229
Jones, Glyn, 162, 170, 180, 210
Jones, Gwyn, 5
Jones, Joan, 208
Jones, John, 133, 165
Jones, Monica, 20

Keating sisters, 228–9, 294
Kent, Duchess of, 141
Kew Gardens, 30
Kidnapped (Robert Louis Stevenson), 144
Kiel University, 133
Kierkegaard, Søren, 30, 304
'Kimla', 63, 83
King Lear (William Shakespeare), 221
Kinnock, Neil, 162
Knight, Alan, 196
Knight, Hester, 186
Korean War, 167
Kreisler, Fritz, 100

Lamb, Henry, 204
Larkin, Philip, 2, 20, 146, 275, 278
Lawrence, D. H., 137
Le Pen, Jean-Marie, 285

Lear, Edward, 184
Leatherhead, 107
Lee, Laurie, 183
Lewis, Alun, 210
Lewis, Dafydd, 281
Lewis, Gwyneth, 254, 311
Lewis, Saunders, 162
Lines, Vincent, 108
Listeners, The (Walter de la Mare), 276
Liverpool, 77, 183
Llanbedrog, 290
Llandaff, 98, 99, 100, 130
Llandinam, 65, 181
Llandudno, 90, 230
Llandyssul, 65
Llanfaelrhys, 229
Llanfechain, 183
Llangollen, 151, 159
Llanpumsaint, 277
Llansilin, 122
Llantwit Major, 73
Lleyn Peninsula, 4, 91, 225–6, 229, 231, 235, 289
Llywerch Hen, 89
Llwyn Copa, 134, 148, 156, 165
Llyn Coch-hwyad, 200
LMS Railway Company, 63
Lockley, R.M., 145
London Magazine, 212
London School of Economics, 193
Lord, Peter, 111
Lowell, Robert, 13
Ludlow, 100

Macdonald, John, 116
Macdonald, Marianne, 21, 62
Machynlleth, 191, 205, 223, 286
Macmillan publishers, 278, 299
Maelgwyn, 60, 218
Mair, Margaret, 196, 207, 224
Mallaig, 115, 117
Manafon, 7, 14, 93, 99, 120, 122–3, 130–3, 135–40, 142–54, 181, 216, 227, 269; Gwydion on, 35–7, 43; influence of on Thomas's poetry, 174, 179, 188, 215; parishioners, 189–91, 201; pastoral duties, 301; poetry reading, 176; remembering, 30; stipend at, 88; Thomas remembered, 194; Thomas returns to, 171–2; Tommy Thomas at, 83
Mappin, Hubert, 200, 202, 207
Mappin and Webb, 200
Marchant, Dr John, 117
Marina, Duchess of Kent, 141
Masefield, John, 54, 210, 211
Mathias, Roland, 168
Mathrafal, 122–3
Medici Society, 110, 269
Meibion Glyndwr, 29, 283–7

Memoirs (Elsi Thomas), 225
Menzies, John, 140
Merchant Navy, 66
Meredith-Morris, Thomas James, 119, 120
Merionethshire, 189
Merthyr Tydfil, 64
Mickleham, 109
Milan, 132
Miles, Bethan, 67
Millais, John Everett, 71
Miller, Henry, 183
Missouri, 101
Mitchell, Julian, 212
Mix, Tom, 84
Modern Welsh Poetry (ed. Keidrych Rhys), 127
Montagu's harriers, 205
Montaillou (Emannuel Le Roy LaDurie), 44
Montgomery Printing Press, 182
Montgomeryshire, 75, 122, 130, 175, 183, 234
Moorey, Ann, 75, 107, 139, 144, 266, 268, 294
Moreton Hall, Chirk, 107, 110, 222
Morgan, Bishop, 220
Morgan, Geraint, 193
Morgan, Gwyn King, 125
Morgan, Professor Prys, 212
Morris, Jan, 306, 314
Morris, Lord, 93
Mother's Union, 301
Motion, Andrew, 20, 315
Mountain Ash, 64
Mountains of Wales, The (various), 269
Mountbatten, Earl, 79
Mowat, John, 78, 130, 156, 221, 263, 270, 272, 312–13
Mowat, Peggy, 78–9, 150, 228, 231, 265, 270–7, 312–13
Mr Nobody (Jenny Rees), 95
Munich, 103, 162
Mynydd Mawr, 235
Mytton-Davies, Cynric, 14, 22, 182

Nantmor, 262
National Eisteddfod, 267
National Library of Wales, 51, 202, 213
National Museum of Wales, 181
National Service, 191
National Trust, 229
Navy Lark, The (BBC), 202
Neale, Joy, 194, 197
New Quay, 40
New Testament, 302
New Welsh Review, 32, 94
Newtown, 131, 152
Nightingale, Benedict, 216
No Direction (James Hanley), 183
Norris, Leslie, 179

North Wales and the Marches (W.J. Gruffydd), 185
North West Frontier, 192

Oldcastle, Sir John, 303
Oldie, 232, 288
Ormond, John, 302, 303
O'Sullivan, Seamus, 55, 118
Oswestry, 106, 107, 173
Owen, Goronwy, 220
Owen, H.D., 163, 165
Owen, John, 284
Owen, Wilfred, 19–20, 50
Oxford University, 67, 90, 99, 253

Packwood prep school, 150
Parry, Gareth, 288–9
Peacock, Thomas Love, 42
Pears, Peter, 181
Peck, Gregory, 193
Penarth, 163, 164
Penguin Book of Religious Verse, 307
Penguin Modern Classics, 253
Penrhos Feilw, 80
Pentrefelin Church, 1
Penybelan, John Jones, 163
Pierce, Thomas Jones, 293
Place in the Mind, A (Gerallt Jones), 226, 229
Plaid Cymru, 285
Planet: Ned Thomas in, 285–6; R.S. Thomas interviewed, 65, 88, 93, 97, 103, 170, 181, 200, 210, 270, 287, 303
Plas-yn-Rhiw, 228
Plath, Sylvia, 276
Ploughman, The (Iolo Goch), 128
Poetry London, 183
Poetry Review, 296
Poetry Wales, 125, 133, 170, 179, 285
Port Talbot, 65
Porth Hotel, Llandyssul, 65
Porthmadog, 267, 313
Portmeirion, 242, 310, 314
Powell, Michael, 185
Powers, Alan, 141
Powys, 122
Prelude, The (William Wordsworth), 300
Pressburger, Emeric, 185
Price-Owen, Molly, 215, 251, 301–4, 305, 309
Priory Clinic, 92
Pritchard, Rev. Bill, 99, 120, 131, 172, 176
Prix de Rome, 42, 105
Producers, The (Mel Brooks), 195
Pryce-Jones, Alan, 182, 210
Prys-Jones, A.G., 210
Prys-Williams, Barbara, 197
Psycho (Alfred Hitchcock), 83
Pugh, Cordera, 196
Pugh, Elfyn, 205, 206
Pugh, Major General Lewis, 192–4, 198, 224

Pwllheli, 44, 226, 265, 273, 281
Pwllheli Grammar School, 240

Queen's Gold Medal for Poetry, 4, 54

RAF, 227
Ramsey Island, 117, 206
Rare Bird, A (BBC), 200
Rawlins, Monica, 203
Rebecca Riots, 286
Rees, Goronwy, 95, 161
Rees, Iaon Bowen, 269
Rees, Jenny, 95
Resurrection, the, 302–3
Rhys, Keidrych, 126, 127, 159, 161
Richards, Dorothy, 138
Ricks, Christopher, 185
Roberts, Lynette, 181–2
Roberts, Mary, 239
Robertson, Canon Thomas, 90
Robinson, Peter, 254
Rodin, Auguste, 111
Rogers, Philip, 180
Rolling Stones, 10
Roman Empire, 60
Romania, 68
Rome, 231
Ross, Alan, 183
Round the Horne (BBC), 202
Royal Academy, 106
Royal College of Art, 42, 105
Royal Watercolour Society, 138
RSPB, 199
R.S. Thomas, Priest and Poet (BBC), 302
Rupert Hart-Davis (Philip Ziegler), 187
Rylands, Denise, 110

Sabellianism, 156
Sage, Lorna, 119, 120–1, 192
St Hywyn church, 5
St Michael and All Angels, Manafon, 131
St Michael's Theological College, 99
Salt, Dr C.E., 140
Sassnitz, 63
Sassoon, Siegfried, 20
Sarn, 16, 31, 33–5, 39, 261–6, 269–70, 277, 286, 294
Schopenhauer, Arthur, 212, 213, 304
Sea Wolves, The (Andrew V. McLaglen), 193
Second World War, 103, 208
Serf, The (Roy Campbell), 128
Seven Years in Tibet (Heinrich Harrer), 184
Severn, River, 132
Shakespeare, William, 276
Sharp, William, 114
Shrewsbury, 100, 101, 219
Shropshire, 104
Simla, 191
Simon, Glyn, 98, 237
Simon, Robin, 98

Skelton, John, 89
Slade School of Fine Art, 111, 228
Snowdon, 300
Snowdonia, 262
Soay, 115
Soho Square, 184
South Stack lighthouse, 80
Spain, 205
Spencer, Stanley, 112, 202, 204
Spender, Stephen, 187, 211
Spoleto, 211
Stanley-Wrench, Margaret, 203
Stapledon, George, 156
Stedall, Jonathan, 187
Stevens, Wallace, 8, 191, 242, 276
Swansea University, 313
Swift, Jonathan, 61

Take It From Here (BBC), 114
Taliesin, 167
Tal-y-Lyn, 243
Taylor, A.J.P., 100
Taylor, Elizabeth, 147
Thailand, 34
Themen und Bolder in der Dichtung von Ronald Stuart Thomas (Gisela Chan Man Fong), 133
Thomas, Betty (second wife), 64, 70, 202, 310, 312, 313, 314
Thomas, Dafydd Elis, 285–6
Thomas, Dylan, 48, 71–2, 127, 158, 160, 210, 276
Thomas, Edmund (uncle), 66
Thomas, Edward, 50
Thomas, Elsi (first wife): appeal of R.S. to, 43; as artist, 105–6, 109–13, 140–4; background 21, 107; car, 114–15; death, 46, 263, 273, 293; Eglwys Fach, 190–1, 195; her family, 38; friends, 270; grandson speaks of, 29; ill health, 13–14, 137, 234, 267; life at Aberdaron, 6–7; love of poetry, 42; Manafon, 136–7, 140; marriage and relationship, 32, 118–19, 221, 248, 266, 277, 294–8; personality, 42, 107, 109, 243; popularity of, 138; previous relationship, 108; R.S.'s poems, 49–50, 295, 297; Sarn, 264–72, 277; strange atmosphere created by her and R.S., 30, 145; teas, 271; teaching, 110, 139; wedding, 119
Thomas, Gwydion (son): approaches Bloodaxe, 299; baptised, 154; birth, 148, 154; boarding school, 35–6, 150, 151, 223; childhood, 149–51; collating father's papers and possessions, 16–17; divorce, 111; on his father, 23, 32–3, 36–47, 75, 79–80, 93, 94, 102, 261; his father and his future wife, 26; girlfriends, 45, 223–4; on his parents,

204; relationship with father, 44, 46–7; testament on his father, 33–47
Thomas, Gwyn (cousin), 67
Thomas, James (grandfather), 65
Thomas, Meurig Wynn, 313, 314
Thomas, Ned, 285
Thomas, Peggy (mother): on career options for son, 87, 88; death, 238, 255–6; effect of on son, 68, 71–4, 76, 97; poems on, 64, 78–9 216–17; R.S.'s second wife on, 70
Thomas, R.S.
  OPINIONS:
  Bardsey island, 280; contemporary poets, 44, 276, 278; Elizabeth Taylor, 147; Gildas, 61; happiness, 12; Holyhead, 59; modern world, 11–12, 39; Nonconformity, 164, 246; trains, 100
  OTHERS' OPINIONS OF:
  Andrew Motion, 314; Cynric Mytton Davies, 14–15; Donald Allchin, 258; Gareth Williams, 290–2; Glyn Davies, 92; Gwydion Thomas, 23, 32–3, 36–47, 75, 79–80, 93, 94, 102, 261; John Betjeman, 186–7; Jon Gower, 22, 243–4; Lawrence Durrell, 211; Lewis Pugh, 198; Peggy Mowat, 228; Penny Condry, 206; Rhodri Thomas, 27–9, 31; Sharon Young, 25–7, 29–31; Sue Griffiths, 223; Thomas Robertson, 90–1; various, 207–9, 239–44; writers, various, 253–4
  PERSONAL:
  autobiographies, 21–2; belonging nowhere, 64; birdwatching, 200–1, 205, 243, 244; birth, 64, 78; birth of son Gwydion, 148, 154; Bryn Coed, 117; childhood, 71–2, 76, 81–7; CND, 280, 281; daily routine, 8, 40, 139–40, 312; death, 1, 313; death of wife Elsi, 46, 263, 293; dissatisfaction with things, 195; distance maintained, 9–10, 113, 251, 257, 270; drawings, 53–4; eating habits, 268; empathy, lack of, 93; escape, desire to, 54–5; family relationship problems, 28, 38, 46; father, 67, 83–4; foreign travel, a bit of, 205, 309, 310; Gwydion sent to boarding school, 35–6, 43, 150–1; having children, 36; health, 129–30, 166, 206, 271, 299; home ownership, 262, 264; humour, 30, 146, 179, 239, 244, 272, 273; initials, use of, 1, 9; intimacy, fear of, 46; kindness, 158; lack of self-awareness, 30; lacking interest in wife's art, 112, 144; late social breakthrough, 279; life summary, 7; loneliness, 8, 64, 237, 250; marriage to Elsi, 32, 221, 248, 266, 277, 295–8; marries Elsi, 118–19; meets Elsi,

105, 113; Meibion Glyndwr and, 282–7; mementoes, 16–17, 152; mental state of, 80; on the modern world, 11–12; money, 41, 264–5; mother's effect on, 45, 68–74, 76–7, 78–9, 82, 87–8, 216–17, 256; mystical experience, 306–8; obituaries, 2–3, 33; old age, 262, 298; pain, response to, 257; physical appearance, 5–6, 15, 288, 311; privacy, intense need for, 7; relations, 65–8; rudeness, 93; school, 76; second wife, 309–13; shyness, 44; snobbishness, 102; son's similarities to, 74; university, 97–8; valium, 206, 268; voice, 74–6, 161; Welshness, aura of, 12, 37–8, 90–1, 92, 94, 155, 158–63, 166–71, 218–20, 228, 230, 236, 289–90; women and, 29
  AS POET
  BBC performances, 173–5; 'Curtis Langdon', 96–7, 122; first published, 97; Fiona MacLeod, 114–17; Hart-Davis publishes, 184–5, 187–8; humour, 252; imagery, 13; introspection, 216; lectures given, 13; a poetry reading, 172–3; Queen's Gold Medal, 4; reading habits, 44, 102, 213; reputation, 6; subject matter, 6–7; technique, 254
  AS PRIEST
  chides parishioners, 153, 154; first calling, 10–11, 87–8, 98–9; on God, 300; honesty as, 234; mystical experience, 306–8; not a natural priest, 257; on Nonconformity, 164, 246; ordained, 100–1; pacifism, 103, 194, 288; as a preacher, 43; on the Resurrection, 302–3; retirement, 238, 259; theosophy, 103; Toc H, 103; youth club, 156, 231, 301
  WORKS
  Acre of Land, An, 178, 182; 'Afallon', 293; 'Airy Tomb, The', 177–8, 212; 'Anniversary', 27; 'Ap Huw's Testament', 69; 'Aubade', 275–6; Autobiographical Essay, An, 21, 69, 73, 77, 85, 87, 97, 102–4, 115, 144, 159, 231, 245, 258; 'Balance', 304; Between Here and Now, 270, 299; 'Boy's Tale, The', 64; Bread of Truth, The, 212; Collected Poems, 40, 41, 288; 'Countryman, The', 170; 'Death of a Peasant' 176, 178; Echoes Return Slow, The, 22, 77–8, 104, 121, 192, 256, 265, 299, 305, 308; 'Evacuee, The', 178; Experimenting with an Amen, 299; Gwenno the Goat, 47; H'm, 12, 56; 'Island, The', 145, 251–2; 'It Hurts Him to Think', 79; Laboratories of the Spirit, 52; Later Poems 1972–82, 299;

Thomas, R.S. (cont.)
  'Life, A', 302; 'Marged', 244; *Mass for Hard Times*, 296; *Neb*, 21, 23, 68, 72, 73, 79, 81, 82, 85, 92, 97, 99, 102, 128, 131, 144, 164, 166, 190, 195, 205, 213, 227, 233, 235, 245; 'Night and Morning', 186; 'Ninetieth Birthday', 215; *Not That He Brought Flowers*, 212; 'Old Language, The', 159; 'On the Coast', 85; *Paths Gone By, The*, 21, 63, 81, 82, 92, 159, 165, 174; 'Peasant, A', 127–8, 174; *Pieta*, 52, 212; *Poetry for Supper*, 52, 210, 215, 216; 'Priest to his People, A', 129; *Residues*, 314; 'Return, The', 135; 'Salt', 68, 69, 73, 79; *Selected Poems*, 4, 299; *Song at the Year's Turning*, 6, 52, 185, 209–10; 'Song for Gwydion', 178; *Spindrift, Poems and Prose Poems*, 52, 102, *Stones of the Field, The*, 41, 42, 52, 125–9, 173, 177; 'Strangers', 272; 'Survivors, The', 68; 'Swifts', 200; *Tares*, 210; various poems, 217–24, 246–58, 295–8, 305; 'White Tiger, The', 274; *Year in Llŷn, The*, 21
Thomas, Rhodri (grandson), 27–31, 33, 41, 271
Thomas, Tommy (father), 43–5, 62–70, 83–4, 87, 216
Times Literary Supplement, 127
To Kill a Mockingbird (Robert Mulligan), 193
Toc H, 103
Tomlinson, Charles, 276
Tomos, Angharad, 282, 284
Tourtel, Mary, 3
Trawsfynydd, 166, 167
Trearddur Bay, 80
Treece, Henry, 210
Tristan da Cunha, 232
Troy, 123, 292
Tryon, Lord, 211
Tudur Aled, 89
Turner, Graham, 221, 300–1, 312–13
20th-Century Autobiography (Barbara Prys-Williams), 197
Twilight People (Seamus O'Sullivan), 117
Ty Pella, Will, 230
Tynan, Kathleen, 296

Under Milk Wood (Dylan Thomas), 276

Vaughan, Ann, 242
Verlaine, Paul, 89
Vernon, Betty, *see* Thomas, Betty
Vernon, Richard, 310

Wain, John, 187, 253
Wales: A Study in Geography and History (E.G. Bowen), 158
Wales, University of, 139
Wantage, 74
War Office, 166
Waste Land, The (T.S. Eliot), 218
Waterfield, Aubrey, 137
Waters of the Moon, The (N.C. Hunter), 191
Watkins, Alan, 160
Watkins, Vernon, 158, 210
Webb, Harri, 125
Wellington, Duke of, 125
Welsh Language Society, 281, 284
Welsh Nationalist party, 12, 167
Welsh, The (Wyn Griffith), 169
Welshpool, 131, 183, 223
Westminster Abbey, 314
W.H. Smith Poetry Prize, 184
Where No Wounds Were (Goronwy Rees), 161
White, Gilbert, 199
White, T.H., 298
Wigley, Dafydd, 285
Wild Life My Life (Bill Condry), 143
Williams, D.J., 167
Williams, Gareth, 74, 103, 261, 291–2
Williams, Glyn, 285
Williams, Gwyn, 72
Williams, Idris, 273
Williams, Megan, 293
Williams, Waldo, 37, 145, 167
Wimbledon, 107
Wintle, Justin, 21, 33, 73, 75, 239, 280, 293, 309
Wolf Cubs, 153
Wood, Joan, 113, 117, 148
Woodstock, 147
World as Will and Idea (Arthur Schopenhauer), 213
Wormwood Scrubs, 227
Writers of Wales, 289
Wuthering Heights (Emily Brontë), 5, 26, 31
Wyatt, Woodrow, 183

Yeats, W.B., 8, 20, 186, 221, 254, 276
Ynyshir Nature Reserve, 199
Yom Kippur War, 47
Young, Andrew, 184
Young, Sharon (daughter-in-law), 24–7, 31, 47, 112
Young Wales Club, 156

Ziegler, Philip, 79, 184, 187